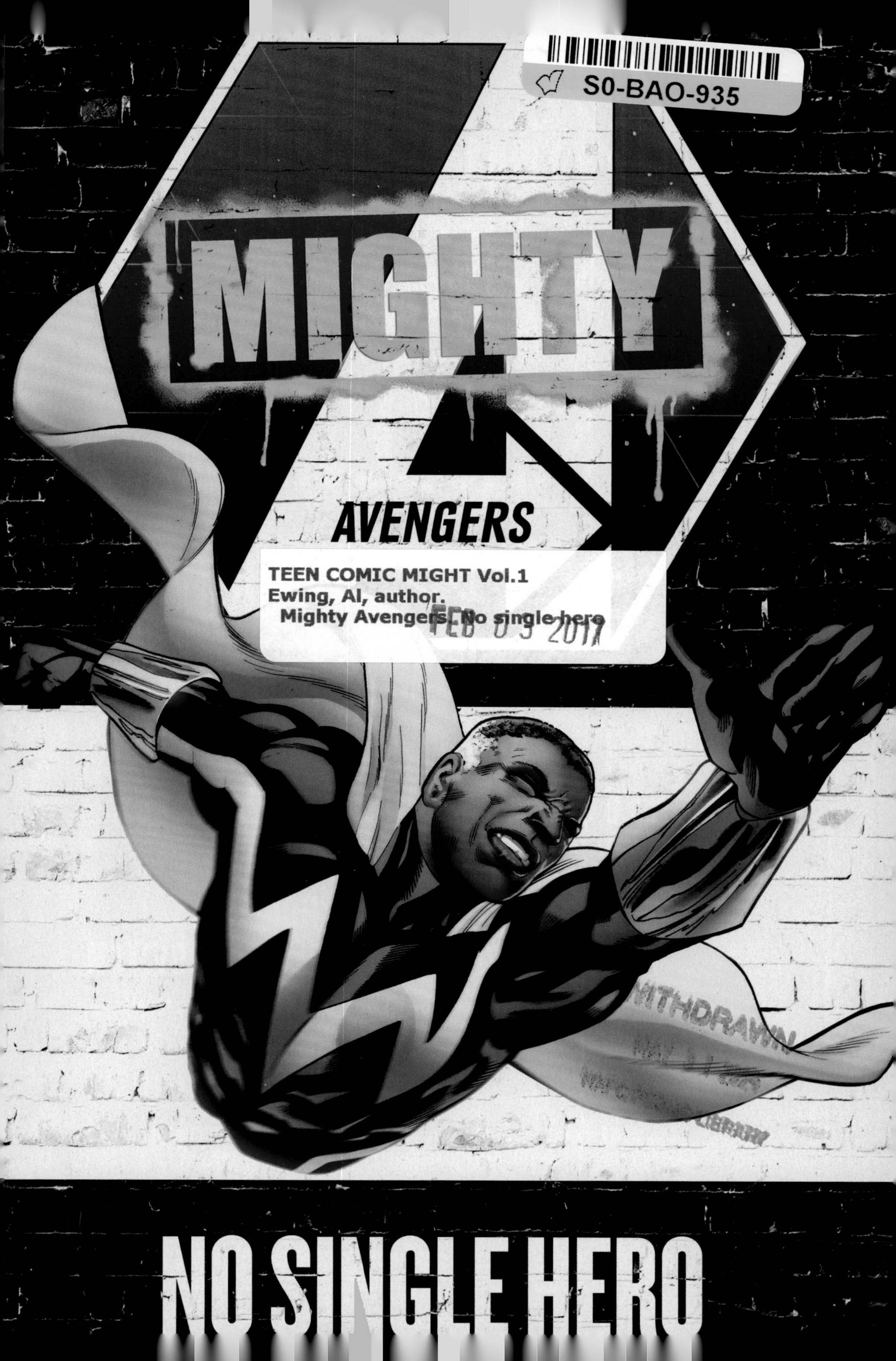
MIGHTY
AVENGERS
NO SINGLE HERO

MIGHTY AVENGERS

NO SINGLE HERO

WRITER **AL EWING** PENCILER **GREG LAND**

INKER **JAY LEISTEN** COLORIST **FRANK D'ARMATA** LETTERER **VC'S CORY PETIT**

COVER ART **GREG LAND**
WITH **LEE DUHIG** (#1), **MORRY HOLLOWELL** (#2)
& **FRANK D'ARMATA** (#3-5)

ASSISTANT EDITOR: **JAKE THOMAS**

EDITORS: **TOM BREVOORT** WITH **LAUREN SANKOVITCH**

COLLECTION EDITOR: **SARAH BRUNSTAD** ASSOCIATE MANAGING EDITOR: **ALEX STARBUCK**
EDITORS, SPECIAL PROJECTS: **JENNIFER GRÜNWALD** & **MARK D. BEAZLEY**
SENIOR EDITOR, SPECIAL PROJECTS: **JEFF YOUNGQUIST**
SVP PRINT, SALES & MARKETING: **DAVID GABRIEL**
BOOK DESIGNER: **RODOLFO MURAGUCHI**

EDITOR IN CHIEF: **AXEL ALONSO** CHIEF CREATIVE OFFICER: **JOE QUESADA**
PUBLISHER: **DAN BUCKLEY** EXECUTIVE PRODUCER: **ALAN FINE**

MIGHTY AVENGERS VOL. 1: NO SINGLE HERO. Contains material originally published in magazine form as MIGHTY AVENGERS #1-3 and #4.INH-5.INH. First printing 2014. ISBN# 978-0-7851-8874-2. Published by MARVEL WORLDWIDE, INC., a subsidiary of MARVEL ENTERTAINMENT, LLC. OFFICE OF PUBLICATION: 135 West 50th Street, New York, NY 10020.

Printed in Canada. ALAN FINE, EVP - Office of the President, Marvel Worldwide, Inc. and EVP & CMO Marvel Characters B.V.; DAN BUCKLEY, Publisher & President - Print, Animation & Digital Divisions; JOE QUESADA, Chief Creative Officer; TOM BREVOORT, SVP of Publishing; DAVID BOGART, SVP of Operations & Procurement, Publishing; C.B. CEBULSKI, SVP of Creator & Content Development; DAVID GABRIEL, SVP Print, Sales & Marketing; JIM O'KEEFE, VP of Operations & Logistics; DAN CARR, Executive Director of Publishing Technology; SUSAN CRESPI, Editorial Operations Manager; ALEX MORALES, Publishing Operations Manager; STAN LEE, Chairman Emeritus. For information regarding advertising in Marvel Comics or on Marvel.com, please contact Niza Disla, Director of Marvel Partnerships, at ndisla@marvel.com. For Marvel subscription inquiries, please call 800-217-9158. **Manufactured between 1/24/2014 and 3/3/2014 by SOLISCO PRINTERS, SCOTT, QC, CANADA.**

10 9 8 7 6 5 4 3 2 1

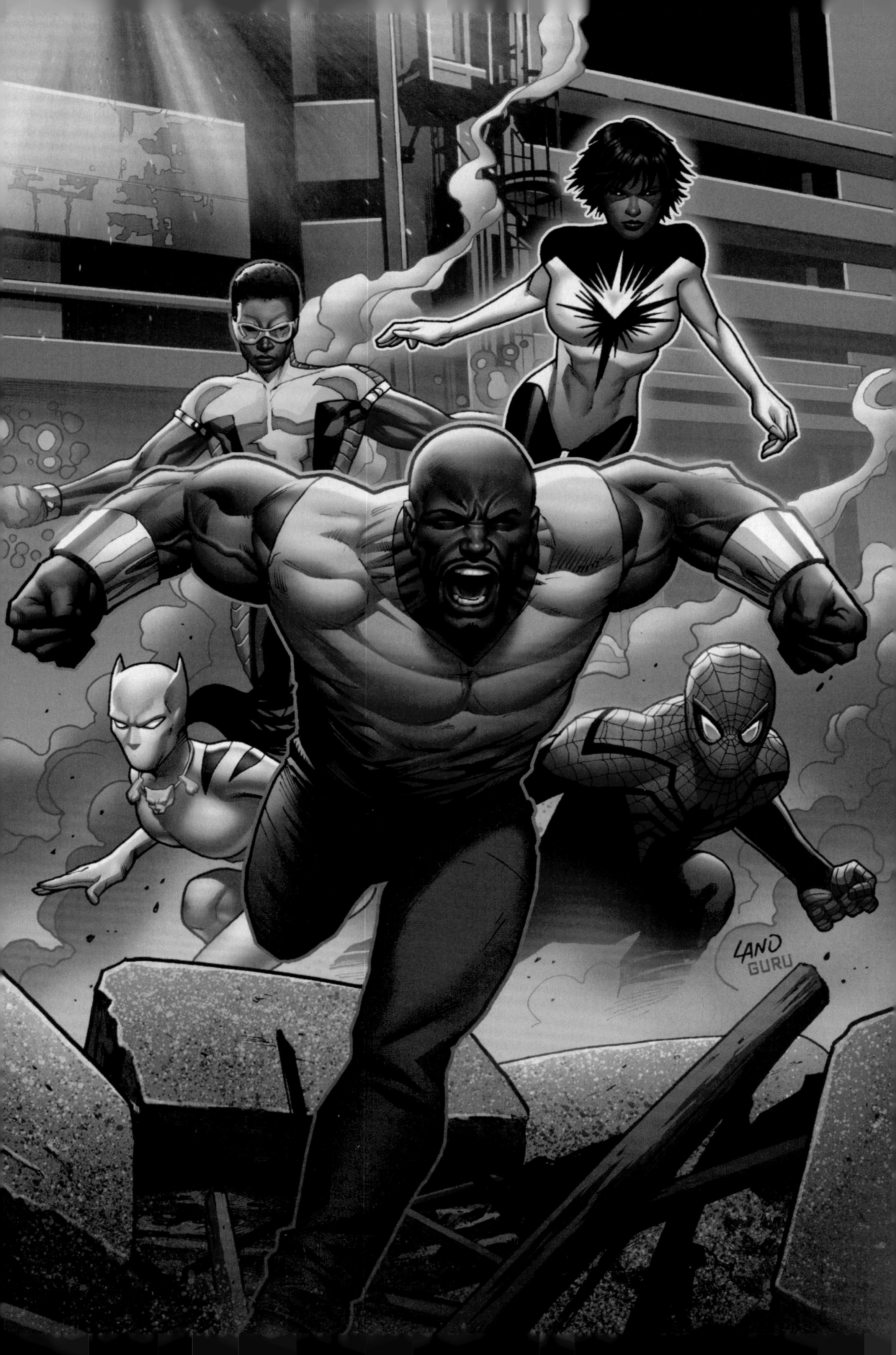
LAND
GURU

WARNING!

The intergalactic marauder Thanos has reportedly been detected in the vicinity of Earth once again!

Not only that, he's come with a group of evil cohorts known as The Black Order. One in particular, **PROXIMA MIDNIGHT**, has been spotted in the greater metropolitan area. If you see her or anyone who may be associated with Thanos and his band of miscreants, please report them immediately to the nearest police officer or super hero.

September 11, 2013

Hey, I'm Luke Cage. I used to lead a team of Avengers, but now I'm looking to focus my time on my family. However, a guy doesn't just stop being a hero, so if you need any help, I've restarted my old business, "HEROES FOR HIRE." I'm strong, I've got unbreakable skin, and I've been at this for a while. My associates, all Avengers Academy graduates, and I are happy to help AND to negotiate, so please don't hesitate to call.

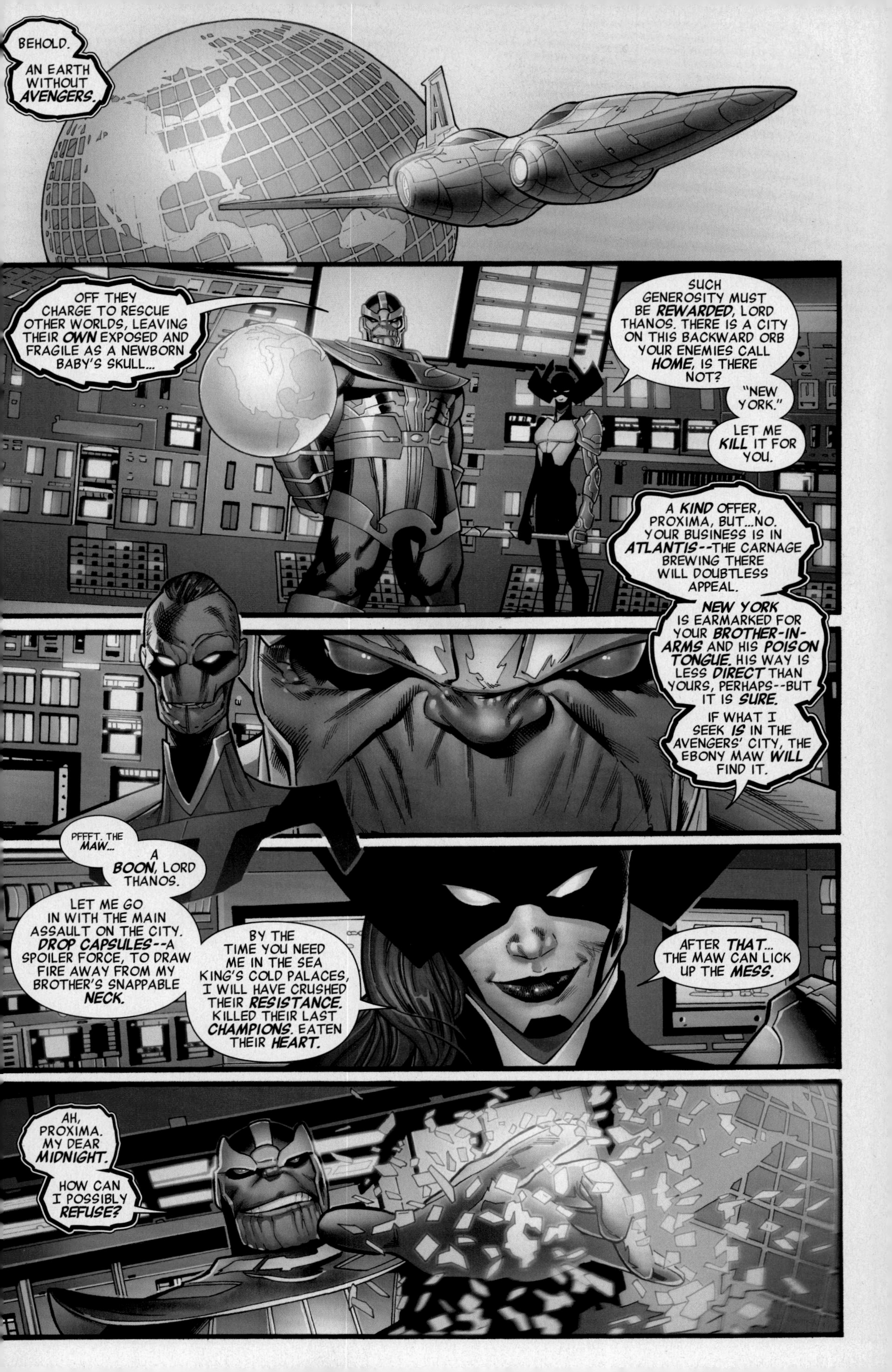
BEHOLD.
AN EARTH WITHOUT AVENGERS.
OFF THEY CHARGE TO RESCUE OTHER WORLDS, LEAVING THEIR OWN EXPOSED AND FRAGILE AS A NEWBORN BABY'S SKULL...
SUCH GENEROSITY MUST BE REWARDED, LORD THANOS. THERE IS A CITY ON THIS BACKWARD ORB YOUR ENEMIES CALL HOME, IS THERE NOT?
"NEW YORK."
LET ME KILL IT FOR YOU.
A KIND OFFER, PROXIMA, BUT...NO. YOUR BUSINESS IS IN ATLANTIS--THE CARNAGE BREWING THERE WILL DOUBTLESS APPEAL.
NEW YORK IS EARMARKED FOR YOUR BROTHER-IN-ARMS AND HIS POISON TONGUE. HIS WAY IS LESS DIRECT THAN YOURS, PERHAPS--BUT IT IS SURE.
IF WHAT I SEEK IS IN THE AVENGERS' CITY, THE EBONY MAW WILL FIND IT.
PFFFT. THE MAW...
A BOON, LORD THANOS.
LET ME GO IN WITH THE MAIN ASSAULT ON THE CITY. DROP CAPSULES--A SPOILER FORCE, TO DRAW FIRE AWAY FROM MY BROTHER'S SNAPPABLE NECK.
BY THE TIME YOU NEED ME IN THE SEA KING'S COLD PALACES, I WILL HAVE CRUSHED THEIR RESISTANCE. KILLED THEIR LAST CHAMPIONS. EATEN THEIR HEART.
AFTER THAT... THE MAW CAN LICK UP THE MESS.
AH, PROXIMA. MY DEAR MIDNIGHT.
HOW CAN I POSSIBLY REFUSE?

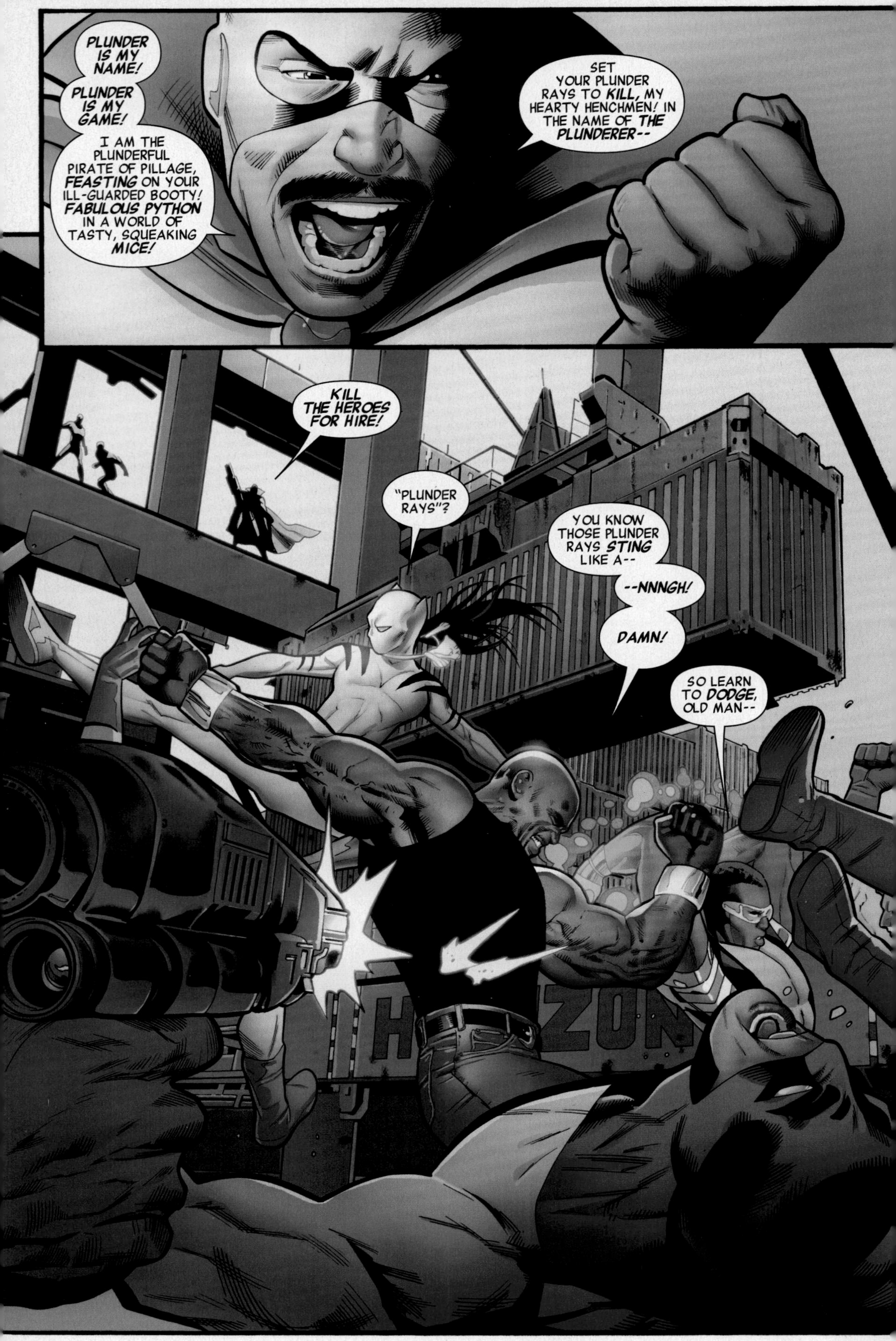
PLUNDER IS MY NAME!
PLUNDER IS MY GAME!
I AM THE PLUNDERFUL PIRATE OF PILLAGE, FEASTING ON YOUR ILL-GUARDED BOOTY! FABULOUS PYTHON IN A WORLD OF TASTY, SQUEAKING MICE!
SET YOUR PLUNDER RAYS TO KILL, MY HEARTY HENCHMEN! IN THE NAME OF THE PLUNDERER--
KILL THE HEROES FOR HIRE!
"PLUNDER RAYS"?
YOU KNOW THOSE PLUNDER RAYS STING LIKE A--
--NNNGH!
DAMN!
SO LEARN TO DODGE, OLD MAN--
HZON

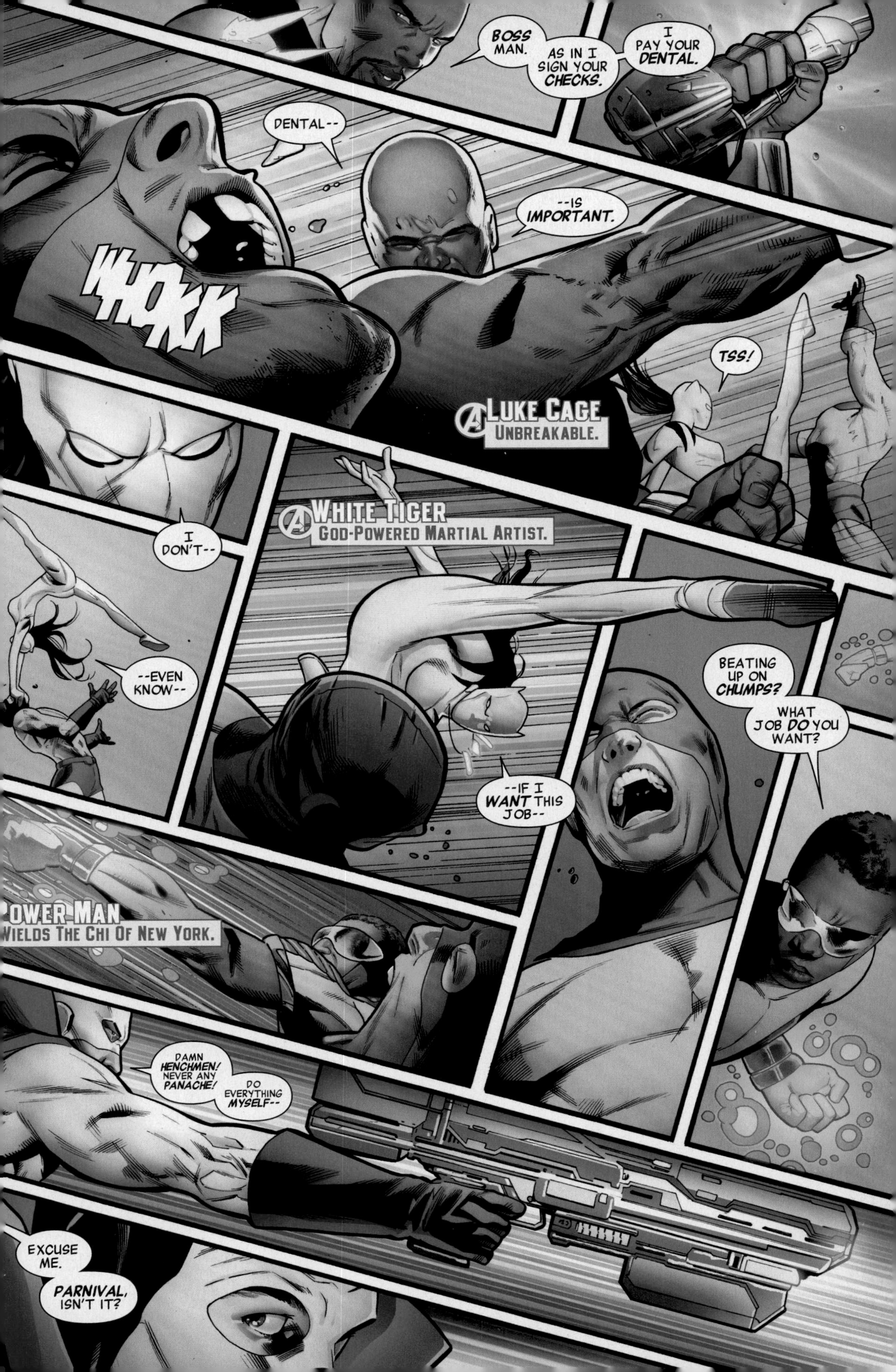
BOSS MAN.
AS IN I SIGN YOUR CHECKS.
I PAY YOUR DENTAL.
DENTAL--
--IS IMPORTANT.
WHOKK
TSS!
LUKE CAGE
UNBREAKABLE.
I DON'T--
--EVEN KNOW--
WHITE TIGER
GOD-POWERED MARTIAL ARTIST.
--IF I WANT THIS JOB--
BEATING UP ON CHUMPS?
WHAT JOB DO YOU WANT?
OWER MAN
WIELDS THE CHI OF NEW YORK.
DAMN HENCHMEN! NEVER ANY PANACHE!
DO EVERYTHING MYSELF--
EXCUSE ME.
PARNIVAL, ISN'T IT?

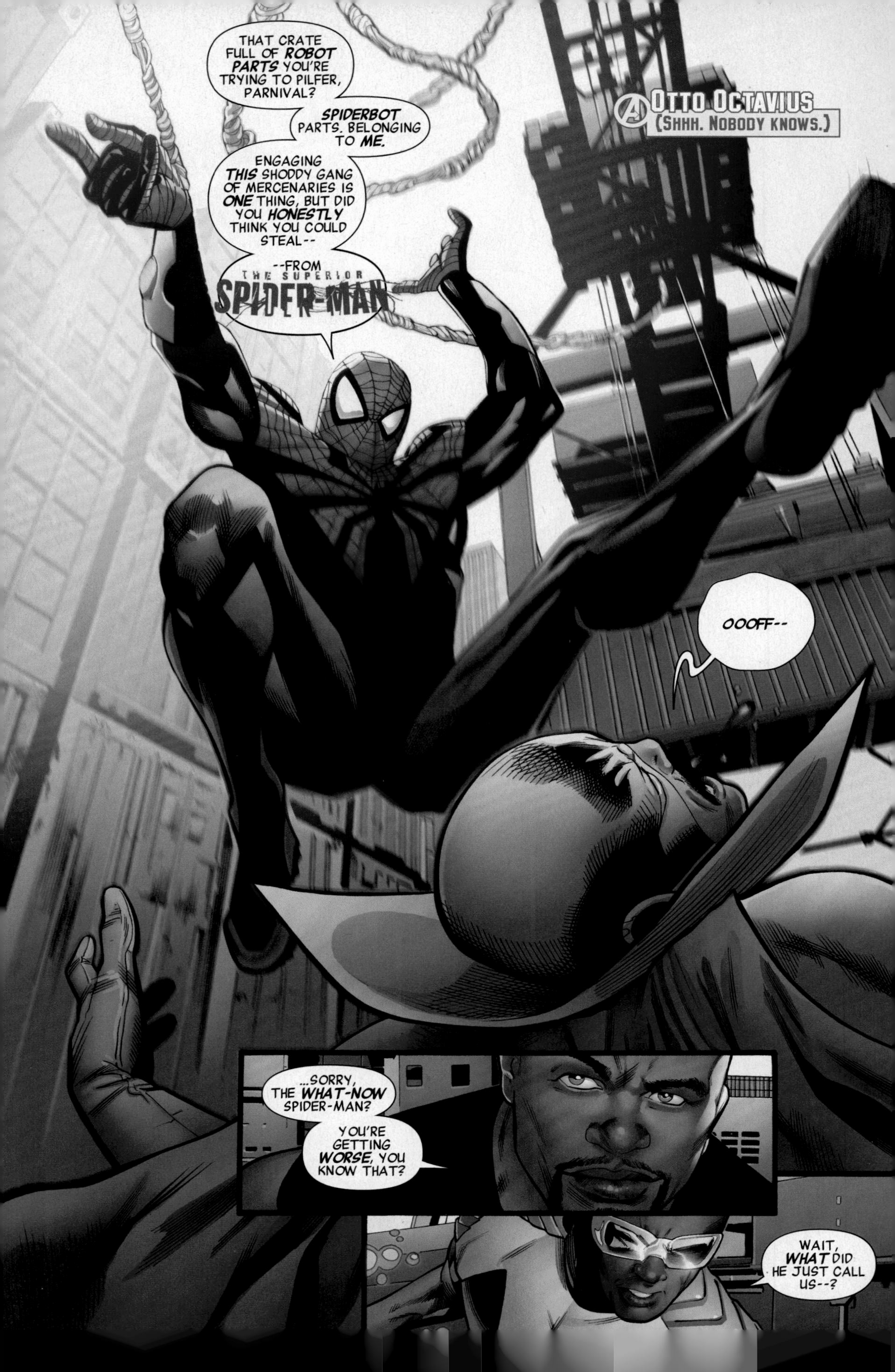
THAT CRATE FULL OF ROBOT PARTS YOU'RE TRYING TO PILFER, PARNIVAL?
SPIDERBOT PARTS. BELONGING TO ME.
ENGAGING THIS SHODDY GANG OF MERCENARIES IS ONE THING, BUT DID YOU HONESTLY THINK YOU COULD STEAL--
--FROM THE SUPERIOR SPIDER-MAN
OTTO OCTAVIUS
(SHHH. NOBODY KNOWS.)
OOOFF--
...SORRY, THE WHAT-NOW SPIDER-MAN?
YOU'RE GETTING WORSE, YOU KNOW THAT?
WAIT, WHAT DID HE JUST CALL US--?

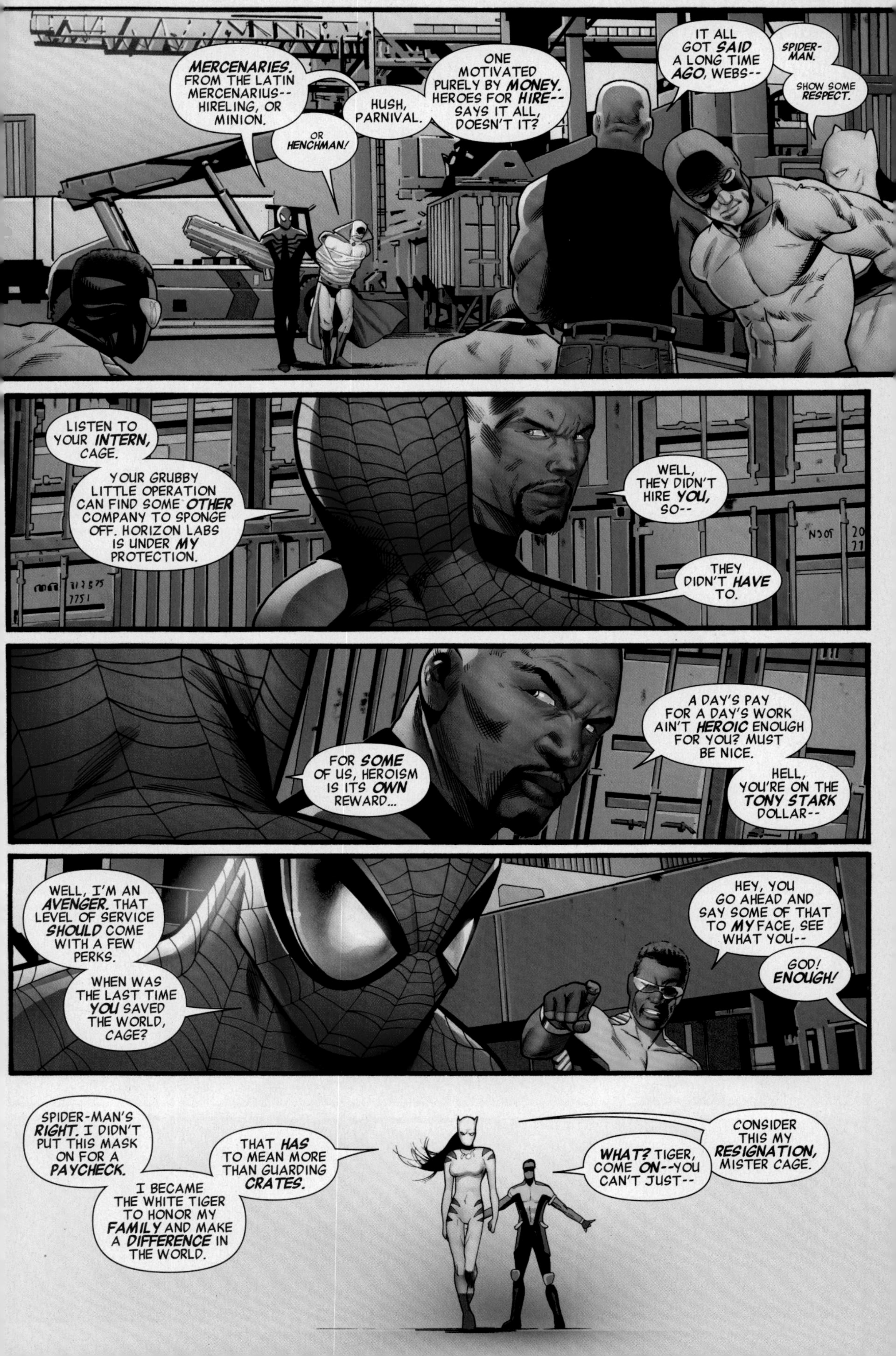
MERCENARIES. FROM THE LATIN MERCENARIUS-- HIRELING, OR MINION.
OR HENCHMAN!
HUSH, PARNIVAL.
ONE MOTIVATED PURELY BY MONEY. HEROES FOR HIRE-- SAYS IT ALL, DOESN'T IT?
IT ALL GOT SAID A LONG TIME AGO, WEBS--
SPIDER-MAN.
SHOW SOME RESPECT.
LISTEN TO YOUR INTERN, CAGE.
YOUR GRUBBY LITTLE OPERATION CAN FIND SOME OTHER COMPANY TO SPONGE OFF. HORIZON LABS IS UNDER MY PROTECTION.
WELL, THEY DIDN'T HIRE YOU, SO--
THEY DIDN'T HAVE TO.
FOR SOME OF US, HEROISM IS ITS OWN REWARD...
A DAY'S PAY FOR A DAY'S WORK AIN'T HEROIC ENOUGH FOR YOU? MUST BE NICE.
HELL, YOU'RE ON THE TONY STARK DOLLAR--
WELL, I'M AN AVENGER. THAT LEVEL OF SERVICE SHOULD COME WITH A FEW PERKS.
WHEN WAS THE LAST TIME YOU SAVED THE WORLD, CAGE?
HEY, YOU GO AHEAD AND SAY SOME OF THAT TO MY FACE, SEE WHAT YOU--
GOD! ENOUGH!
SPIDER-MAN'S RIGHT. I DIDN'T PUT THIS MASK ON FOR A PAYCHECK.
I BECAME THE WHITE TIGER TO HONOR MY FAMILY AND MAKE A DIFFERENCE IN THE WORLD.
THAT HAS TO MEAN MORE THAN GUARDING CRATES.
CONSIDER THIS MY RESIGNATION, MISTER CAGE.
WHAT? TIGER, COME ON--YOU CAN'T JUST--

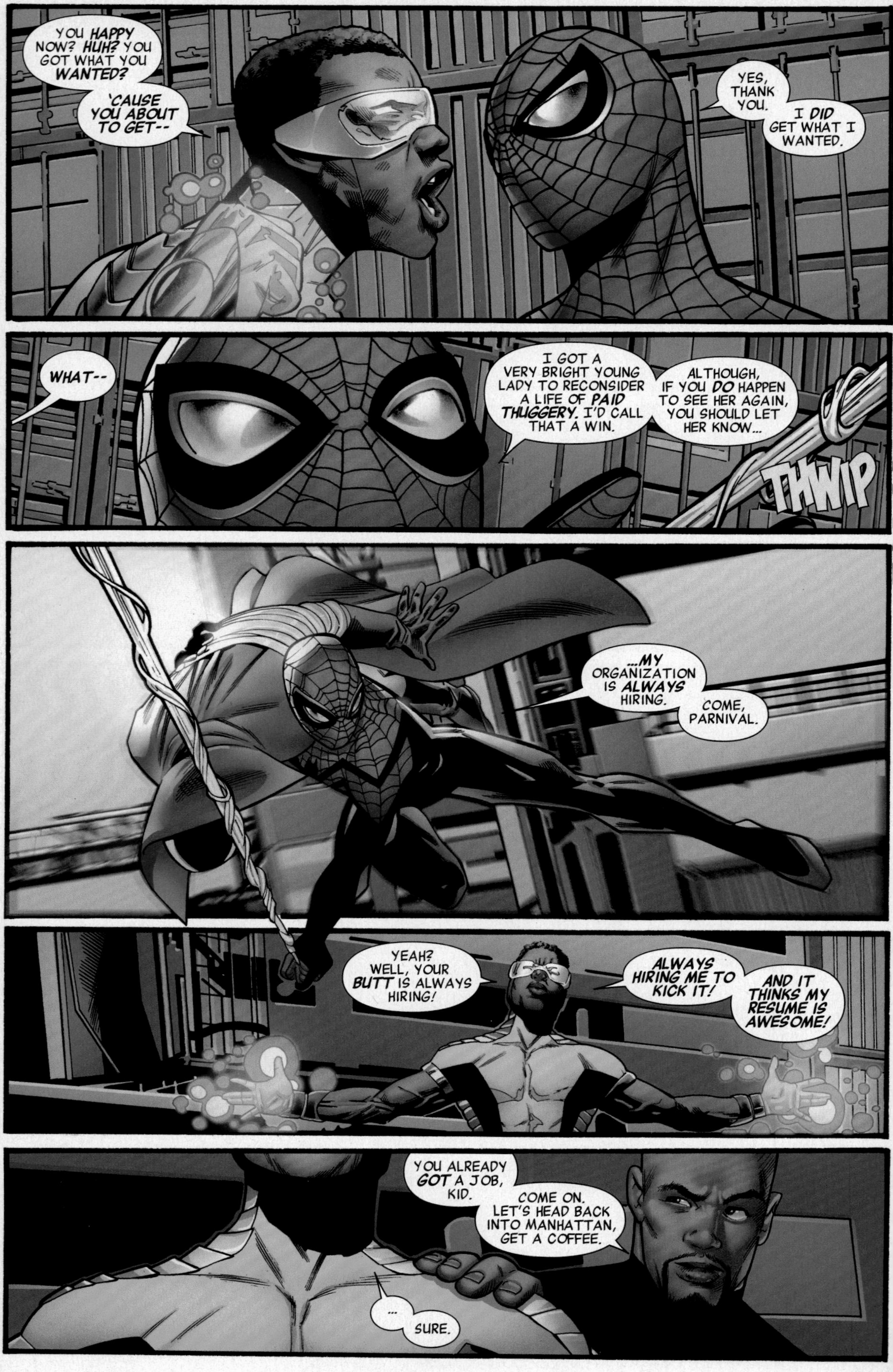
YOU HAPPY NOW? HUH? YOU GOT WHAT YOU WANTED?
'CAUSE YOU ABOUT TO GET--
YES, THANK YOU.
I DID GET WHAT I WANTED.
WHAT--
I GOT A VERY BRIGHT YOUNG LADY TO RECONSIDER A LIFE OF PAID THUGGERY. I'D CALL THAT A WIN.
ALTHOUGH, IF YOU DO HAPPEN TO SEE HER AGAIN, YOU SHOULD LET HER KNOW...
THWIP
...MY ORGANIZATION IS ALWAYS HIRING.
COME, PARNIVAL.
YEAH? WELL, YOUR BUTT IS ALWAYS HIRING!
ALWAYS HIRING ME TO KICK IT!
AND IT THINKS MY RESUME IS AWESOME!
YOU ALREADY GOT A JOB, KID.
COME ON. LET'S HEAD BACK INTO MANHATTAN, GET A COFFEE.
...
SURE.

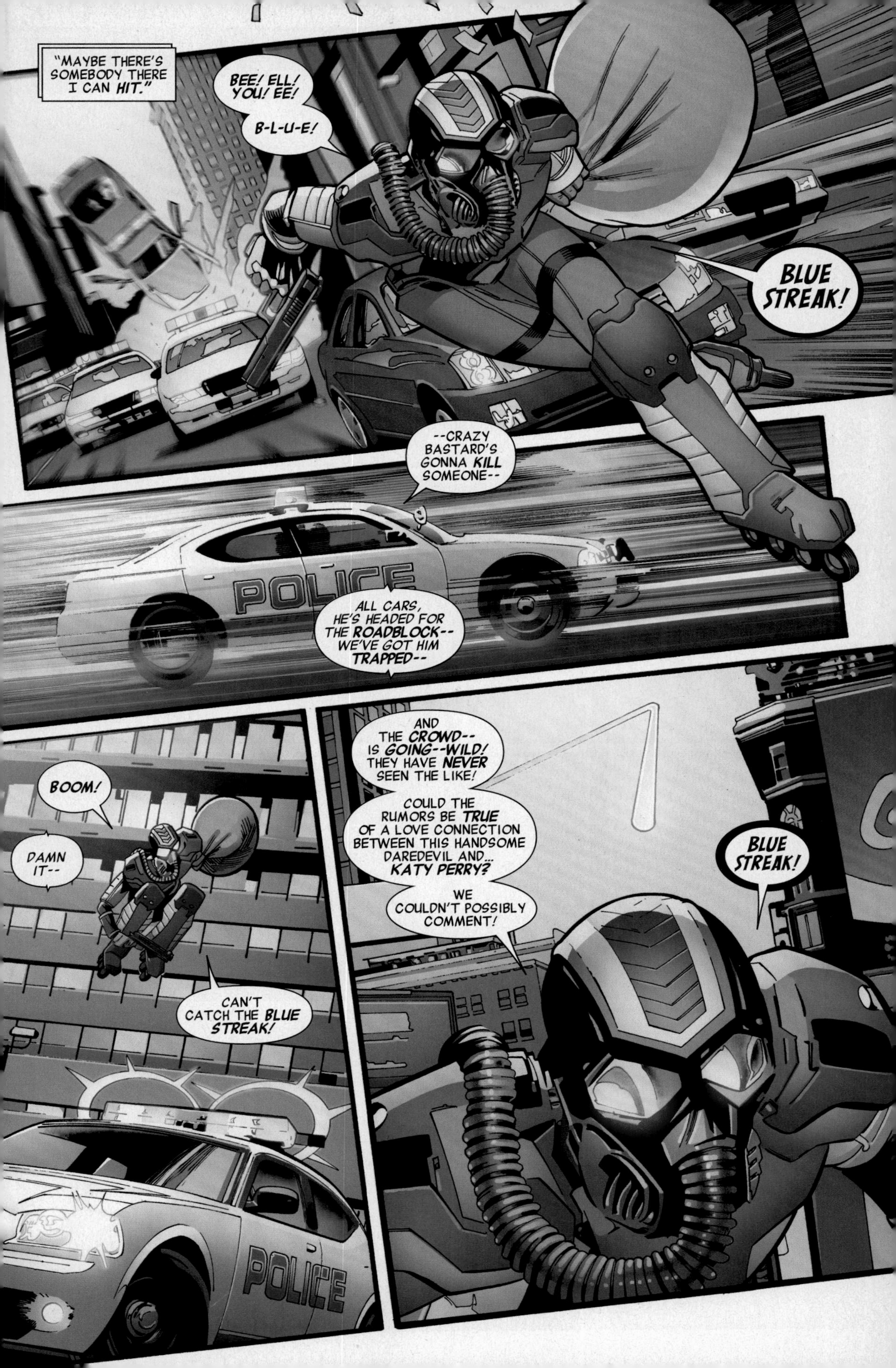
"MAYBE THERE'S SOMEBODY THERE I CAN HIT."
BEE! ELL! YOU! EE!
B-L-U-E!
BLUE STREAK!
--CRAZY BASTARD'S GONNA KILL SOMEONE--
POLICE
ALL CARS, HE'S HEADED FOR THE ROADBLOCK-- WE'VE GOT HIM TRAPPED--
BOOM!
DAMN IT--
CAN'T CATCH THE BLUE STREAK!
POLICE
AND THE CROWD-- IS GOING--WILD! THEY HAVE NEVER SEEN THE LIKE!
COULD THE RUMORS BE TRUE OF A LOVE CONNECTION BETWEEN THIS HANDSOME DAREDEVIL AND... KATY PERRY?
WE COULDN'T POSSIBLY COMMENT!
BLUE STREAK!

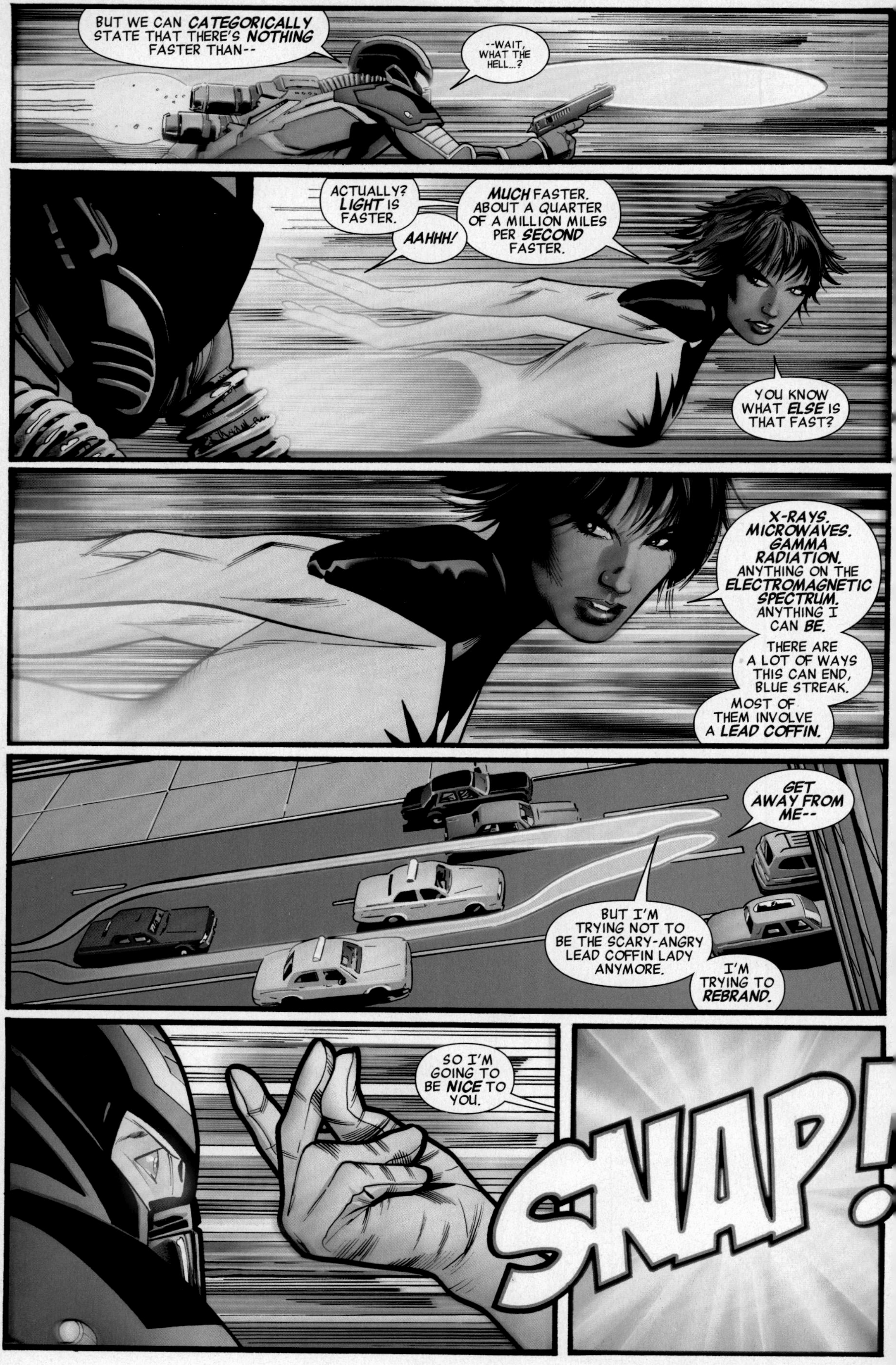
BUT WE CAN CATEGORICALLY STATE THAT THERE'S NOTHING FASTER THAN--
--WAIT, WHAT THE HELL...?
ACTUALLY? LIGHT IS FASTER.
AAHHH!
MUCH FASTER. ABOUT A QUARTER OF A MILLION MILES PER SECOND FASTER.
YOU KNOW WHAT ELSE IS THAT FAST?
X-RAYS. MICROWAVES. GAMMA RADIATION. ANYTHING ON THE ELECTROMAGNETIC SPECTRUM. ANYTHING I CAN BE.
THERE ARE A LOT OF WAYS THIS CAN END, BLUE STREAK.
MOST OF THEM INVOLVE A LEAD COFFIN.
GET AWAY FROM ME--
BUT I'M TRYING NOT TO BE THE SCARY-ANGRY LEAD COFFIN LADY ANYMORE.
I'M TRYING TO REBRAND.
SO I'M GOING TO BE NICE TO YOU.
SNAP!

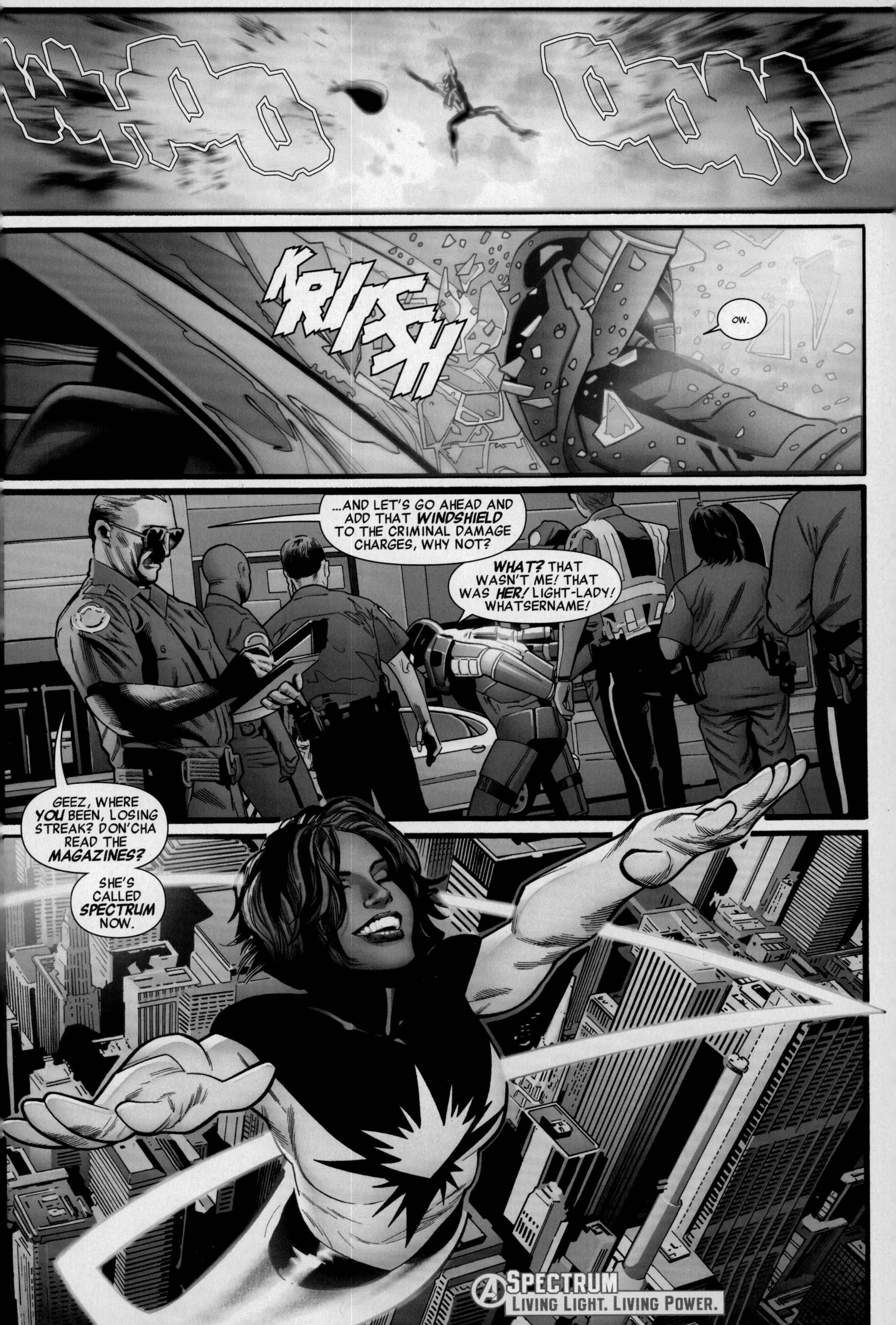
WHOOOM
KRISH
OW.
...AND LET'S GO AHEAD AND ADD THAT WINDSHIELD TO THE CRIMINAL DAMAGE CHARGES, WHY NOT?
WHAT? THAT WASN'T ME! THAT WAS HER! LIGHT-LADY! WHATSERNAME!
GEEZ, WHERE YOU BEEN, LOSING STREAK? DON'CHA READ THE MAGAZINES?
SHE'S CALLED SPECTRUM NOW.
SPECTRUM
LIVING LIGHT. LIVING POWER.

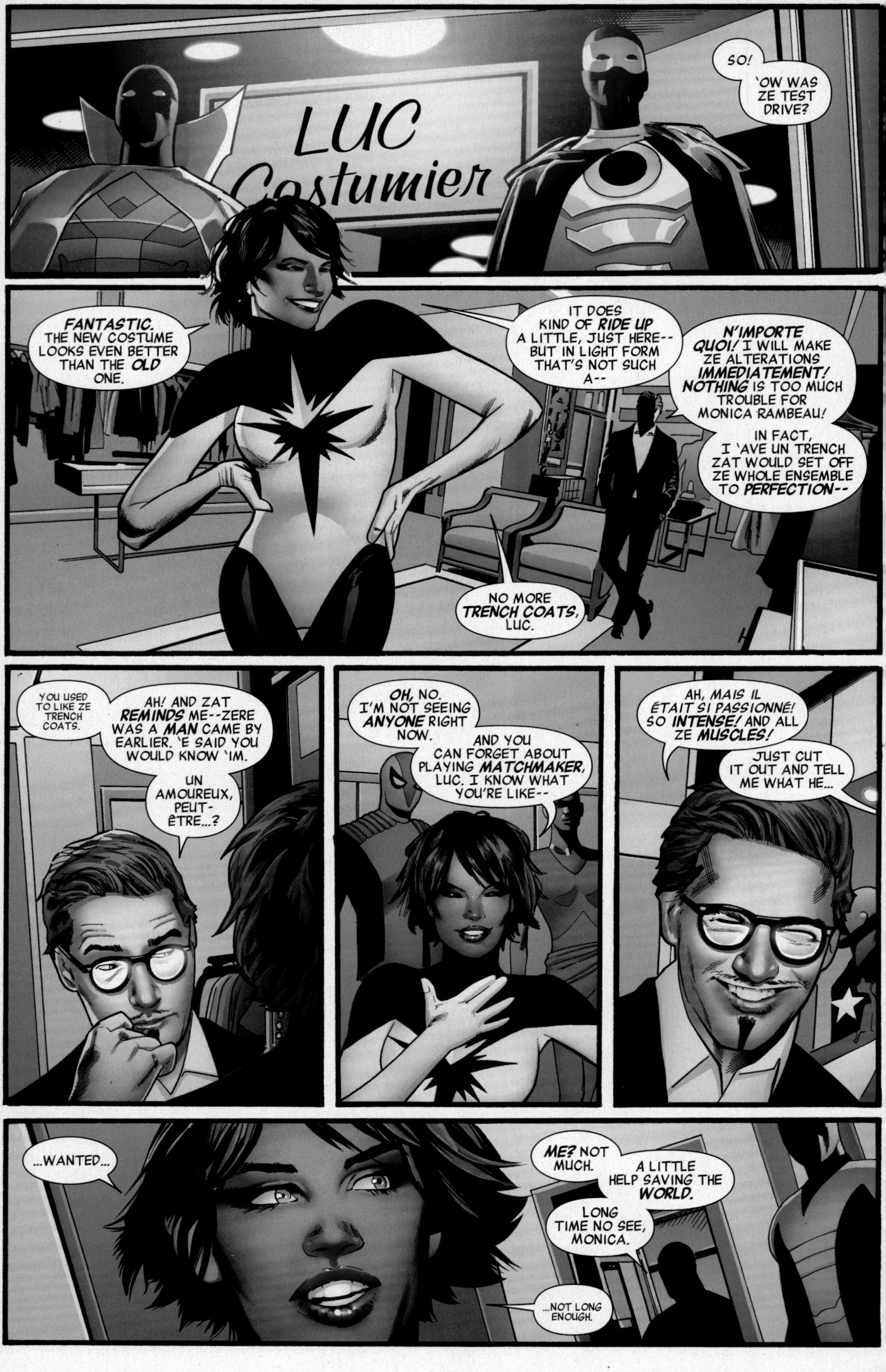

LUC Costumier
SO!
'OW WAS ZE TEST DRIVE?
FANTASTIC. THE NEW COSTUME LOOKS EVEN BETTER THAN THE OLD ONE.
IT DOES KIND OF RIDE UP A LITTLE, JUST HERE-- BUT IN LIGHT FORM THAT'S NOT SUCH A--
N'IMPORTE QUOI! I WILL MAKE ZE ALTERATIONS IMMEDIATEMENT! NOTHING IS TOO MUCH TROUBLE FOR MONICA RAMBEAU!
IN FACT, I 'AVE UN TRENCH ZAT WOULD SET OFF ZE WHOLE ENSEMBLE TO PERFECTION--
NO MORE TRENCH COATS, LUC.
YOU USED TO LIKE ZE TRENCH COATS.
AH! AND ZAT REMINDS ME--ZERE WAS A MAN CAME BY EARLIER. 'E SAID YOU WOULD KNOW 'IM.
UN AMOUREUX, PEUT-ÊTRE...?
OH, NO. I'M NOT SEEING ANYONE RIGHT NOW.
AND YOU CAN FORGET ABOUT PLAYING MATCHMAKER, LUC. I KNOW WHAT YOU'RE LIKE--
AH, MAIS IL ÉTAIT SI PASSIONNÉ! SO INTENSE! AND ALL ZE MUSCLES!
JUST CUT IT OUT AND TELL ME WHAT HE...
...WANTED...
ME? NOT MUCH.
A LITTLE HELP SAVING THE WORLD.
LONG TIME NO SEE, MONICA.
...NOT LONG ENOUGH.

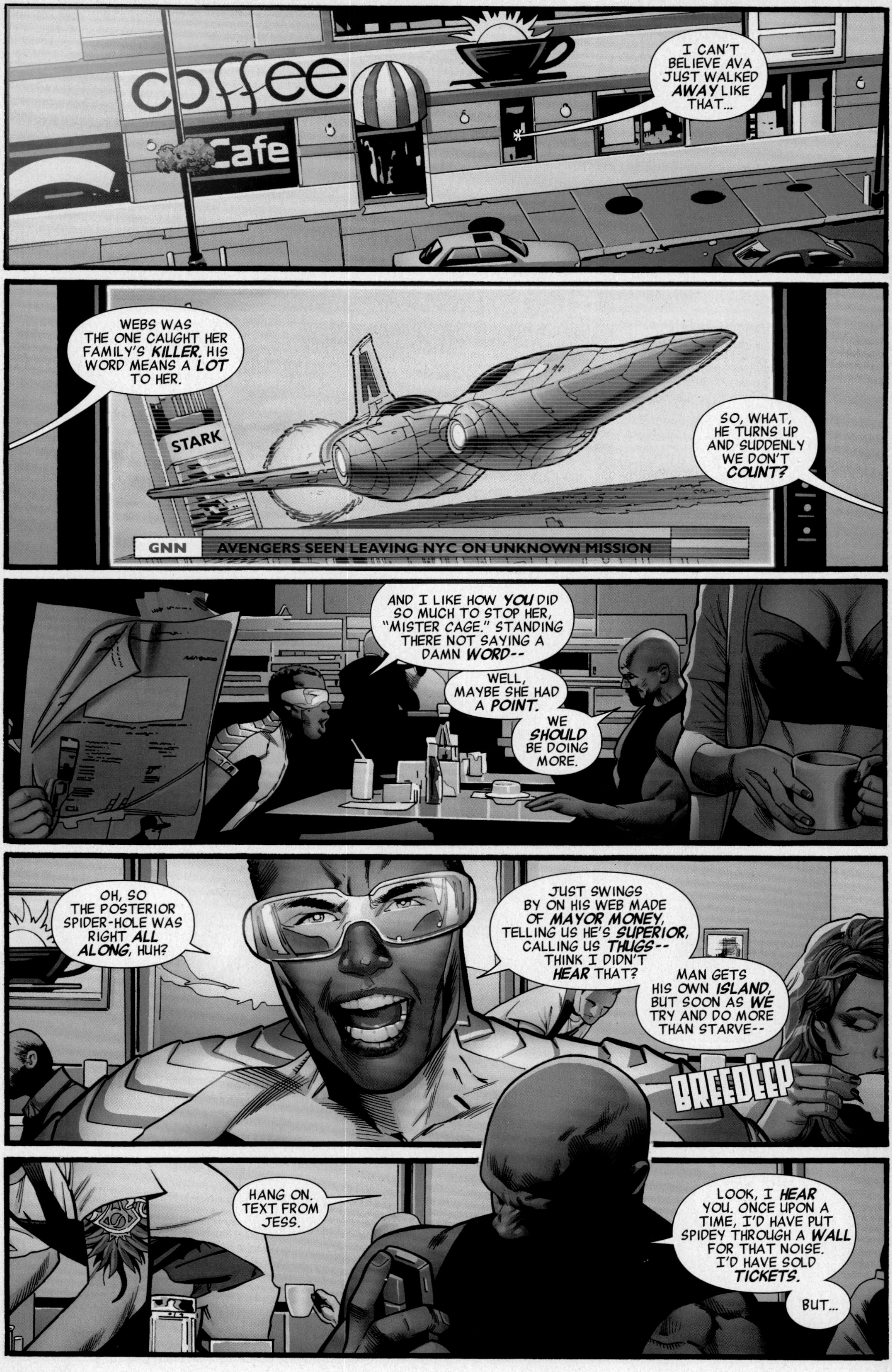
coffee
Cafe
I CAN'T BELIEVE AVA JUST WALKED AWAY LIKE THAT...
WEBS WAS THE ONE CAUGHT HER FAMILY'S KILLER. HIS WORD MEANS A LOT TO HER.
STARK
SO, WHAT, HE TURNS UP AND SUDDENLY WE DON'T COUNT?
GNN
AVENGERS SEEN LEAVING NYC ON UNKNOWN MISSION
AND I LIKE HOW YOU DID SO MUCH TO STOP HER, "MISTER CAGE." STANDING THERE NOT SAYING A DAMN WORD--
WELL, MAYBE SHE HAD A POINT.
WE SHOULD BE DOING MORE.
OH, SO THE POSTERIOR SPIDER-HOLE WAS RIGHT ALL ALONG, HUH?
JUST SWINGS BY ON HIS WEB MADE OF MAYOR MONEY, TELLING US HE'S SUPERIOR, CALLING US THUGS-- THINK I DIDN'T HEAR THAT?
MAN GETS HIS OWN ISLAND, BUT SOON AS WE TRY AND DO MORE THAN STARVE--
BREEDEEP
HANG ON. TEXT FROM JESS.
LOOK, I HEAR YOU. ONCE UPON A TIME, I'D HAVE PUT SPIDEY THROUGH A WALL FOR THAT NOISE. I'D HAVE SOLD TICKETS.
BUT...

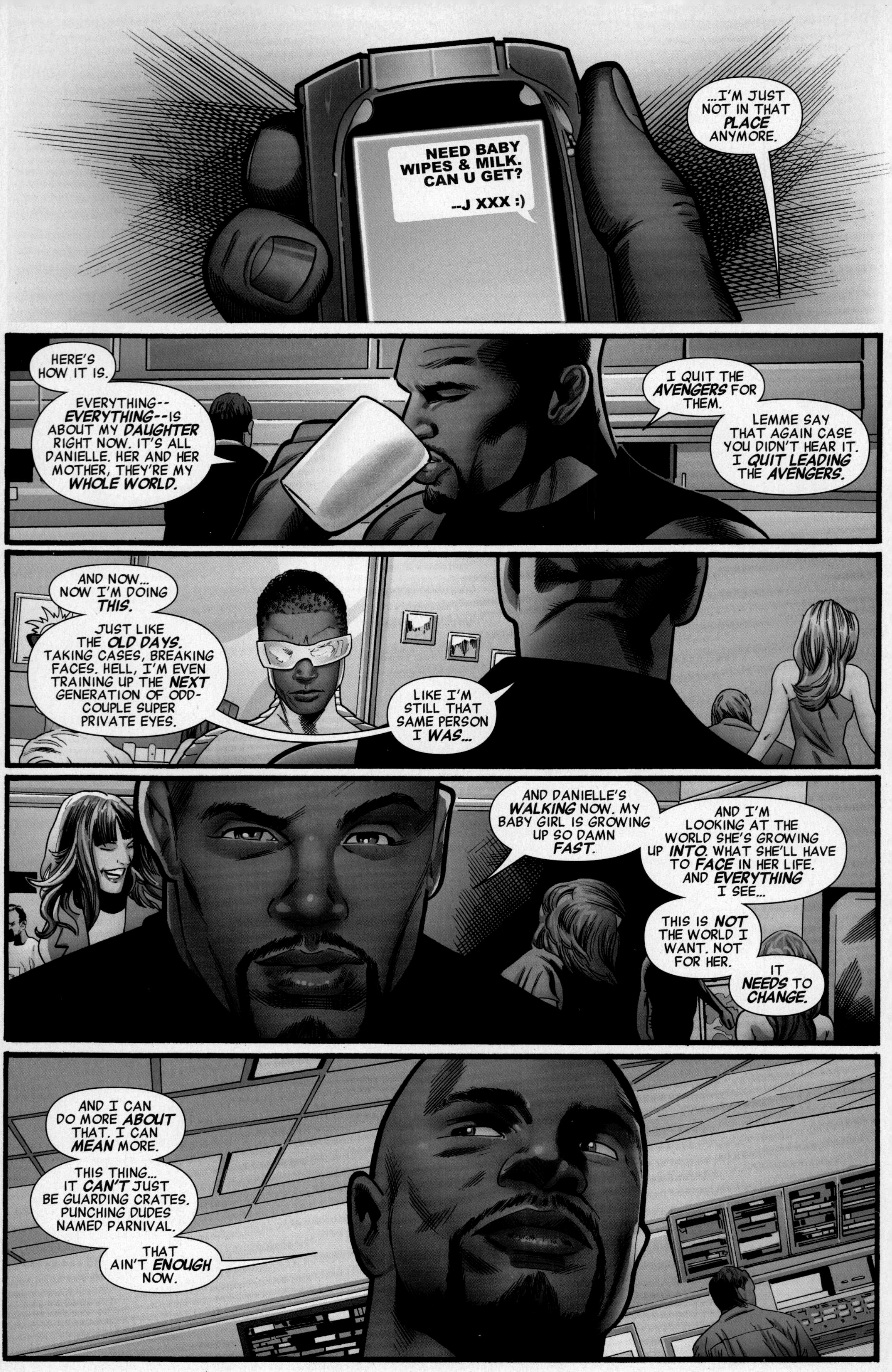
NEED BABY WIPES & MILK. CAN U GET? --J XXX :)
...I'M JUST NOT IN THAT PLACE ANYMORE.
HERE'S HOW IT IS.
EVERYTHING-- EVERYTHING--IS ABOUT MY DAUGHTER RIGHT NOW. IT'S ALL DANIELLE. HER AND HER MOTHER, THEY'RE MY WHOLE WORLD.
I QUIT THE AVENGERS FOR THEM.
LEMME SAY THAT AGAIN CASE YOU DIDN'T HEAR IT. I QUIT LEADING THE AVENGERS.
AND NOW... NOW I'M DOING THIS.
JUST LIKE THE OLD DAYS. TAKING CASES, BREAKING FACES. HELL, I'M EVEN TRAINING UP THE NEXT GENERATION OF ODD-COUPLE SUPER PRIVATE EYES.
LIKE I'M STILL THAT SAME PERSON I WAS...
AND DANIELLE'S WALKING NOW. MY BABY GIRL IS GROWING UP SO DAMN FAST.
AND I'M LOOKING AT THE WORLD SHE'S GROWING UP INTO. WHAT SHE'LL HAVE TO FACE IN HER LIFE. AND EVERYTHING I SEE...
THIS IS NOT THE WORLD I WANT. NOT FOR HER.
IT NEEDS TO CHANGE.
AND I CAN DO MORE ABOUT THAT. I CAN MEAN MORE.
THIS THING... IT CAN'T JUST BE GUARDING CRATES. PUNCHING DUDES NAMED PARNIVAL.
THAT AIN'T ENOUGH NOW.

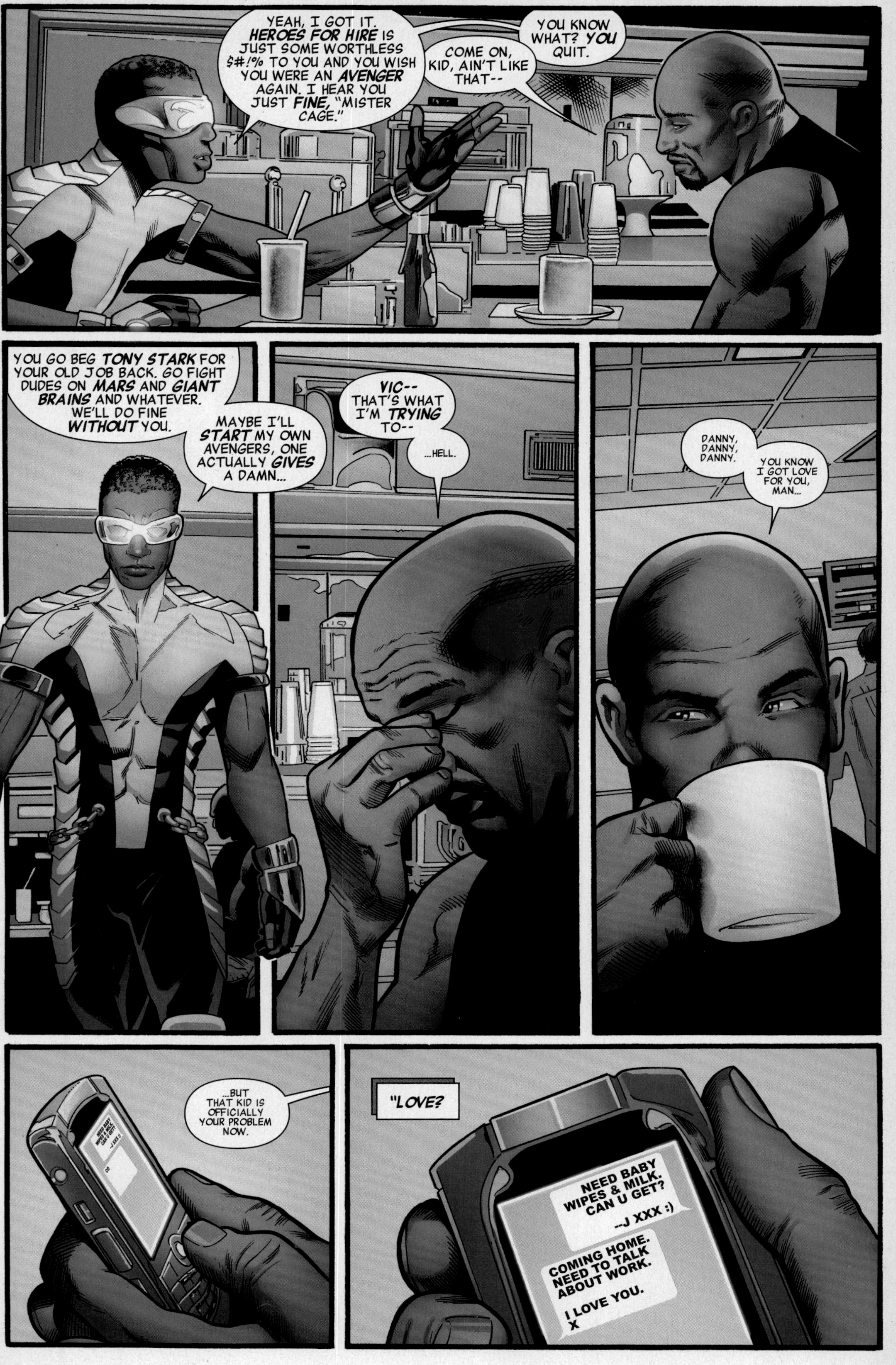
YEAH, I GOT IT. HEROES FOR HIRE IS JUST SOME WORTHLESS $#!% TO YOU AND YOU WISH YOU WERE AN AVENGER AGAIN. I HEAR YOU JUST FINE, "MISTER CAGE."
COME ON, KID, AIN'T LIKE THAT--
YOU KNOW WHAT? YOU QUIT.
YOU GO BEG TONY STARK FOR YOUR OLD JOB BACK. GO FIGHT DUDES ON MARS AND GIANT BRAINS AND WHATEVER. WE'LL DO FINE WITHOUT YOU.
MAYBE I'LL START MY OWN AVENGERS, ONE ACTUALLY GIVES A DAMN...
VIC-- THAT'S WHAT I'M TRYING TO--
...HELL.
DANNY, DANNY, DANNY.
YOU KNOW I GOT LOVE FOR YOU, MAN...
...BUT THAT KID IS OFFICIALLY YOUR PROBLEM NOW.
"LOVE?
NEED BABY WIPES & MILK. CAN U GET?
--J XXX :)
COMING HOME. NEED TO TALK ABOUT WORK.
I LOVE YOU.
X

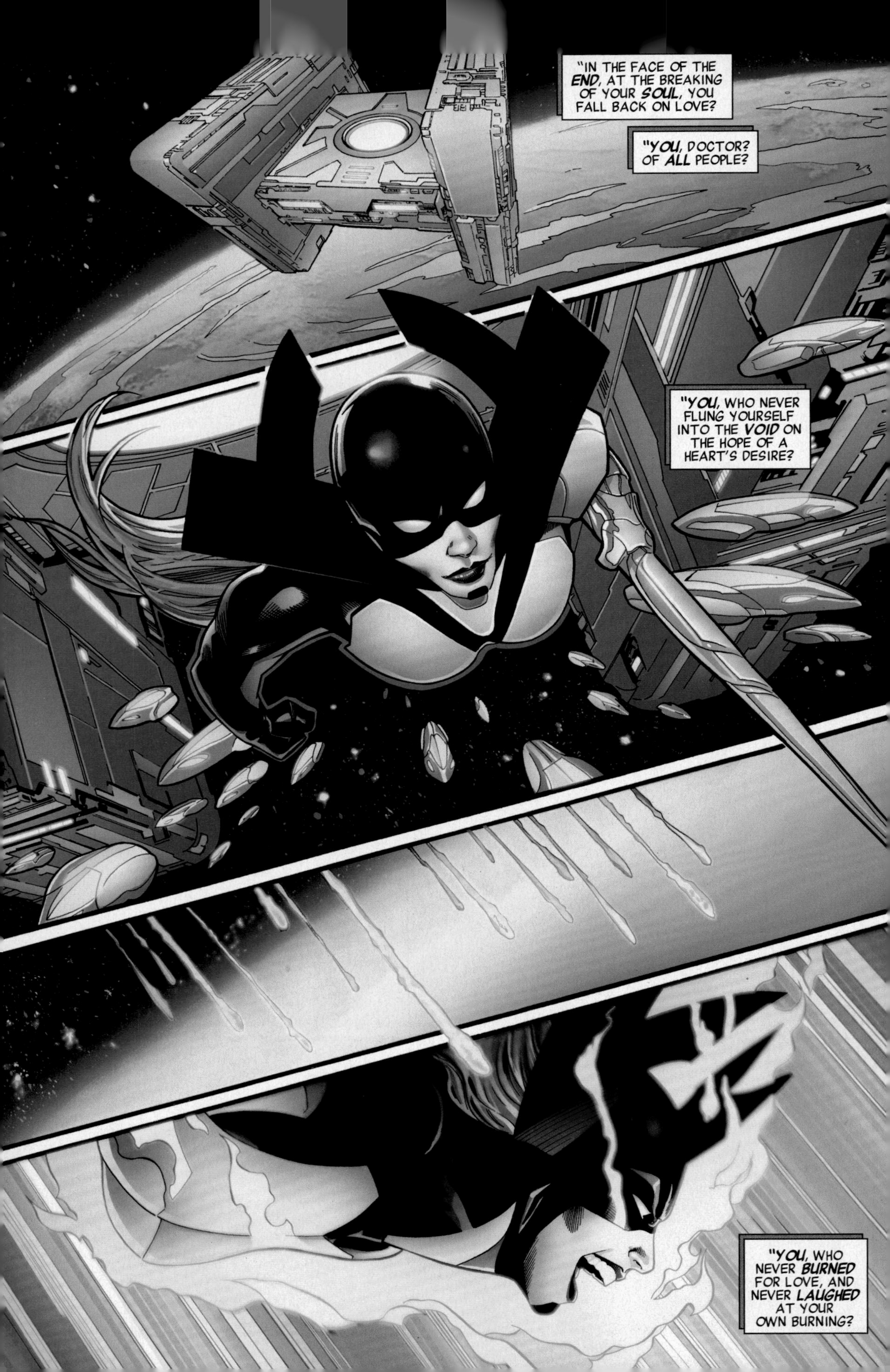
"IN THE FACE OF THE END, AT THE BREAKING OF YOUR SOUL, YOU FALL BACK ON LOVE?
"YOU, DOCTOR? OF ALL PEOPLE?
"YOU, WHO NEVER FLUNG YOURSELF INTO THE VOID ON THE HOPE OF A HEART'S DESIRE?
"YOU, WHO NEVER BURNED FOR LOVE, AND NEVER LAUGHED AT YOUR OWN BURNING?

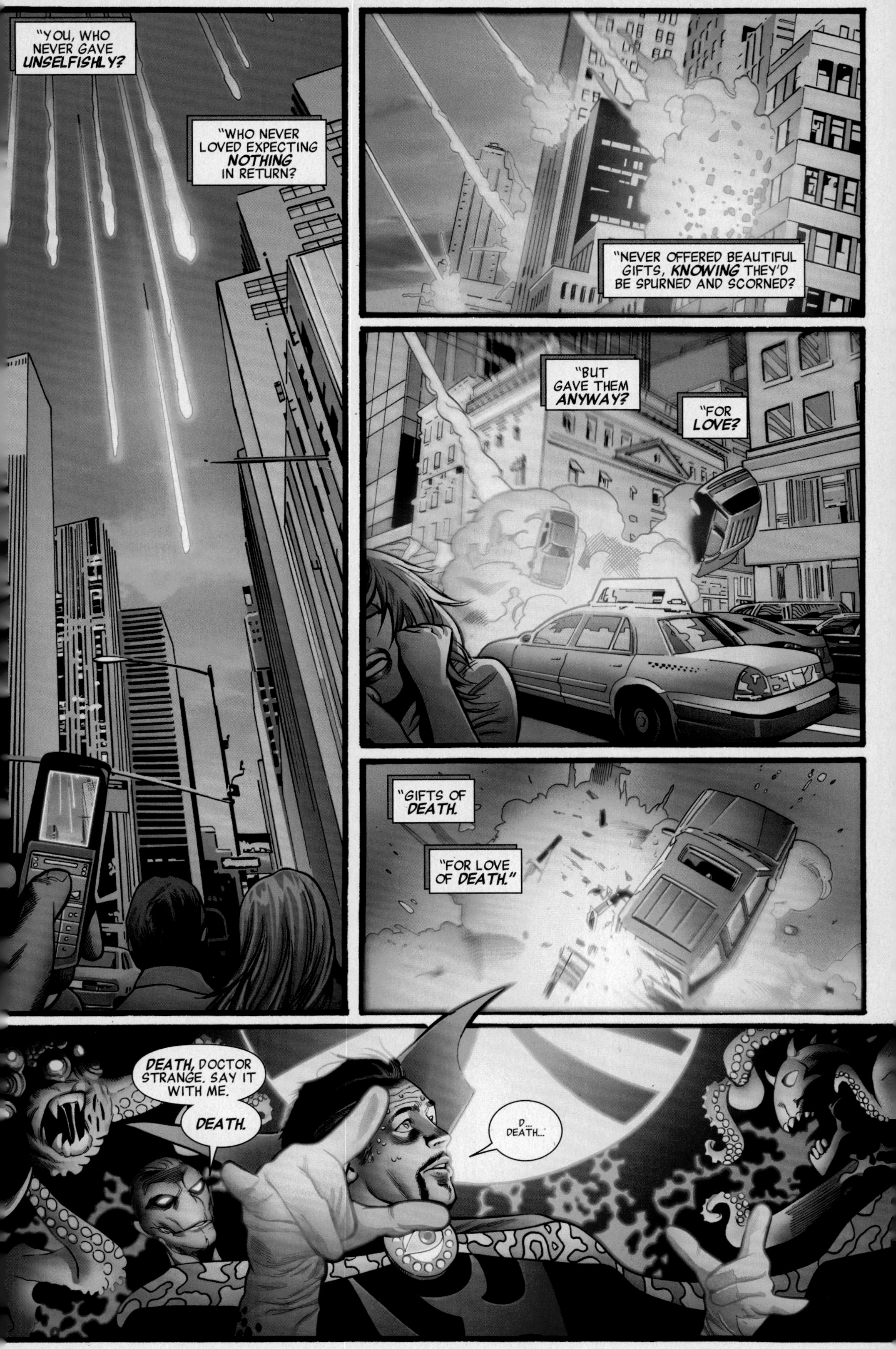
"YOU, WHO NEVER GAVE UNSELFISHLY?
"WHO NEVER LOVED EXPECTING NOTHING IN RETURN?
"NEVER OFFERED BEAUTIFUL GIFTS, KNOWING THEY'D BE SPURNED AND SCORNED?
"BUT GAVE THEM ANYWAY?
"FOR LOVE?
"GIFTS OF DEATH.
"FOR LOVE OF DEATH."
DEATH, DOCTOR STRANGE. SAY IT WITH ME.
DEATH.
D... DEATH...

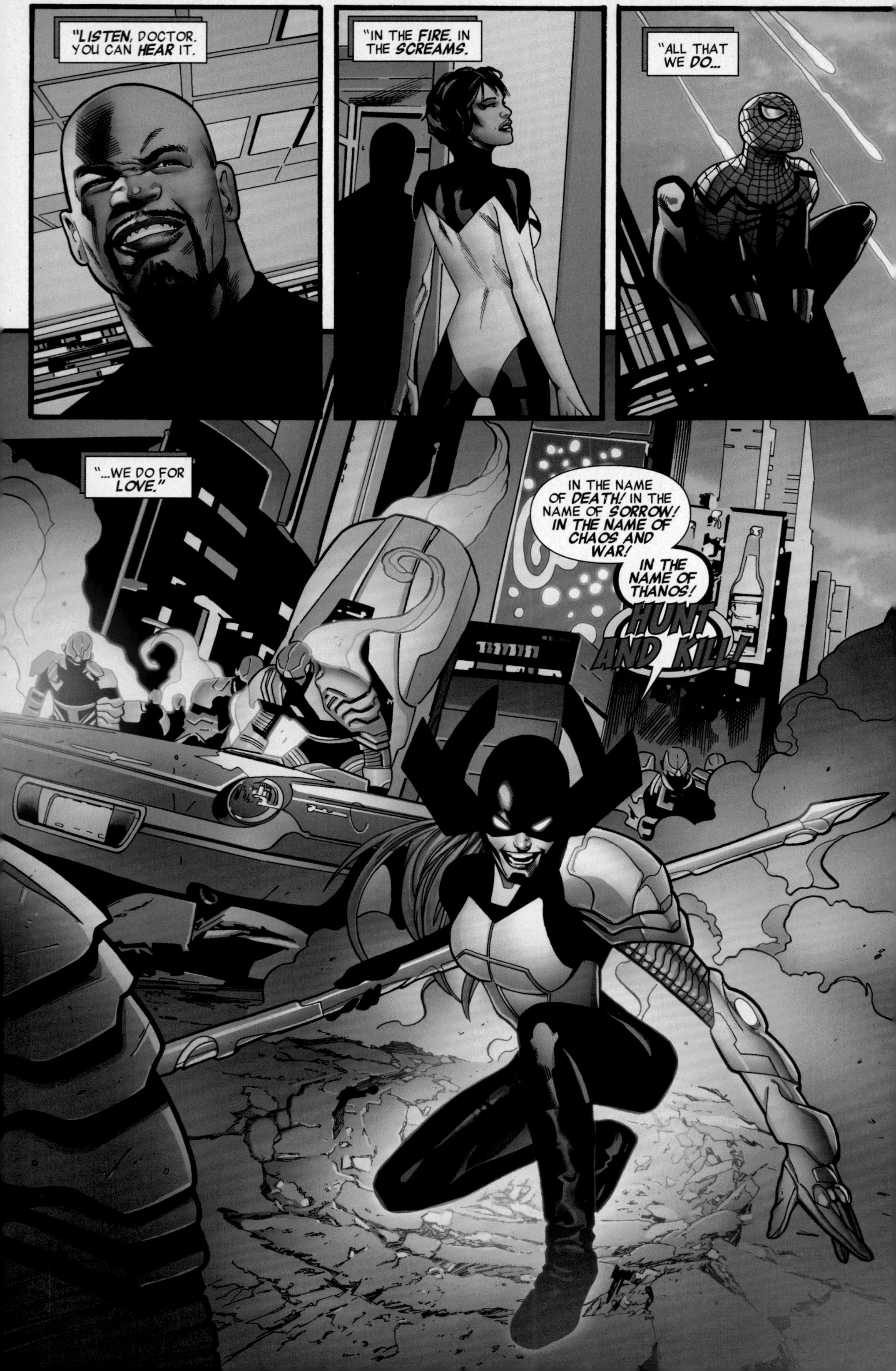
"LISTEN, DOCTOR. YOU CAN HEAR IT.
"IN THE FIRE. IN THE SCREAMS.
"ALL THAT WE DO...
"...WE DO FOR LOVE."
IN THE NAME OF DEATH! IN THE NAME OF SORROW! IN THE NAME OF CHAOS AND WAR!
IN THE NAME OF THANOS! HUNT AND KILL!

...WAS THAT AN EXPLOSION?

EXPLOSIONS-- PLURAL. A COUPLE OF BLOCKS AWAY, TIMES SQUARE OR THEREABOUTS.

PEOPLE ARE GOING TO NEED HELP.

COMING?

WE HAVE OTHER PRIORITIES--

WRONG ANSWER. I DON'T HAVE TIME FOR YOUR ONE-TRACK MIND RIGHT NOW.

IF YOU WANT MY HELP WITH YOUR "PRIORITIES"--YOU HELP ME WITH THIS.

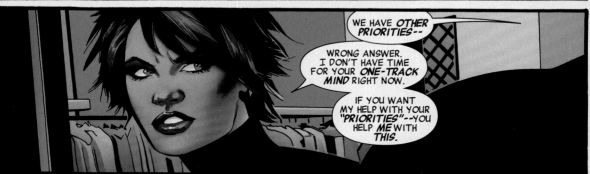

IT'S NOT THAT SIMPLE. I CAN'T BE SEEN TO BE IN-COUNTRY RIGHT NOW.

IF THEY FIND OUT I'M HERE--

OH, YOU NEED A SECRET IDENTITY?

YOU'RE IN A COSTUME SHOP, GENIUS.

SUIT UP.

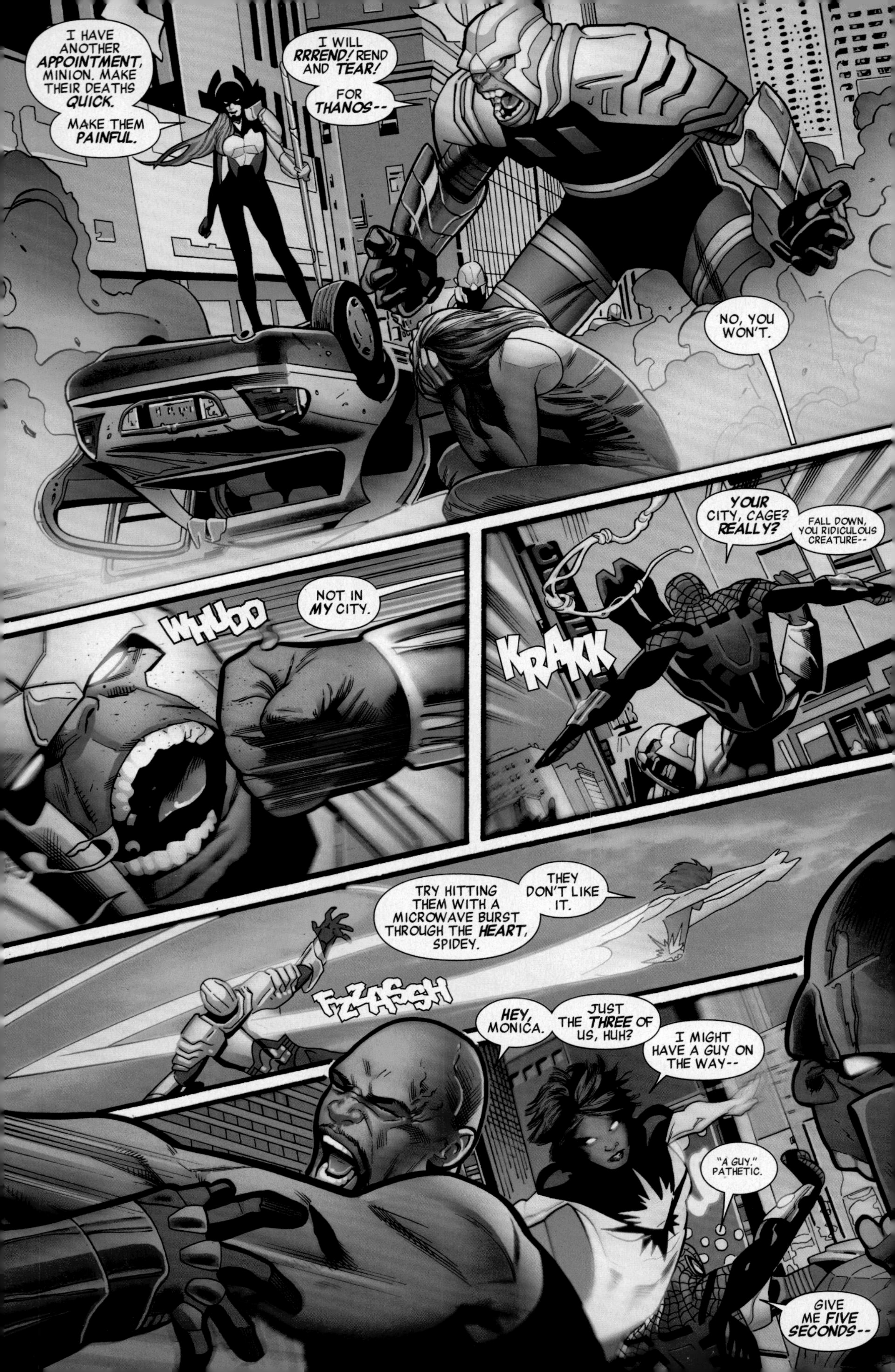

I HAVE ANOTHER APPOINTMENT, MINION. MAKE THEIR DEATHS QUICK.
MAKE THEM PAINFUL.
I WILL RRREND! REND AND TEAR!
FOR THANOS--
NO, YOU WON'T.
WHUDD
NOT IN MY CITY.
YOUR CITY, CAGE? REALLY?
FALL DOWN, YOU RIDICULOUS CREATURE--
KRAKK
THEY DON'T LIKE IT.
TRY HITTING THEM WITH A MICROWAVE BURST THROUGH THE HEART, SPIDEY.
FZZASSH
HEY, MONICA.
JUST THE THREE OF US, HUH?
I MIGHT HAVE A GUY ON THE WAY--
"A GUY." PATHETIC.
GIVE ME FIVE SECONDS--

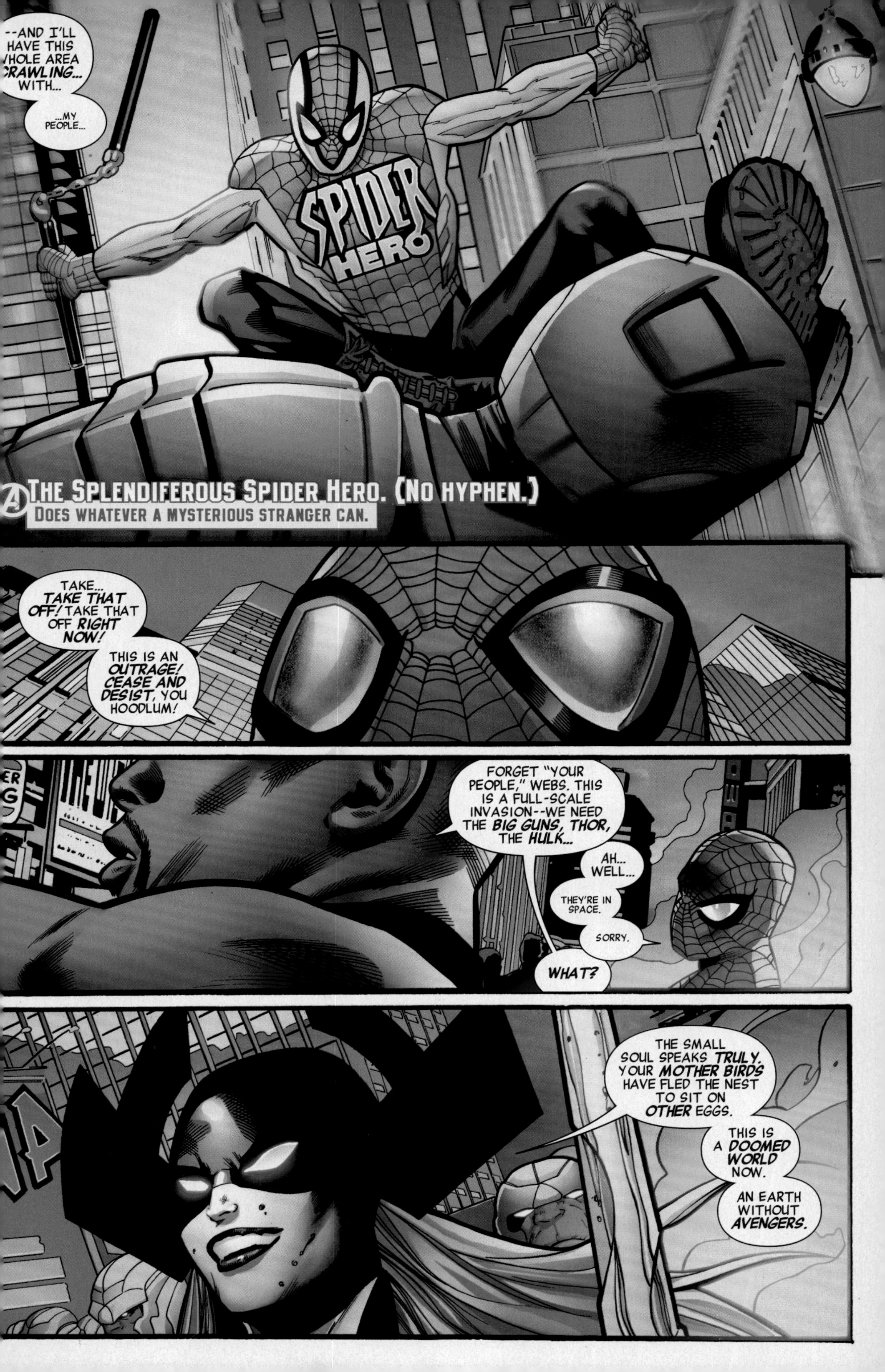
--AND I'LL HAVE THIS WHOLE AREA CRAWLING... WITH...
...MY PEOPLE...
THE SPLENDIFEROUS SPIDER HERO. (NO HYPHEN.)
DOES WHATEVER A MYSTERIOUS STRANGER CAN.
SPIDER HERO
TAKE... TAKE THAT OFF! TAKE THAT OFF RIGHT NOW!
THIS IS AN OUTRAGE! CEASE AND DESIST, YOU HOODLUM!
FORGET "YOUR PEOPLE," WEBS. THIS IS A FULL-SCALE INVASION--WE NEED THE BIG GUNS, THOR, THE HULK...
AH... WELL...
THEY'RE IN SPACE.
SORRY.
WHAT?
THE SMALL SOUL SPEAKS TRULY. YOUR MOTHER BIRDS HAVE FLED THE NEST TO SIT ON OTHER EGGS.
THIS IS A DOOMED WORLD NOW.
AN EARTH WITHOUT AVENGERS.

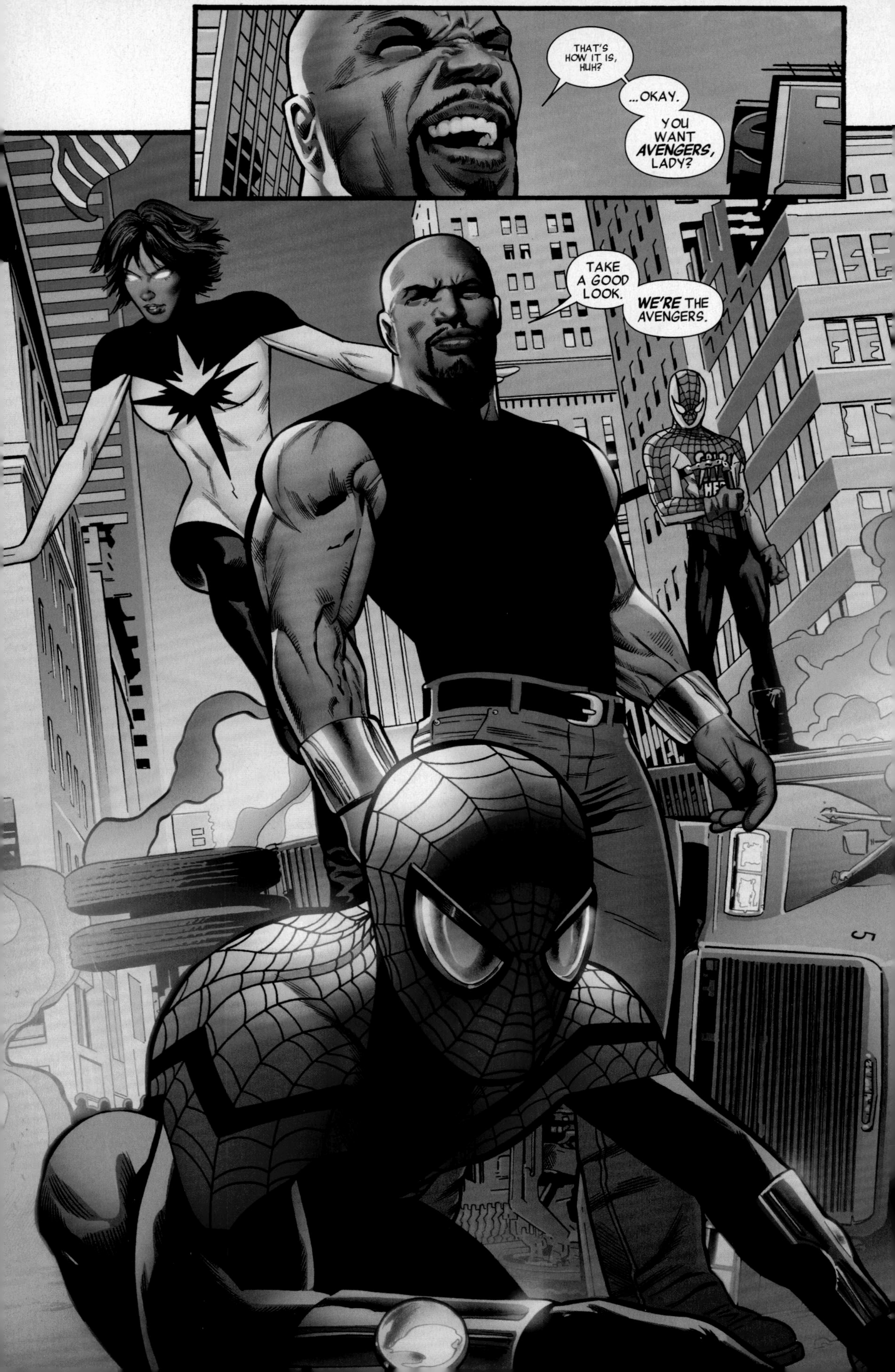
THAT'S HOW IT IS, HUH?
...OKAY.
YOU WANT AVENGERS, LADY?
TAKE A GOOD LOOK.
WE'RE THE AVENGERS.

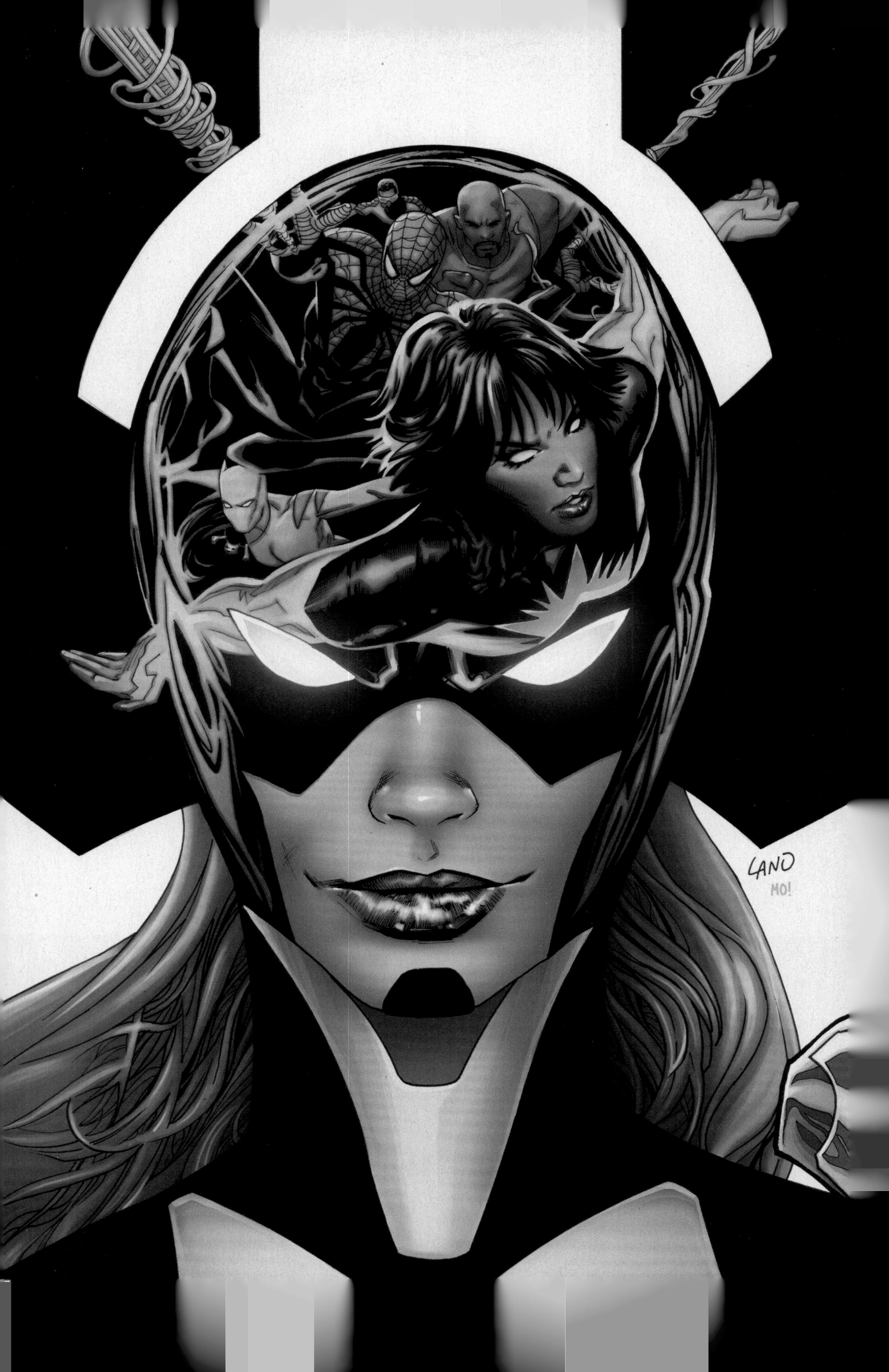
LANO
MO!

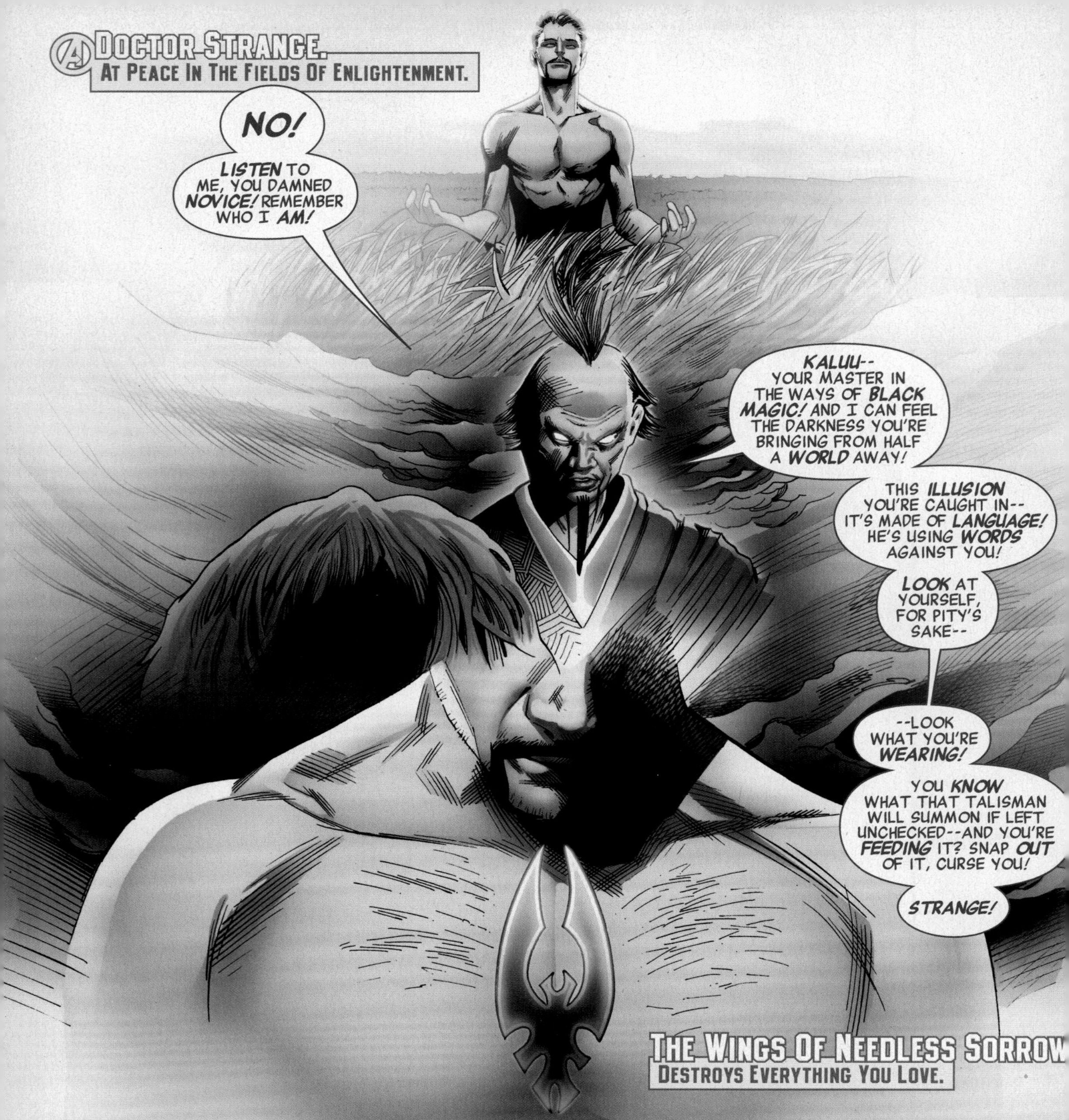
DOCTOR STRANGE.
AT PEACE IN THE FIELDS OF ENLIGHTENMENT.
NO!
LISTEN TO ME, YOU DAMNED NOVICE! REMEMBER WHO I AM!
KALUU-- YOUR MASTER IN THE WAYS OF BLACK MAGIC! AND I CAN FEEL THE DARKNESS YOU'RE BRINGING FROM HALF A WORLD AWAY!
THIS ILLUSION YOU'RE CAUGHT IN-- IT'S MADE OF LANGUAGE! HE'S USING WORDS AGAINST YOU!
LOOK AT YOURSELF, FOR PITY'S SAKE--
--LOOK WHAT YOU'RE WEARING!
YOU KNOW WHAT THAT TALISMAN WILL SUMMON IF LEFT UNCHECKED--AND YOU'RE FEEDING IT? SNAP OUT OF IT, CURSE YOU!
STRANGE!
THE WINGS OF NEEDLESS SORROW
DESTROYS EVERYTHING YOU LOVE.

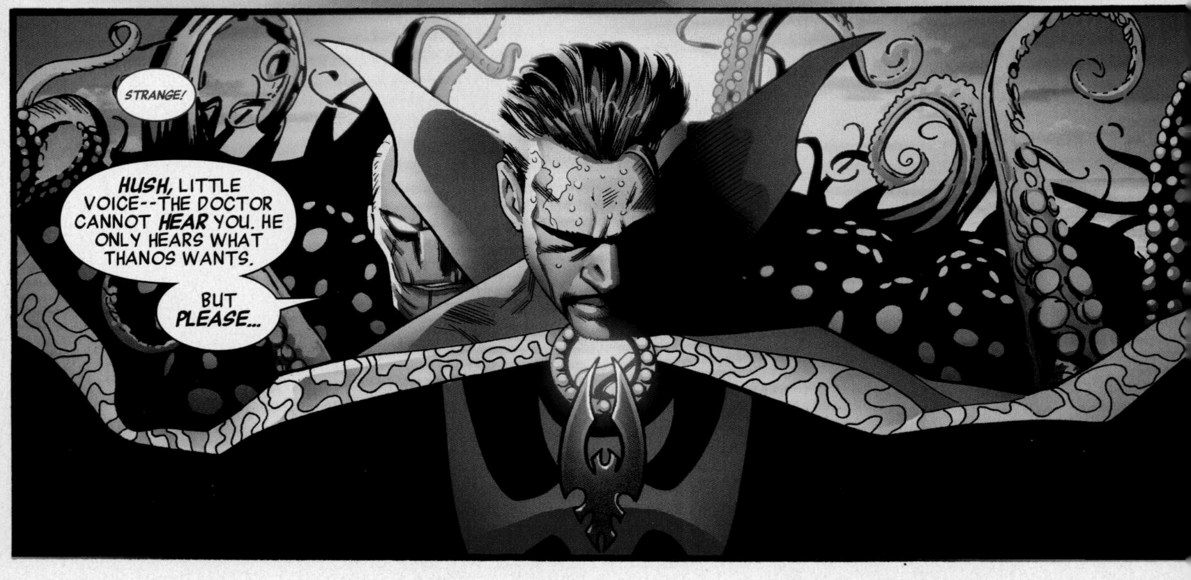
STRANGE!
HUSH, LITTLE VOICE--THE DOCTOR CANNOT HEAR YOU. HE ONLY HEARS WHAT THANOS WANTS.
BUT PLEASE...

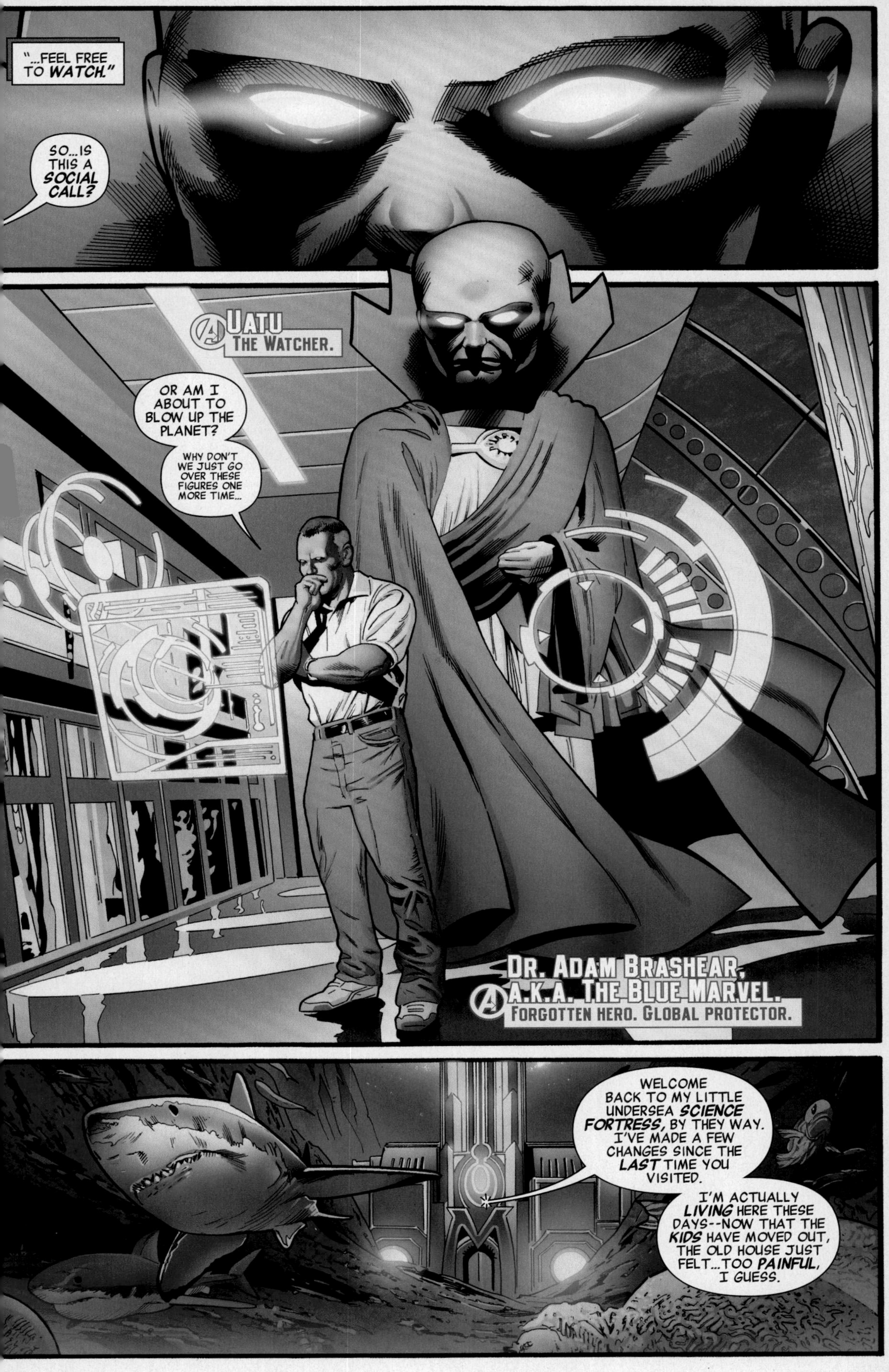
"...FEEL FREE TO WATCH."
SO...IS THIS A SOCIAL CALL?
UATU THE WATCHER.
OR AM I ABOUT TO BLOW UP THE PLANET?
WHY DON'T WE JUST GO OVER THESE FIGURES ONE MORE TIME...
DR. ADAM BRASHEAR, A.K.A. THE BLUE MARVEL.
FORGOTTEN HERO. GLOBAL PROTECTOR.
WELCOME BACK TO MY LITTLE UNDERSEA SCIENCE FORTRESS, BY THEY WAY. I'VE MADE A FEW CHANGES SINCE THE LAST TIME YOU VISITED.
I'M ACTUALLY LIVING HERE THESE DAYS--NOW THAT THE KIDS HAVE MOVED OUT, THE OLD HOUSE JUST FELT...TOO PAINFUL, I GUESS.

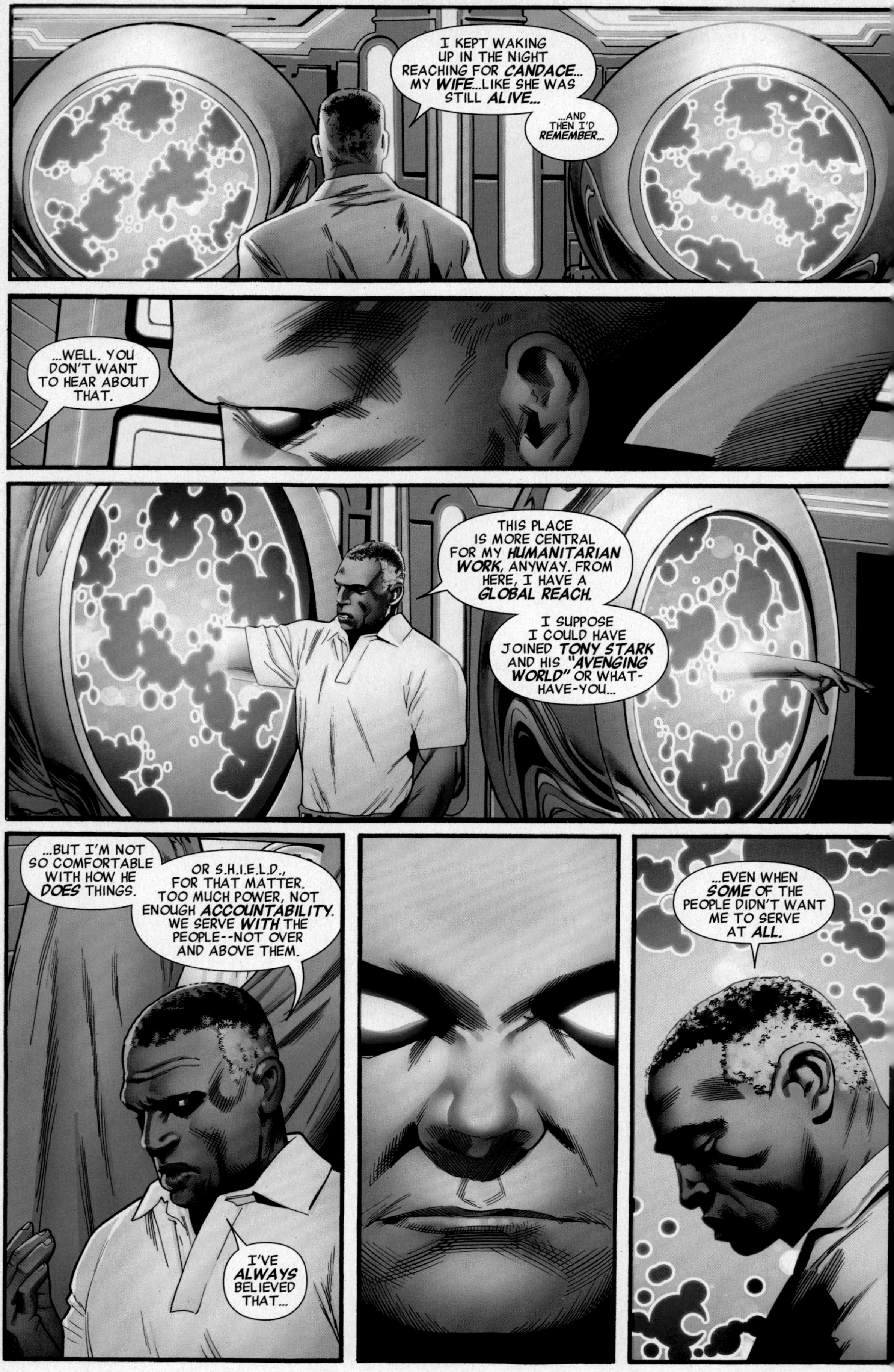
I KEPT WAKING UP IN THE NIGHT REACHING FOR CANDACE... MY WIFE...LIKE SHE WAS STILL ALIVE...
...AND THEN I'D REMEMBER...
...WELL. YOU DON'T WANT TO HEAR ABOUT THAT.
THIS PLACE IS MORE CENTRAL FOR MY HUMANITARIAN WORK, ANYWAY. FROM HERE, I HAVE A GLOBAL REACH.
I SUPPOSE I COULD HAVE JOINED TONY STARK AND HIS "AVENGING WORLD" OR WHAT-HAVE-YOU...
...BUT I'M NOT SO COMFORTABLE WITH HOW HE DOES THINGS.
OR S.H.I.E.L.D., FOR THAT MATTER. TOO MUCH POWER, NOT ENOUGH ACCOUNTABILITY. WE SERVE WITH THE PEOPLE--NOT OVER AND ABOVE THEM.
I'VE ALWAYS BELIEVED THAT...
...EVEN WHEN SOME OF THE PEOPLE DIDN'T WANT ME TO SERVE AT ALL.

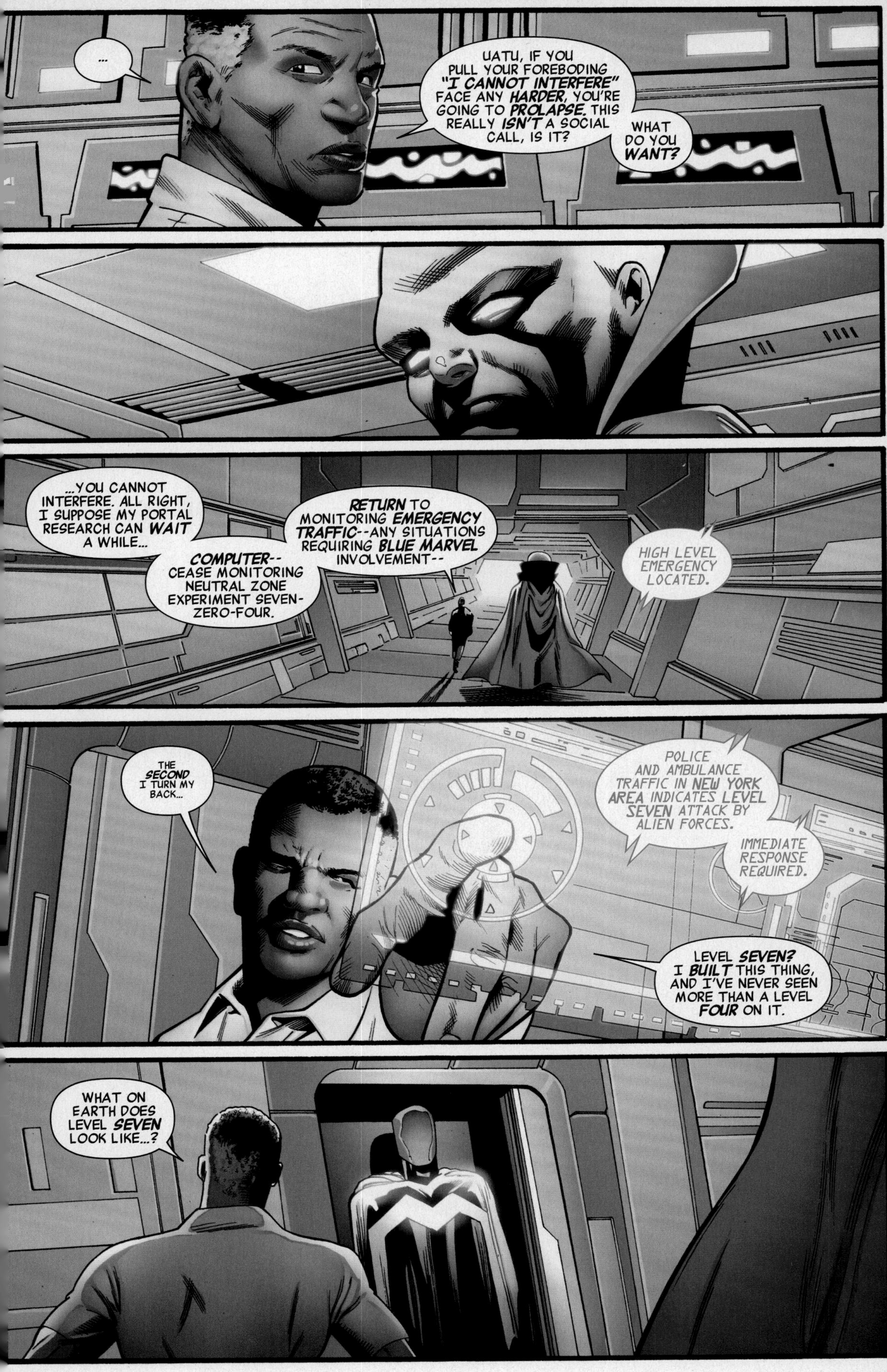
...
UATU, IF YOU PULL YOUR FOREBODING "I CANNOT INTERFERE" FACE ANY HARDER, YOU'RE GOING TO PROLAPSE. THIS REALLY ISN'T A SOCIAL CALL, IS IT?
WHAT DO YOU WANT?
...YOU CANNOT INTERFERE. ALL RIGHT, I SUPPOSE MY PORTAL RESEARCH CAN WAIT A WHILE...
COMPUTER-- CEASE MONITORING NEUTRAL ZONE EXPERIMENT SEVEN-ZERO-FOUR.
RETURN TO MONITORING EMERGENCY TRAFFIC--ANY SITUATIONS REQUIRING BLUE MARVEL INVOLVEMENT--
HIGH LEVEL EMERGENCY LOCATED.
THE SECOND I TURN MY BACK...
POLICE AND AMBULANCE TRAFFIC IN NEW YORK AREA INDICATES LEVEL SEVEN ATTACK BY ALIEN FORCES.
IMMEDIATE RESPONSE REQUIRED.
LEVEL SEVEN? I BUILT THIS THING, AND I'VE NEVER SEEN MORE THAN A LEVEL FOUR ON IT.
WHAT ON EARTH DOES LEVEL SEVEN LOOK LIKE...?

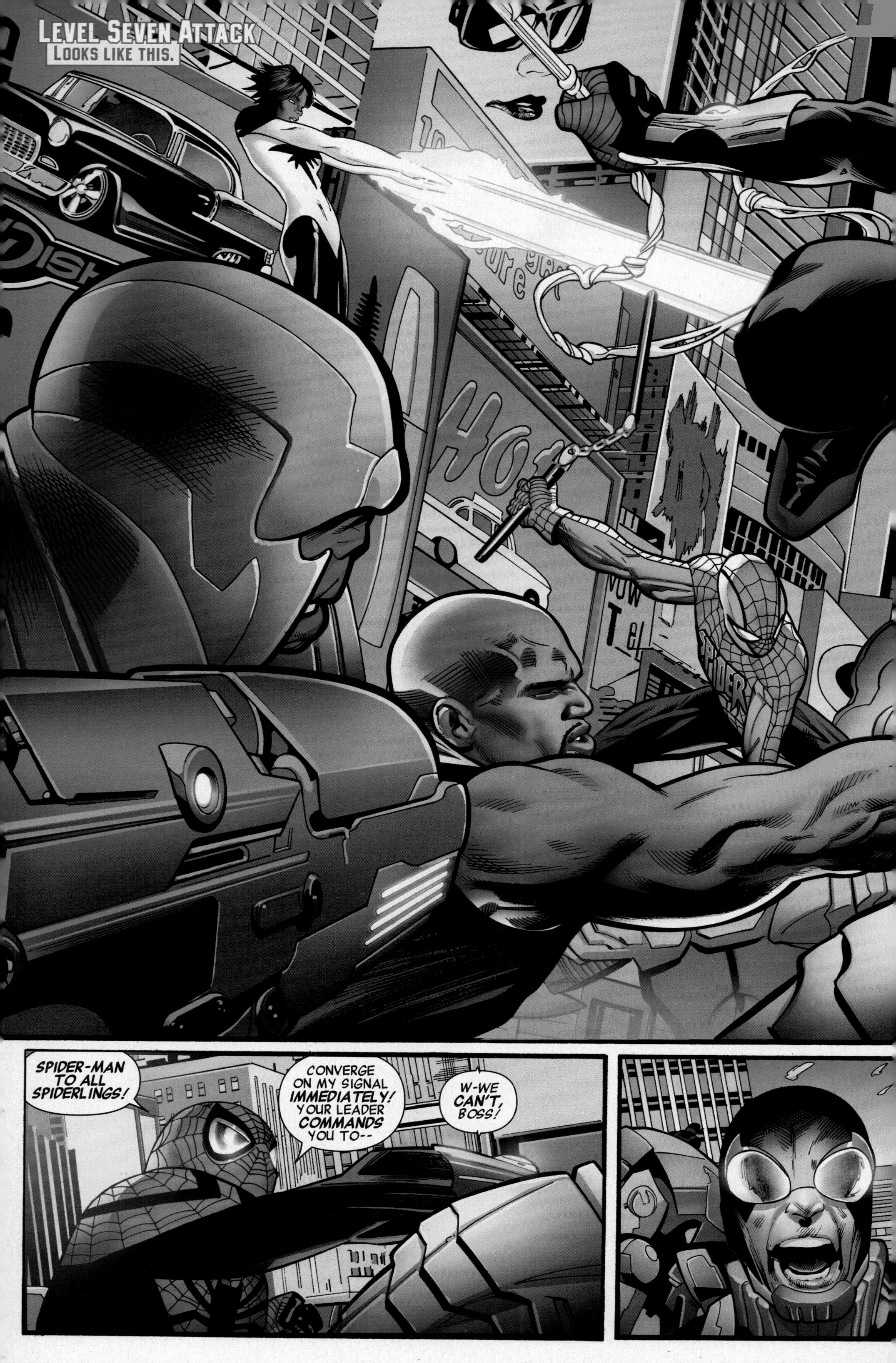
LEVEL SEVEN ATTACK
LOOKS LIKE THIS.
SPIDER-MAN TO ALL SPIDERLINGS!
CONVERGE ON MY SIGNAL IMMEDIATELY! YOUR LEADER COMMANDS YOU TO--
W-WE CAN'T, BOSS!

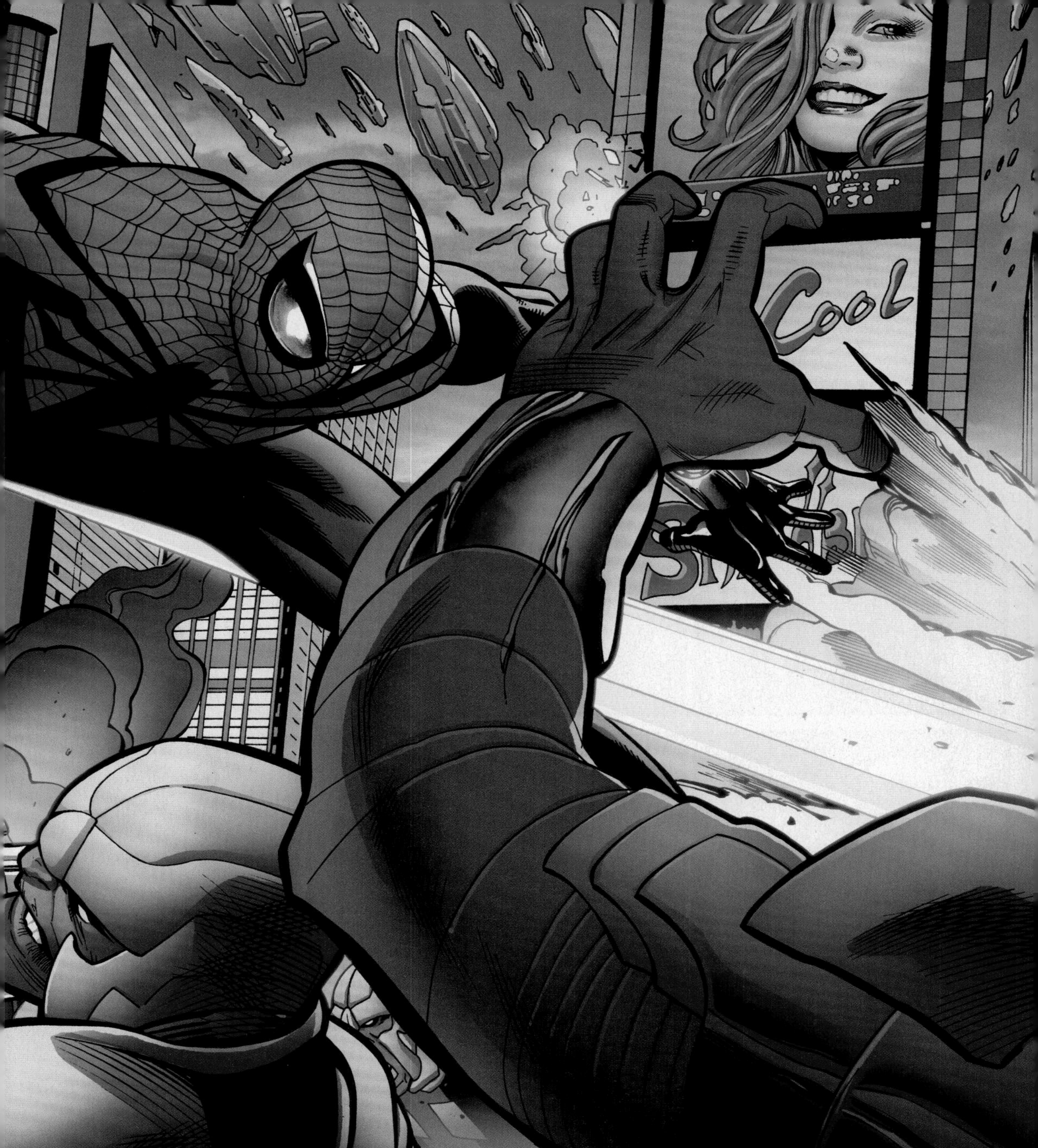
Cool

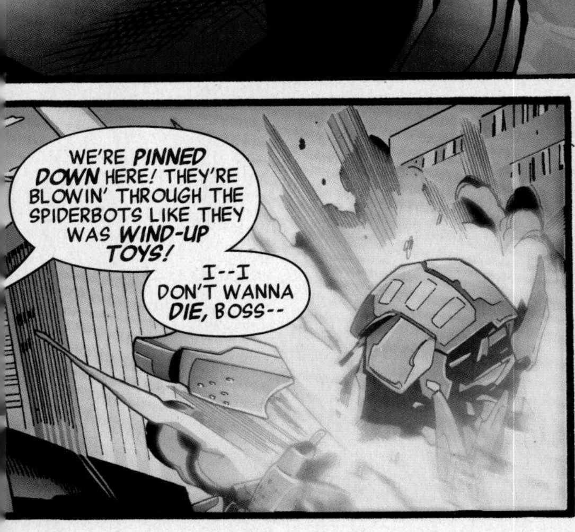
WE'RE **PINNED DOWN** HERE! THEY'RE BLOWIN' THROUGH THE SPIDERBOTS LIKE THEY WAS **WIND-UP TOYS!**
I--I DON'T WANNA **DIE,** BOSS--

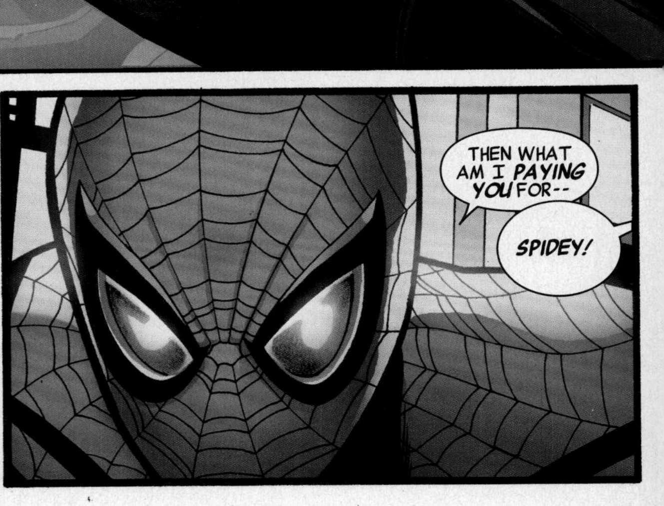
THEN WHAT AM I **PAYING YOU** FOR--
SPIDEY!

PEOPLE ARE DYING HERE! PUT YOUR CELL PHONE AWAY AND GET BACK IN THE FIGHT!
FINE, "SPECTRUM."
BUT NOT BECAUSE YOU TOLD ME TO.
ATURDAY
ONUS
THWIP
ZING
ONCE I'VE DISARMED THESE IGNORAMI, IT'LL BE CHILD'S PLAY TO RENDER THEM--
--HEY!
KRAKK
I WAS JUST ABOUT TO--
--GIVE THEM A LECTURE.
LESS #$%@ MORE HIT, BUGMAN.
ON

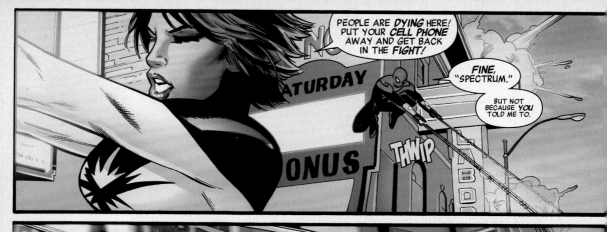

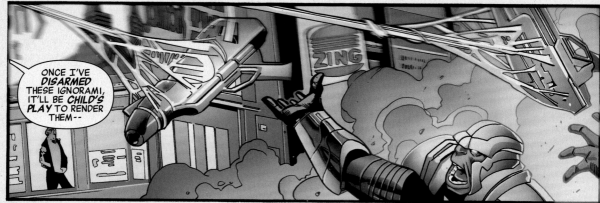

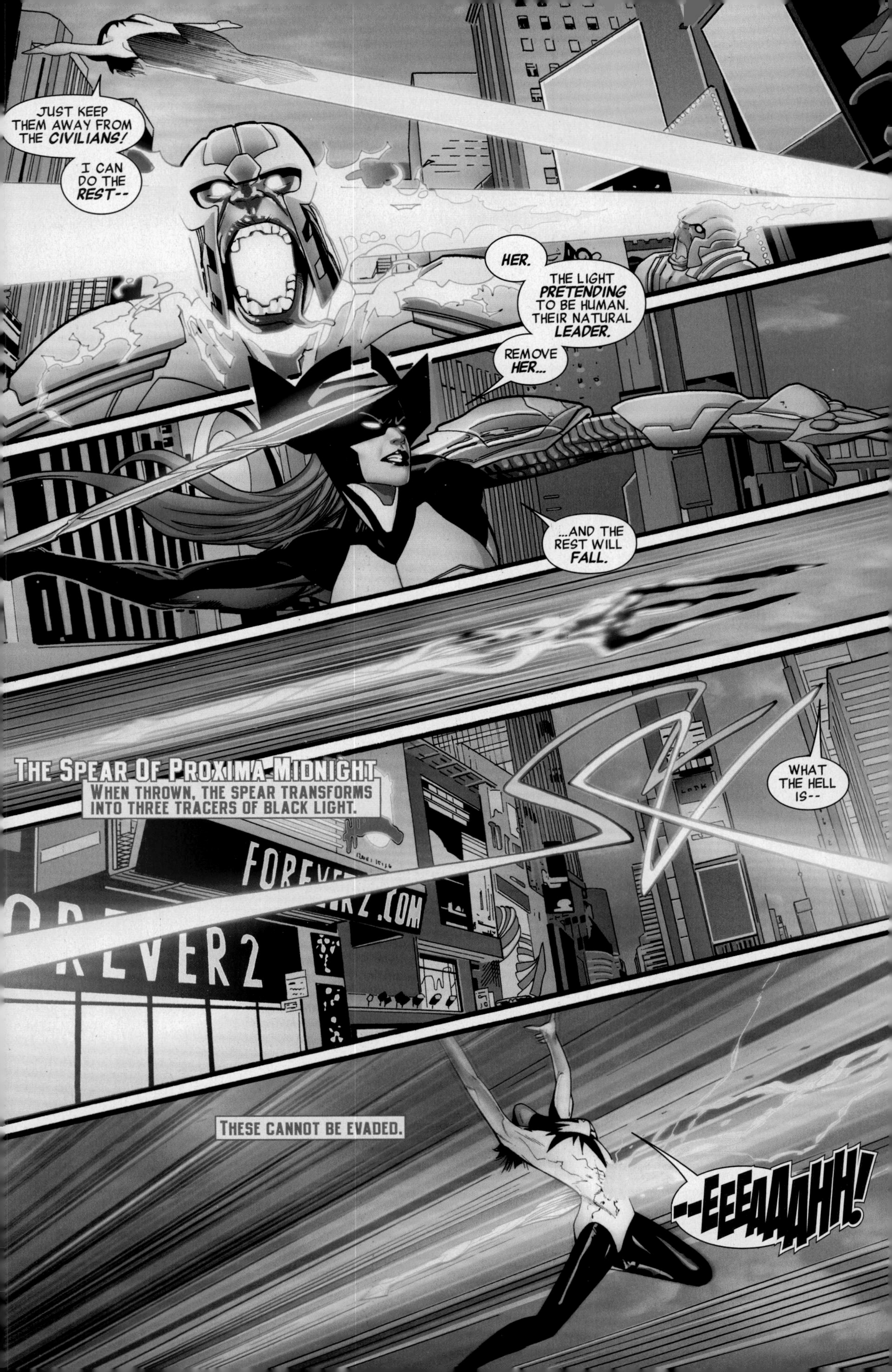
JUST KEEP THEM AWAY FROM THE CIVILIANS!
I CAN DO THE REST--
HER.
THE LIGHT PRETENDING TO BE HUMAN. THEIR NATURAL LEADER.
REMOVE HER...
...AND THE REST WILL FALL.
THE SPEAR OF PROXIMA MIDNIGHT
WHEN THROWN, THE SPEAR TRANSFORMS INTO THREE TRACERS OF BLACK LIGHT.
WHAT THE HELL IS--
FOREVER 2
THESE CANNOT BE EVADED.
--EEEAAAHH!

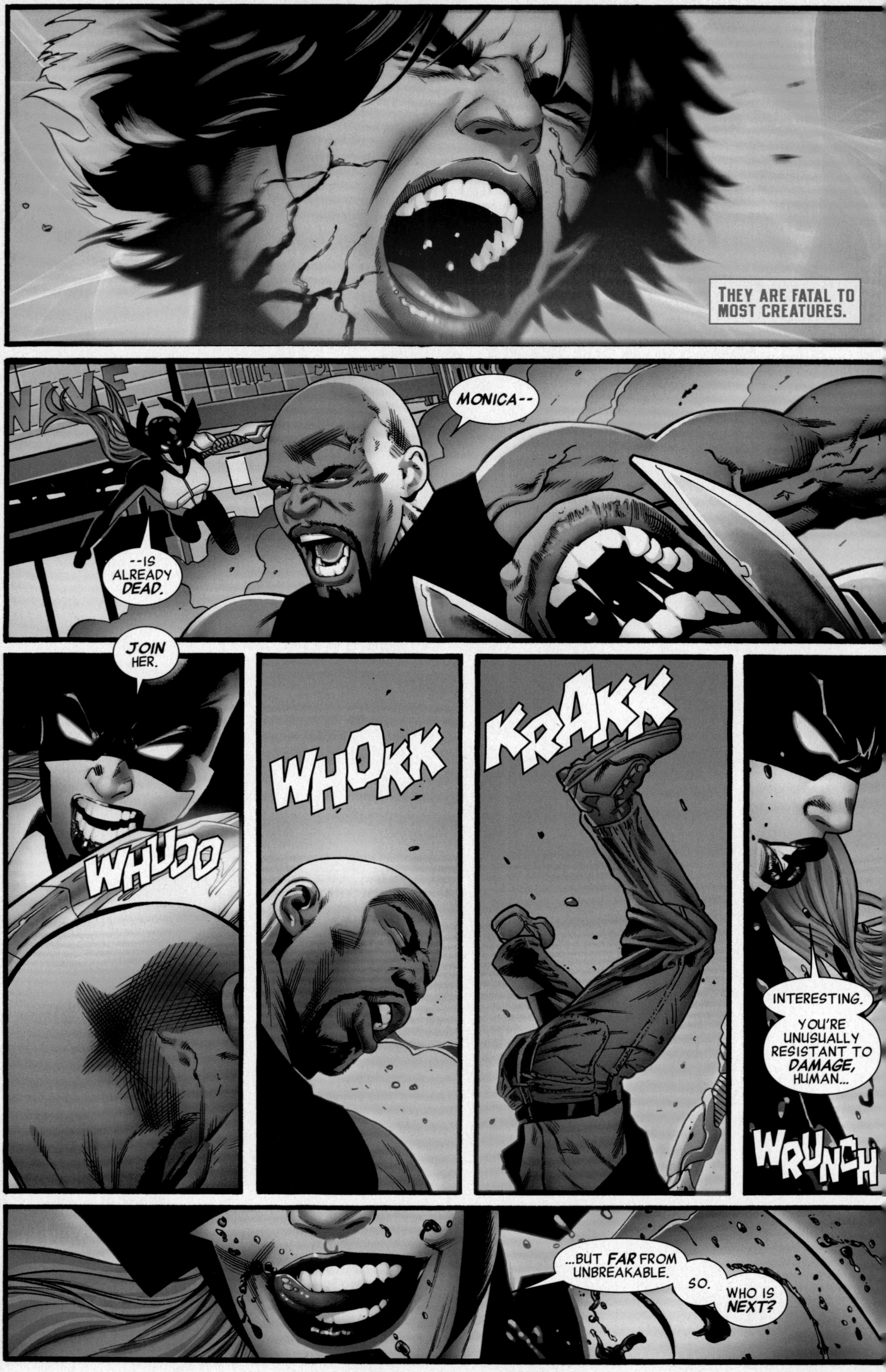
THEY ARE FATAL TO MOST CREATURES.
MONICA--
--IS ALREADY DEAD.
JOIN HER.
WHUDD
WHOKK
KRAKK
INTERESTING.
YOU'RE UNUSUALLY RESISTANT TO DAMAGE, HUMAN...
WRUNCH
...BUT FAR FROM UNBREAKABLE.
SO.
WHO IS NEXT?

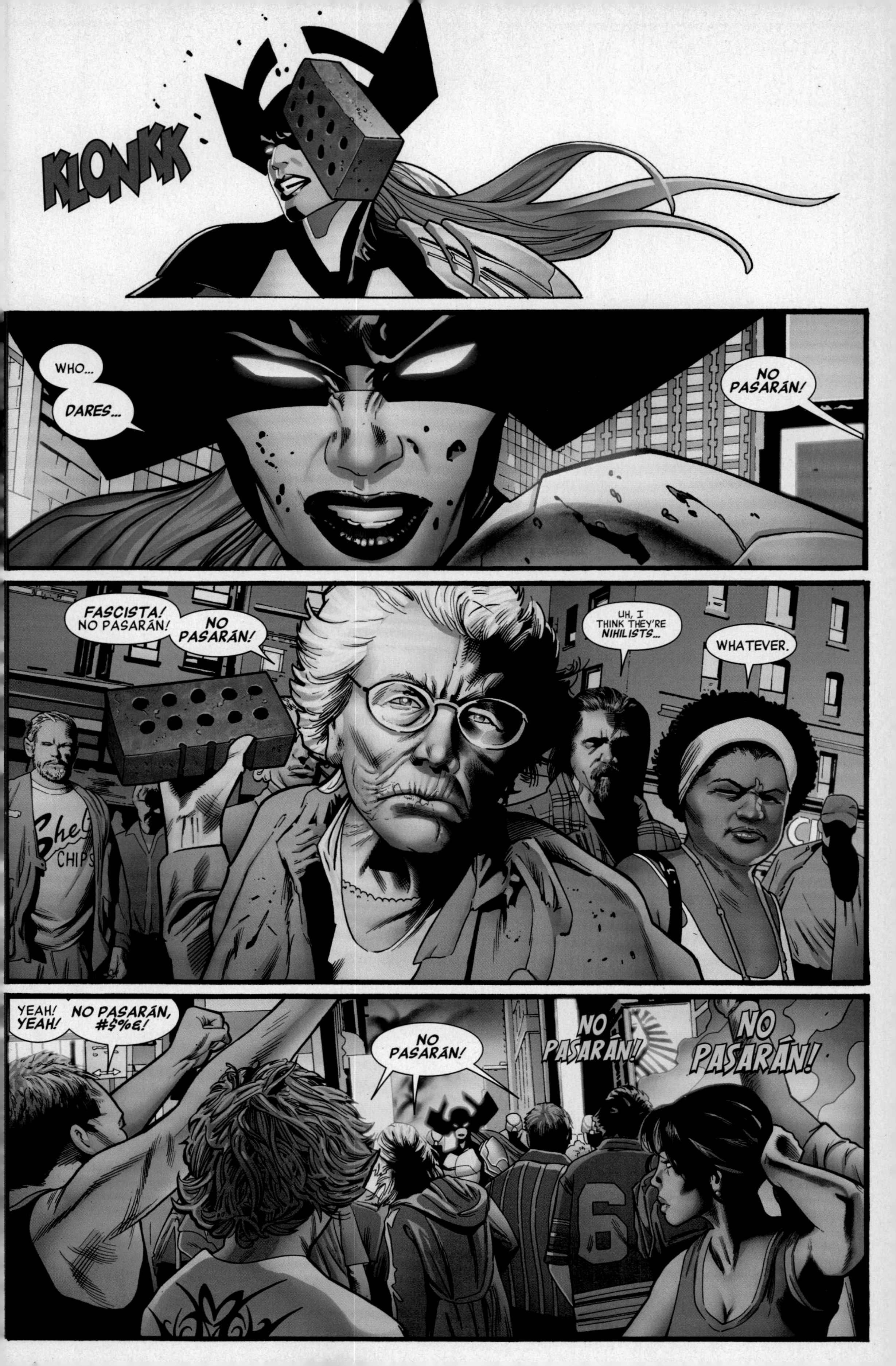
KLONKK
WHO...
DARES...
NO PASARÁN!
FASCISTA! NO PASARÁN!
NO PASARÁN!
UH, I THINK THEY'RE NIHILISTS...
WHATEVER.
SHEL CHIPS
YEAH! YEAH!
NO PASARÁN, #$%&!
NO PASARÁN!
NO PASARÁN!
NO PASARÁN!

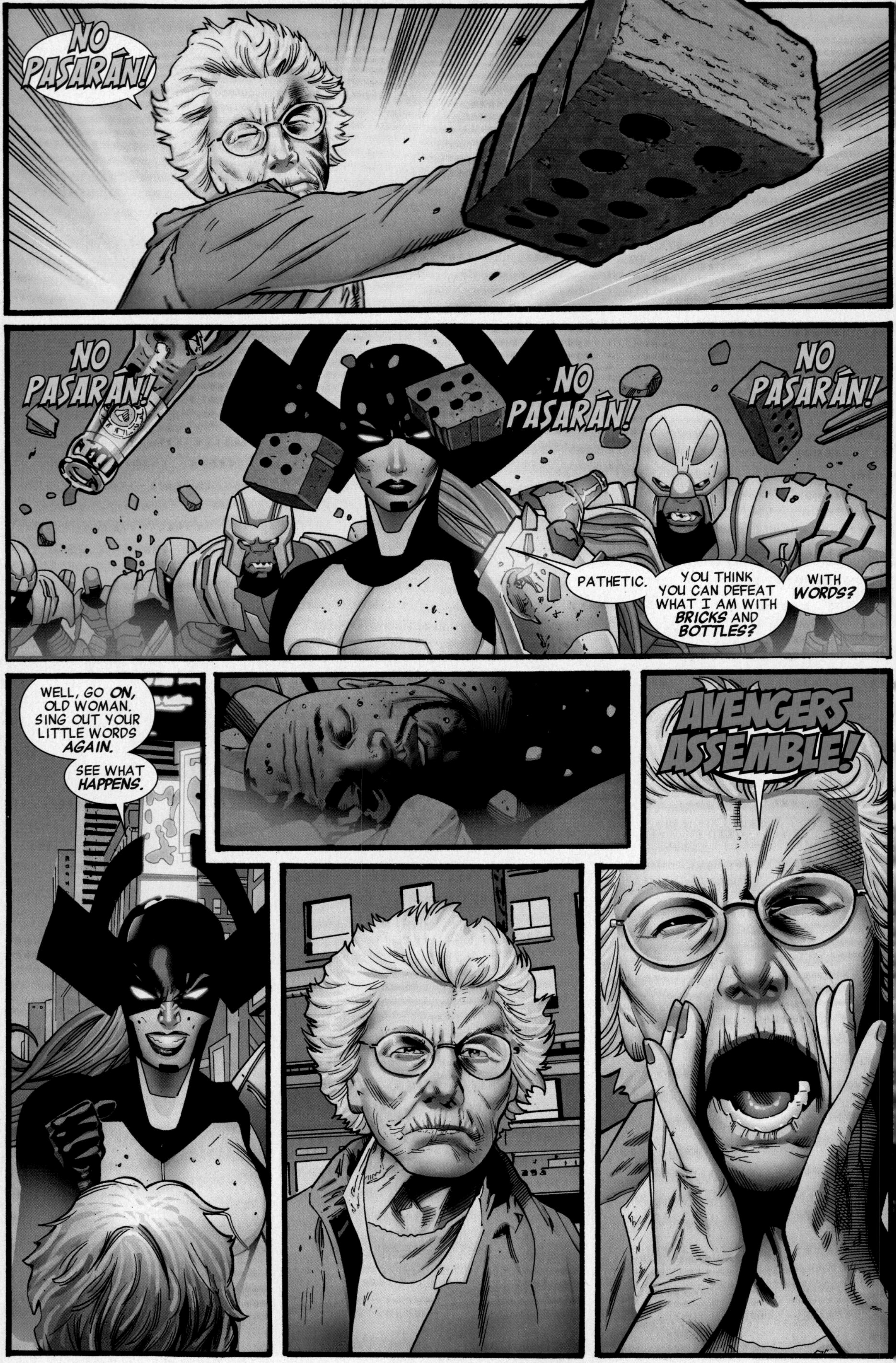

NO PASARÁN!
NO PASARÁN!
NO PASARÁN!
NO PASARÁN!
PATHETIC.
YOU THINK YOU CAN DEFEAT WHAT I AM WITH BRICKS AND BOTTLES?
WITH WORDS?
WELL, GO ON, OLD WOMAN. SING OUT YOUR LITTLE WORDS AGAIN.
SEE WHAT HAPPENS.
AVENGERS ASSEMBLE!

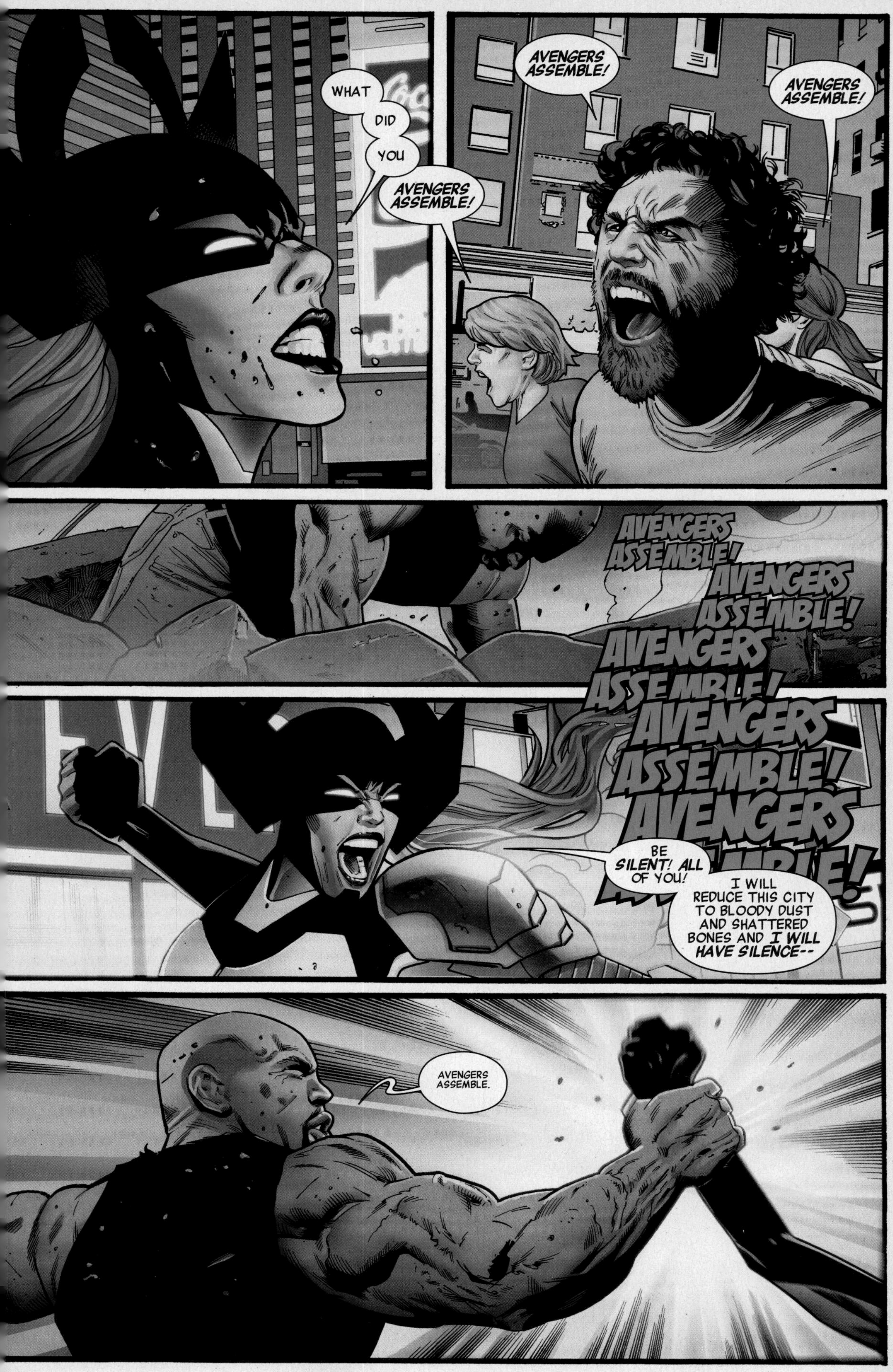
WHAT
DID
YOU
AVENGERS ASSEMBLE!
AVENGERS ASSEMBLE!
AVENGERS ASSEMBLE!
AVENGERS ASSEMBLE!
AVENGERS ASSEMBLE!
AVENGERS ASSEMBLE!
AVENGERS ASSEMBLE!
BE SILENT! ALL OF YOU!
I WILL REDUCE THIS CITY TO BLOODY DUST AND SHATTERED BONES AND I WILL HAVE SILENCE--
AVENGERS ASSEMBLE.

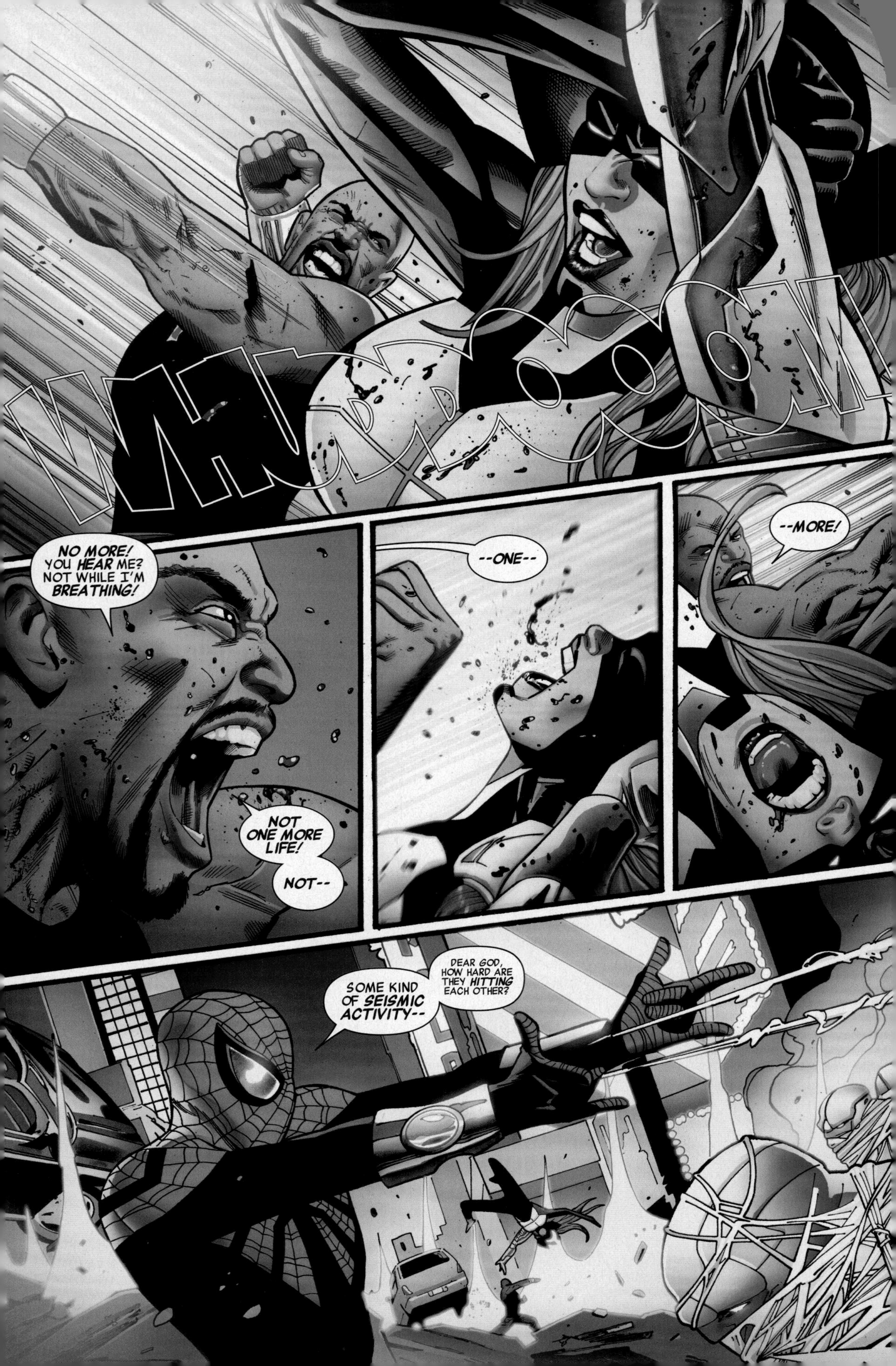
WHUDOOOOM
NO MORE! YOU HEAR ME? NOT WHILE I'M BREATHING!
NOT ONE MORE LIFE!
NOT--
--ONE--
--MORE!
SOME KIND OF SEISMIC ACTIVITY--
DEAR GOD, HOW HARD ARE THEY HITTING EACH OTHER?

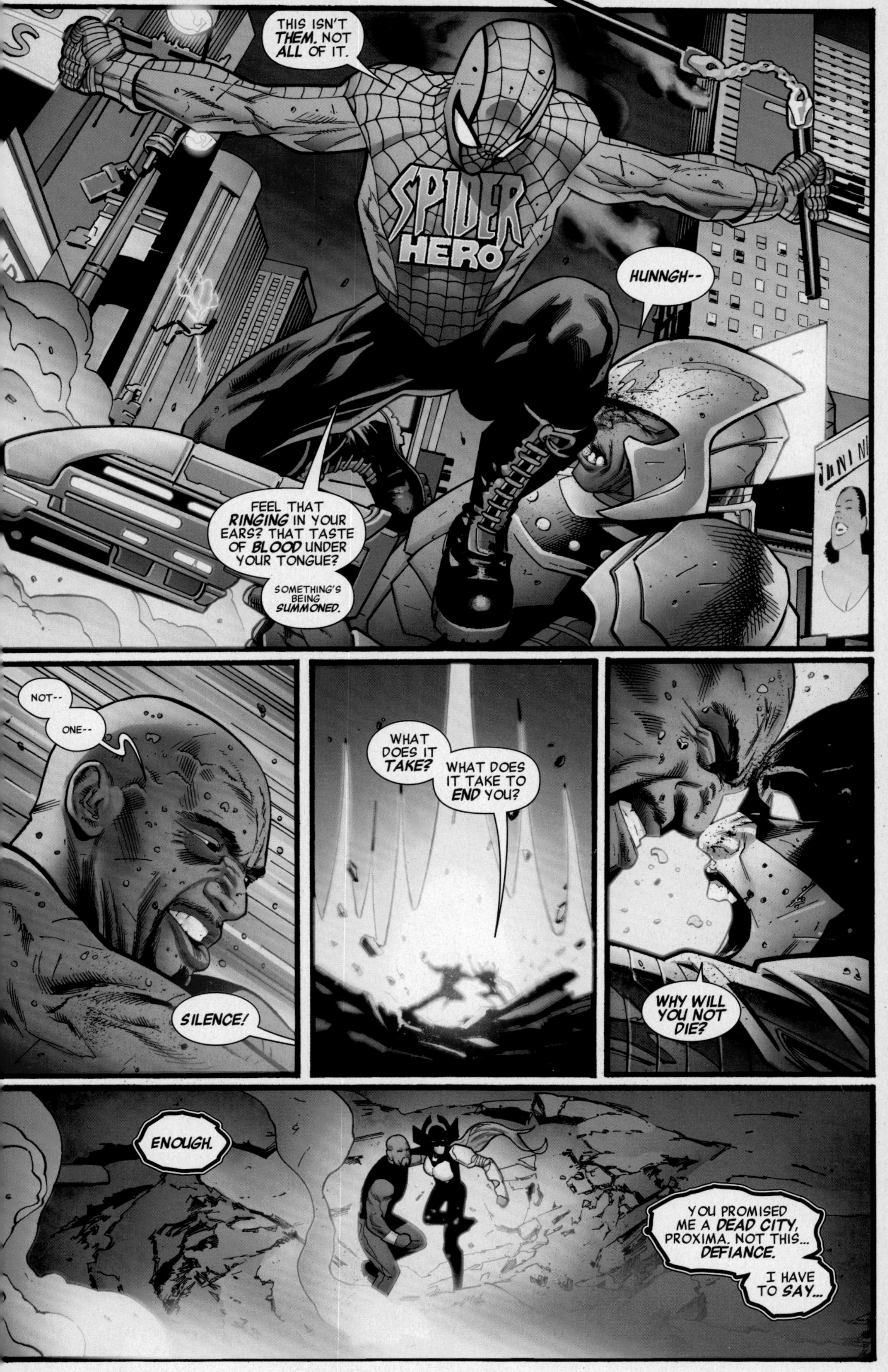
THIS ISN'T THEM. NOT ALL OF IT.
SPIDER HERO
HUNNGH--
FEEL THAT RINGING IN YOUR EARS? THAT TASTE OF BLOOD UNDER YOUR TONGUE?
SOMETHING'S BEING SUMMONED.
NOT--
ONE--
SILENCE!
WHAT DOES IT TAKE?
WHAT DOES IT TAKE TO END YOU?
WHY WILL YOU NOT DIE?
ENOUGH.
YOU PROMISED ME A DEAD CITY, PROXIMA. NOT THIS... DEFIANCE.
I HAVE TO SAY...

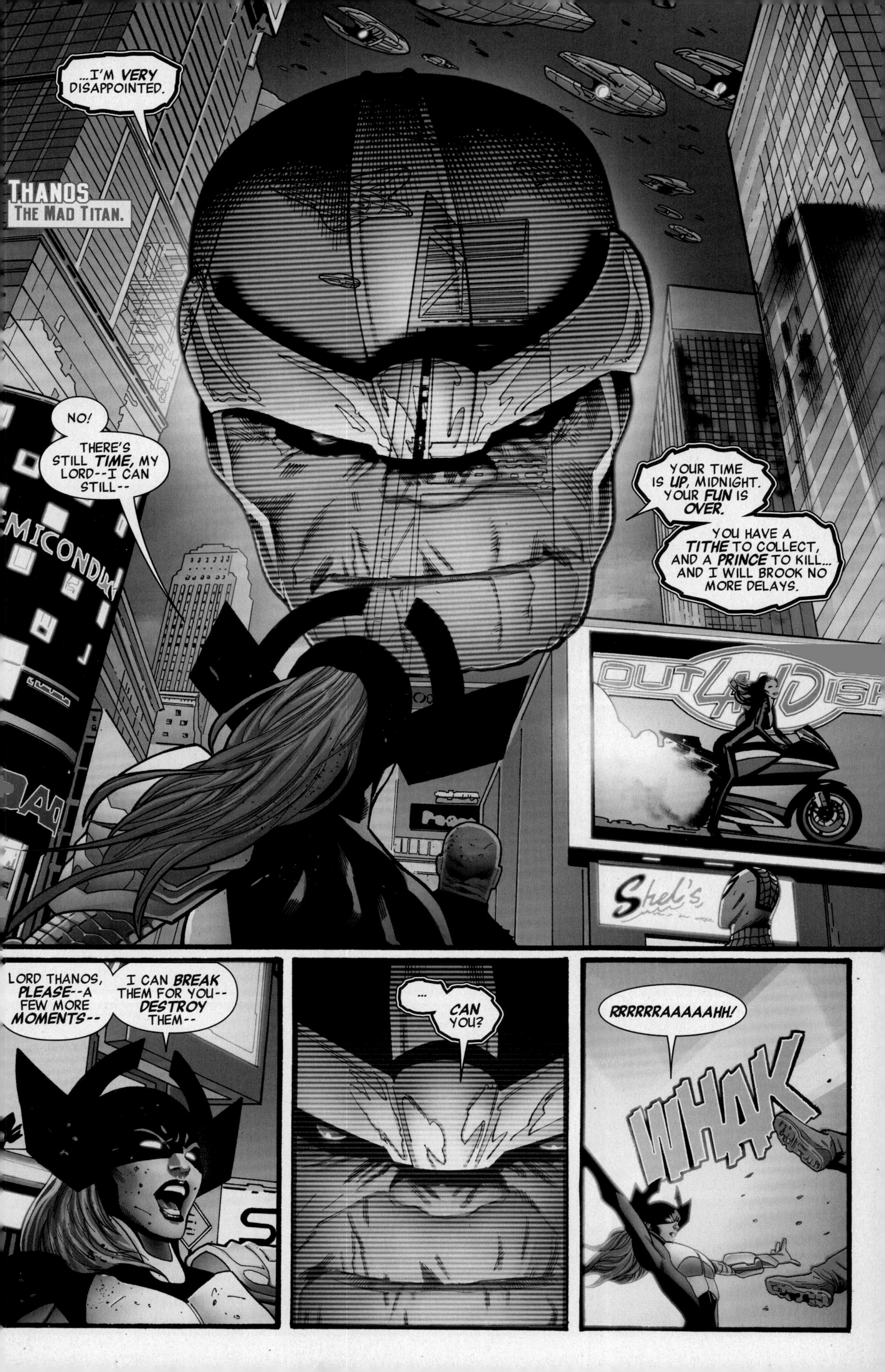

...I'M VERY DISAPPOINTED.
THANOS THE MAD TITAN.
NO!
THERE'S STILL TIME, MY LORD--I CAN STILL--
YOUR TIME IS UP, MIDNIGHT. YOUR FUN IS OVER.
YOU HAVE A TITHE TO COLLECT, AND A PRINCE TO KILL... AND I WILL BROOK NO MORE DELAYS.
LORD THANOS, PLEASE--A FEW MORE MOMENTS--
I CAN BREAK THEM FOR YOU--DESTROY THEM--
... CAN YOU?
RRRRRRAAAAAHH!
WHAK

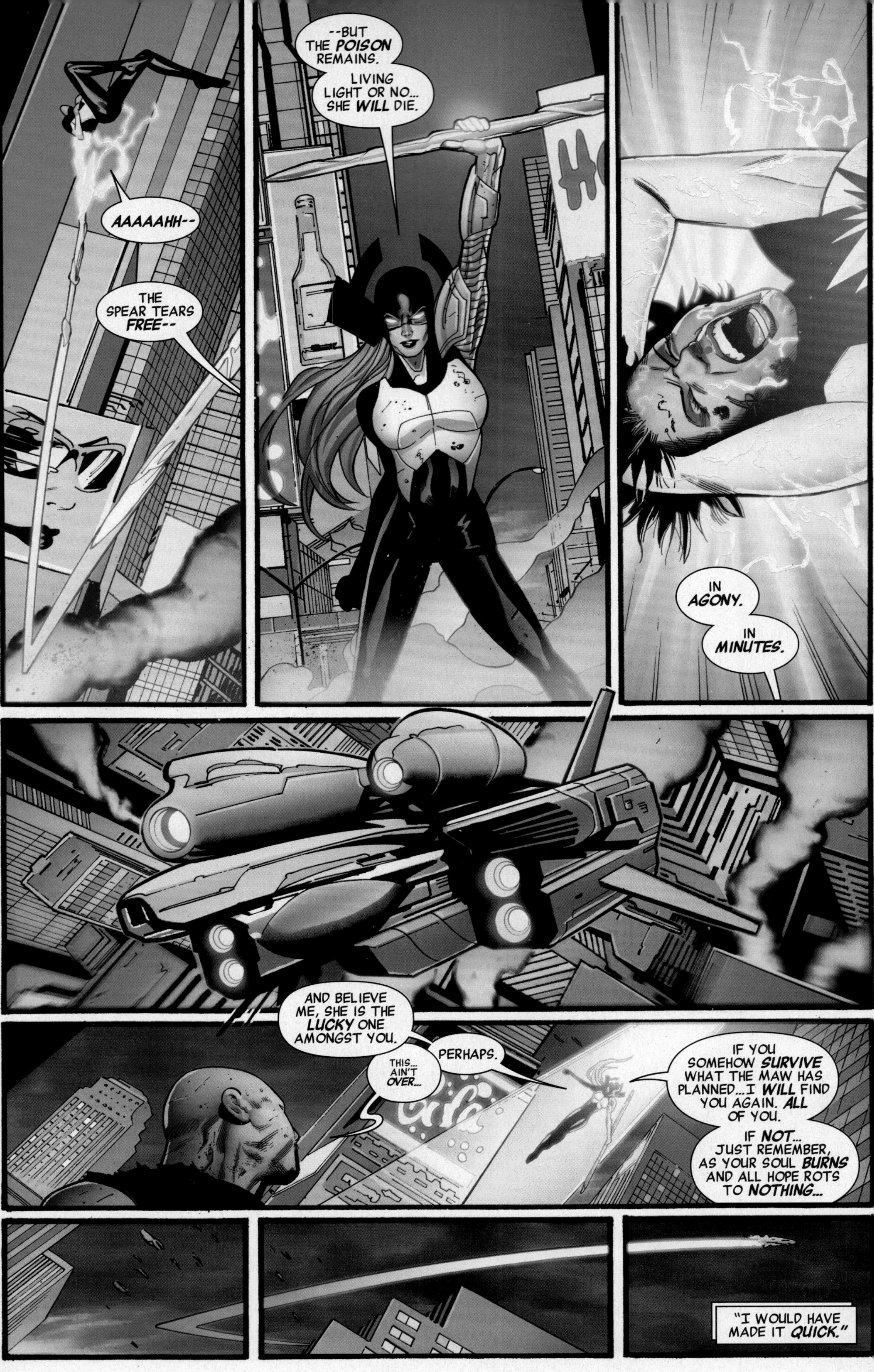
AAAAAHH--
THE SPEAR TEARS FREE--
--BUT THE POISON REMAINS.
LIVING LIGHT OR NO... SHE WILL DIE.
IN AGONY.
IN MINUTES.
AND BELIEVE ME, SHE IS THE LUCKY ONE AMONGST YOU.
PERHAPS.
THIS... AIN'T OVER...
IF YOU SOMEHOW SURVIVE WHAT THE MAW HAS PLANNED...I WILL FIND YOU AGAIN. ALL OF YOU.
IF NOT... JUST REMEMBER, AS YOUR SOUL BURNS AND ALL HOPE ROTS TO NOTHING...
"I WOULD HAVE MADE IT QUICK."

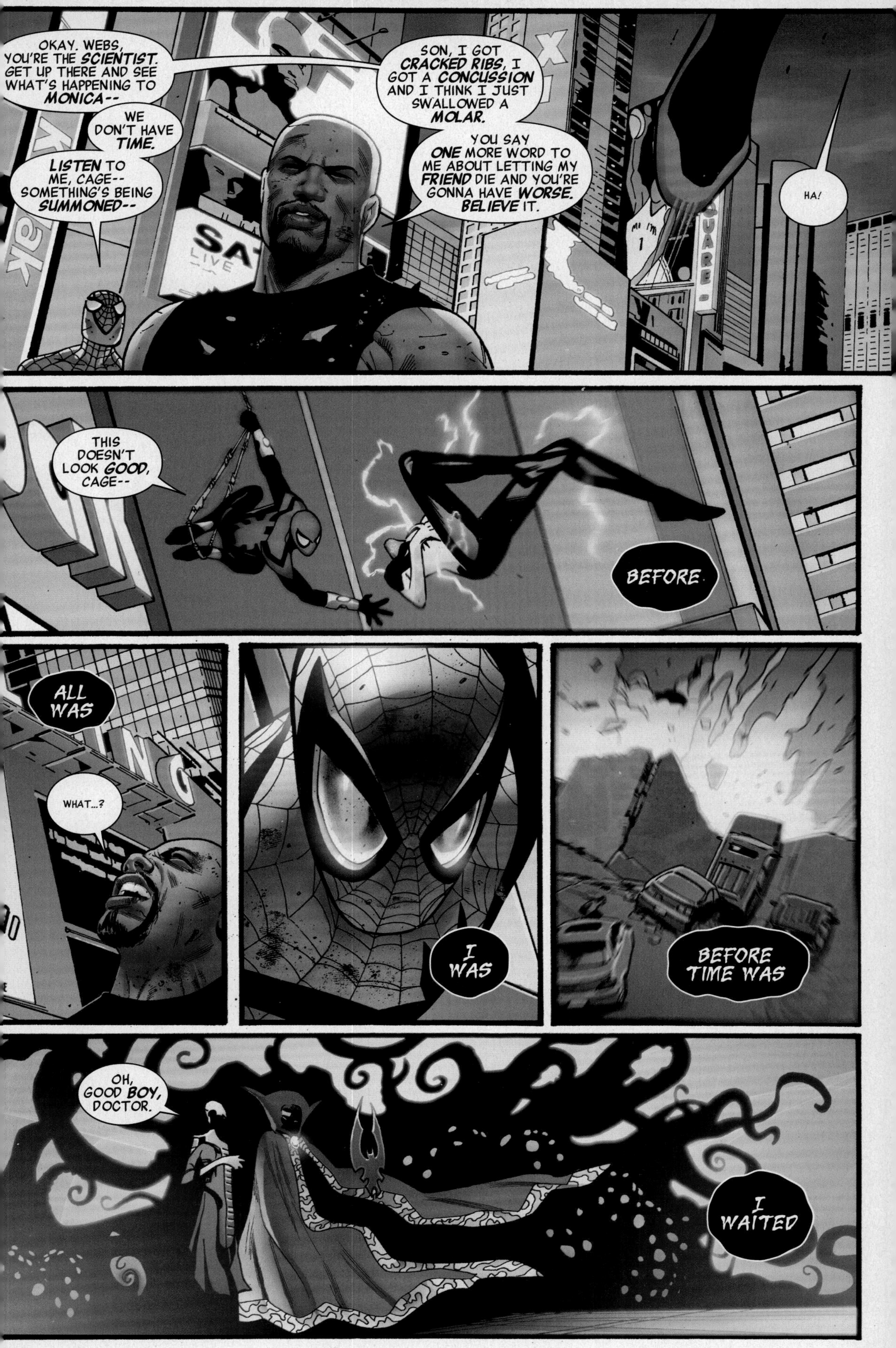
OKAY. WEBS, YOU'RE THE SCIENTIST. GET UP THERE AND SEE WHAT'S HAPPENING TO MONICA--
SON, I GOT CRACKED RIBS, I GOT A CONCUSSION AND I THINK I JUST SWALLOWED A MOLAR.
WE DON'T HAVE TIME.
LISTEN TO ME, CAGE-- SOMETHING'S BEING SUMMONED--
YOU SAY ONE MORE WORD TO ME ABOUT LETTING MY FRIEND DIE AND YOU'RE GONNA HAVE WORSE. BELIEVE IT.
HA!
THIS DOESN'T LOOK GOOD, CAGE--
BEFORE
ALL WAS
WHAT...?
I WAS
BEFORE TIME WAS
OH, GOOD BOY, DOCTOR.
I WAITED

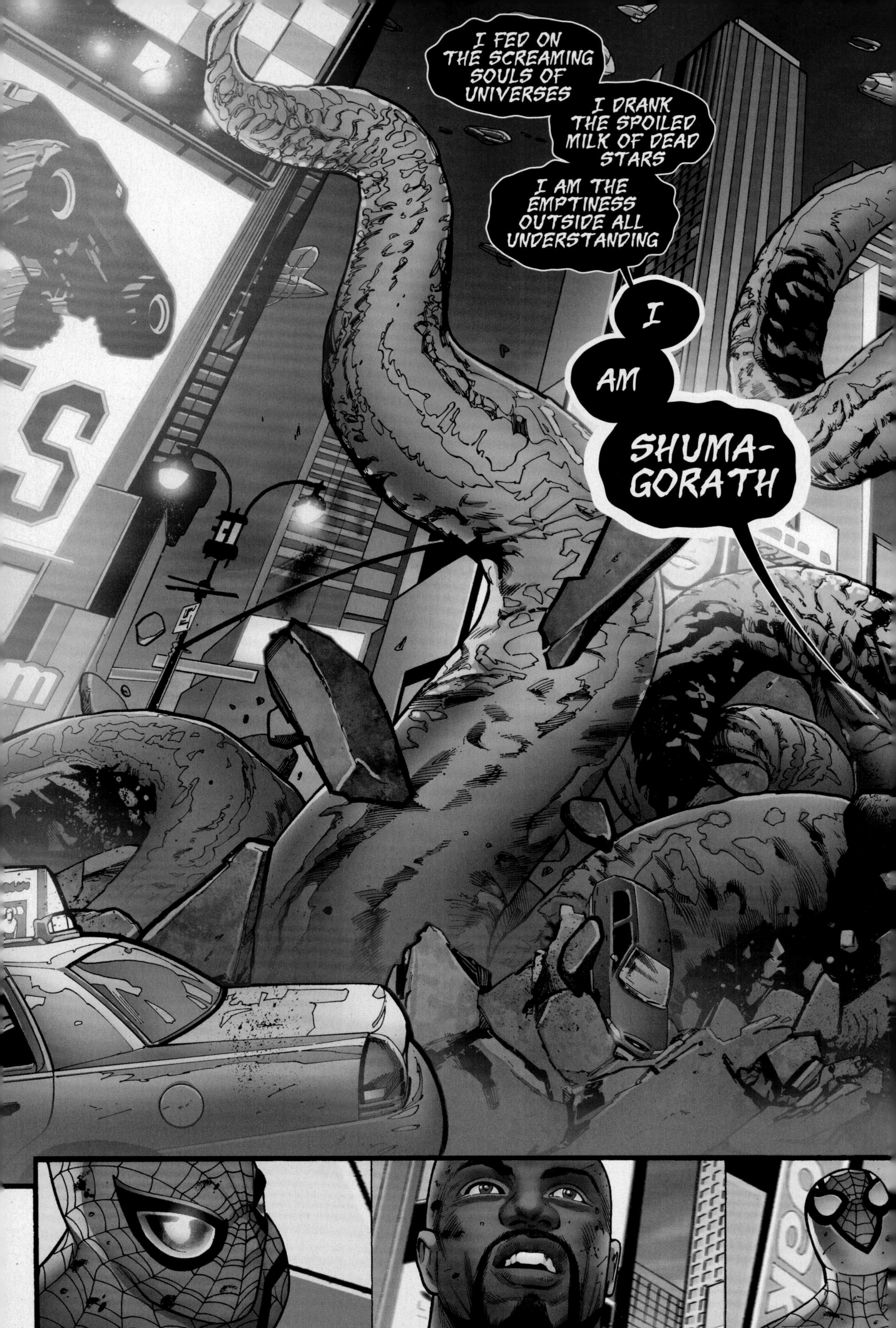
I FED ON THE SCREAMING SOULS OF UNIVERSES
I DRANK THE SPOILED MILK OF DEAD STARS
I AM THE EMPTINESS OUTSIDE ALL UNDERSTANDING
I AM SHUMA-GORATH

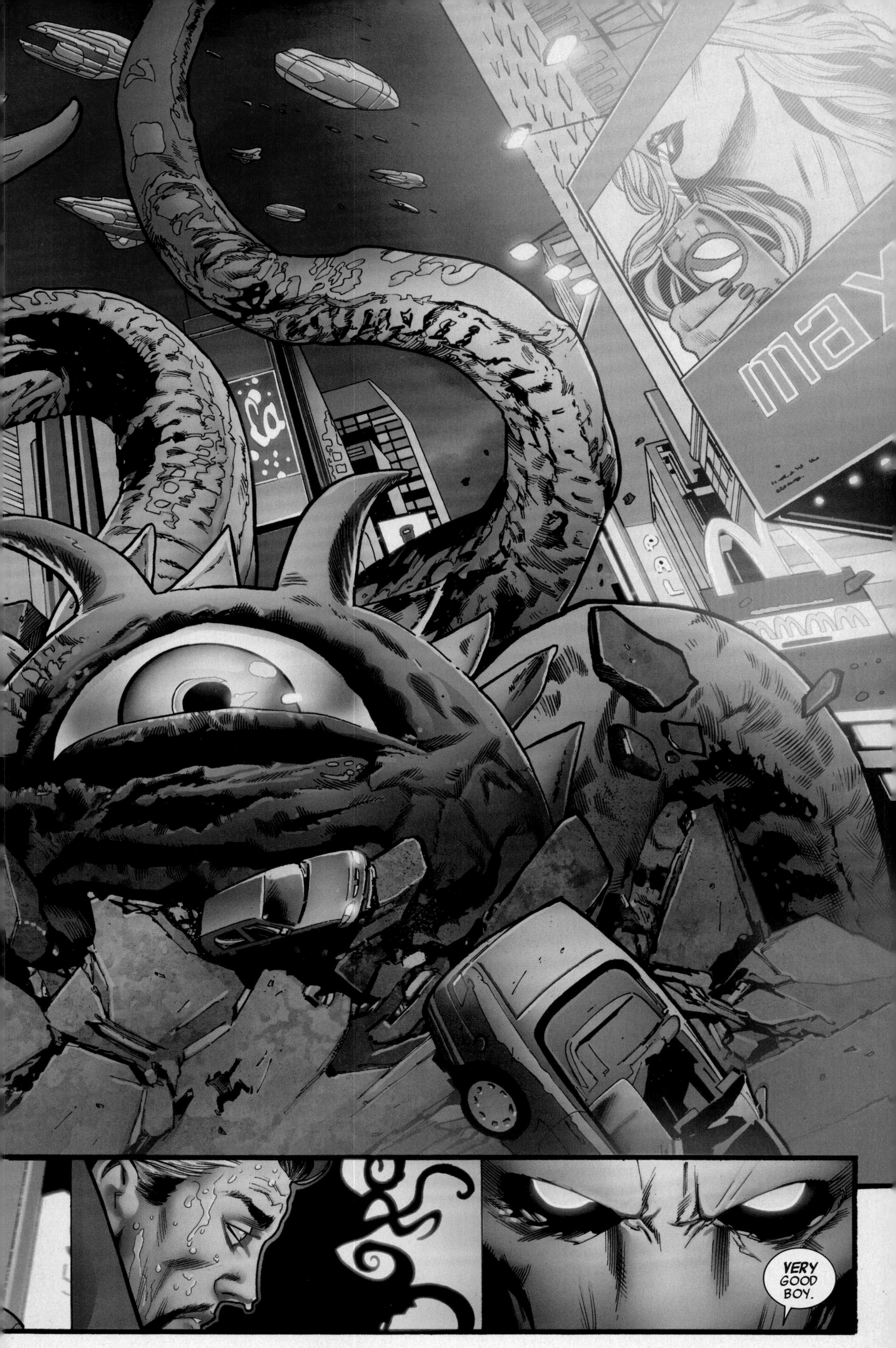
max
VERY GOOD BOY.

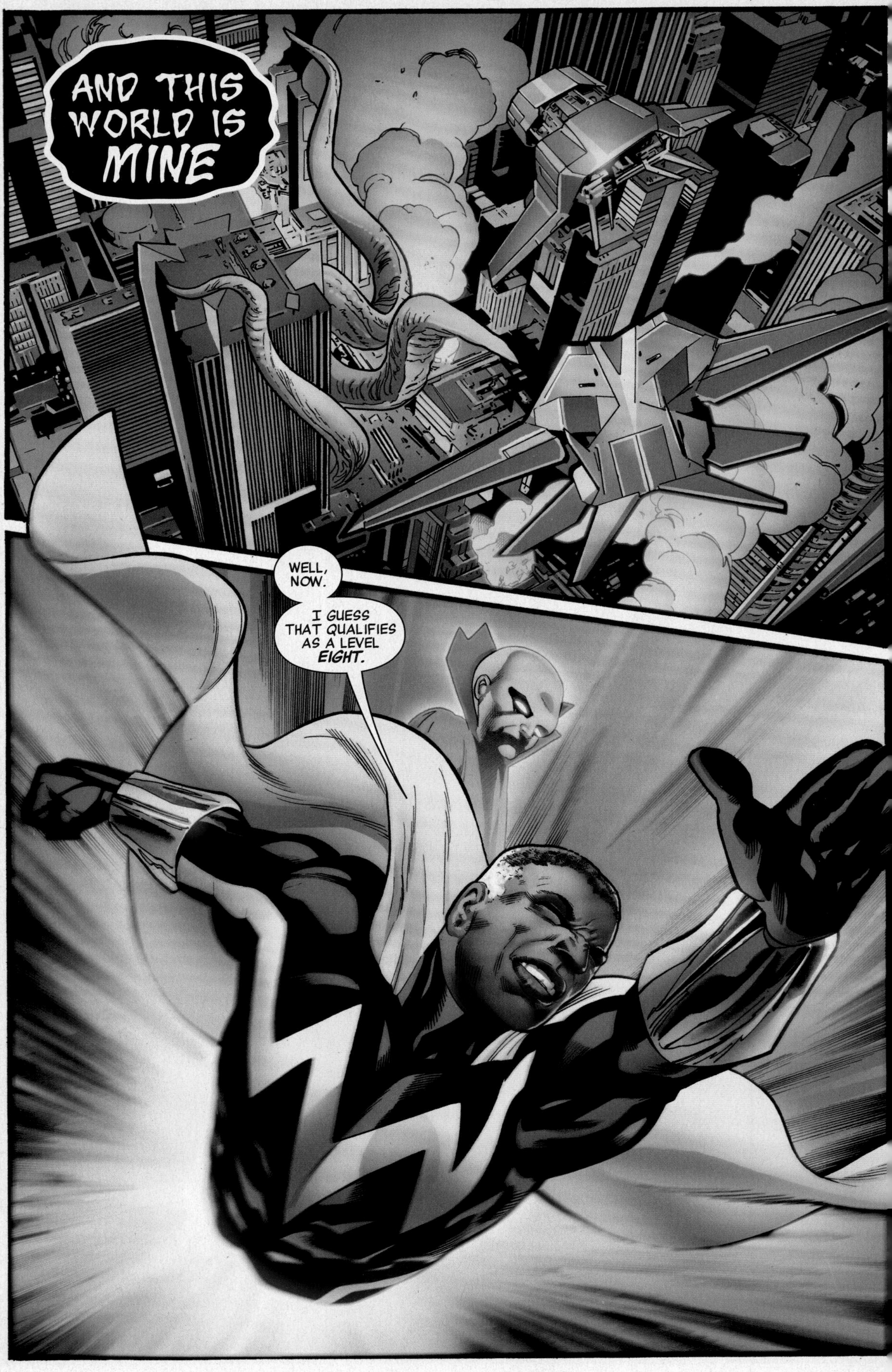
AND THIS WORLD IS MINE
WELL, NOW.
I GUESS THAT QUALIFIES AS A LEVEL EIGHT.

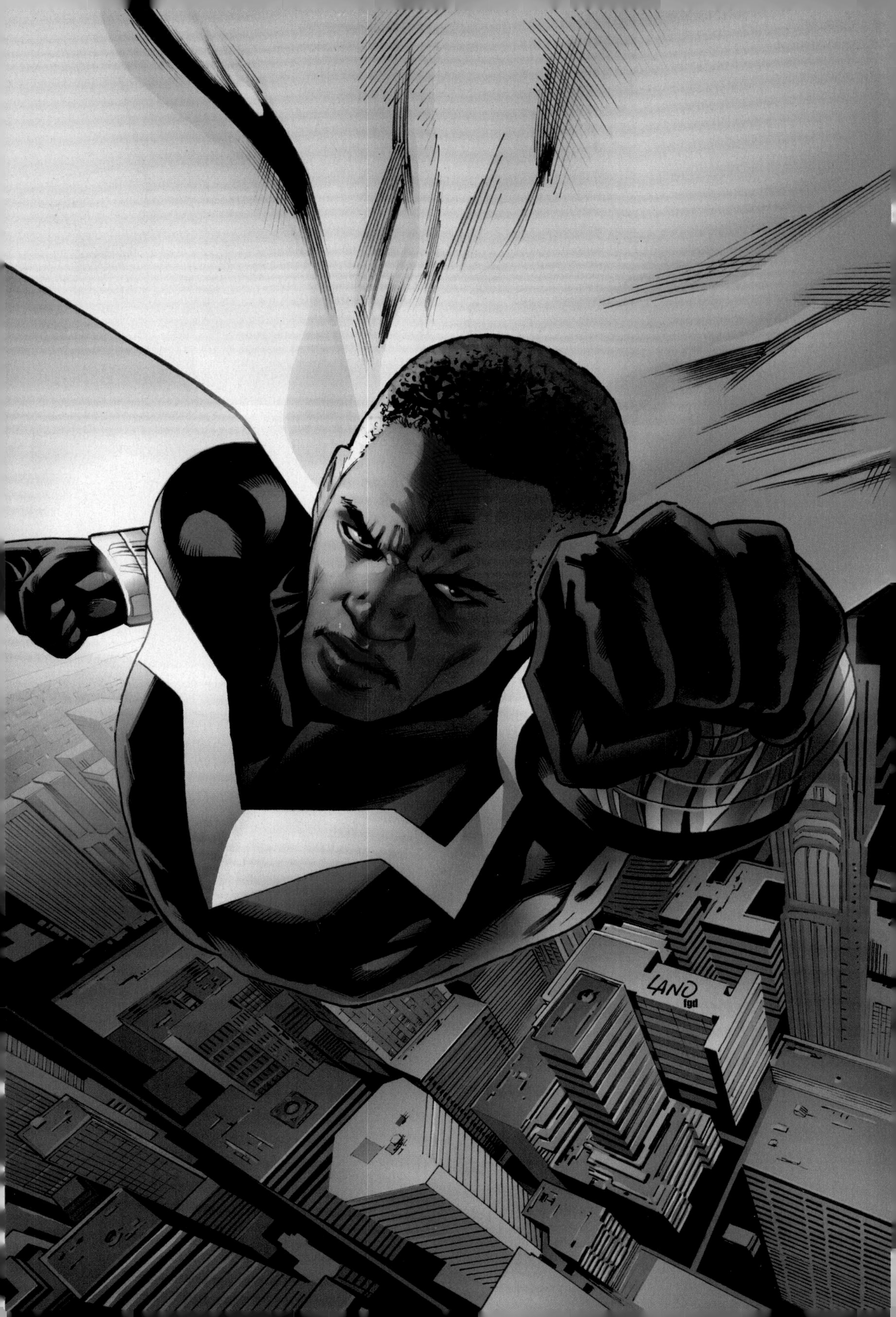
LANO
fgd

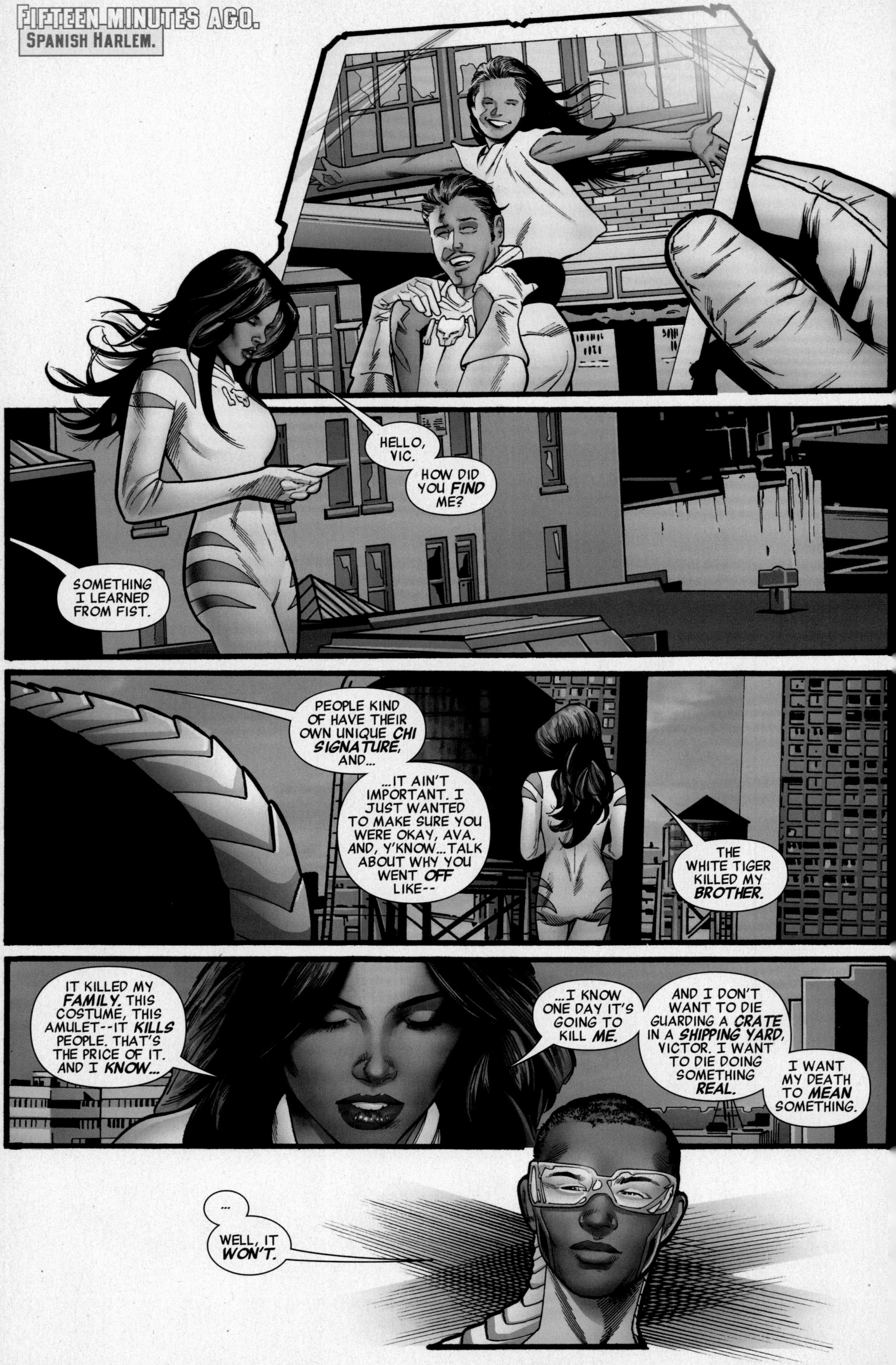
FIFTEEN MINUTES AGO.
SPANISH HARLEM.
HELLO, VIC.
HOW DID YOU FIND ME?
SOMETHING I LEARNED FROM FIST.
PEOPLE KIND OF HAVE THEIR OWN UNIQUE CHI SIGNATURE, AND...
...IT AIN'T IMPORTANT. I JUST WANTED TO MAKE SURE YOU WERE OKAY, AVA. AND, Y'KNOW...TALK ABOUT WHY YOU WENT OFF LIKE--
THE WHITE TIGER KILLED MY BROTHER.
IT KILLED MY FAMILY. THIS COSTUME, THIS AMULET--IT KILLS PEOPLE. THAT'S THE PRICE OF IT. AND I KNOW...
...I KNOW ONE DAY IT'S GOING TO KILL ME.
AND I DON'T WANT TO DIE GUARDING A CRATE IN A SHIPPING YARD, VICTOR. I WANT TO DIE DOING SOMETHING REAL.
I WANT MY DEATH TO MEAN SOMETHING.
...
WELL, IT WON'T.

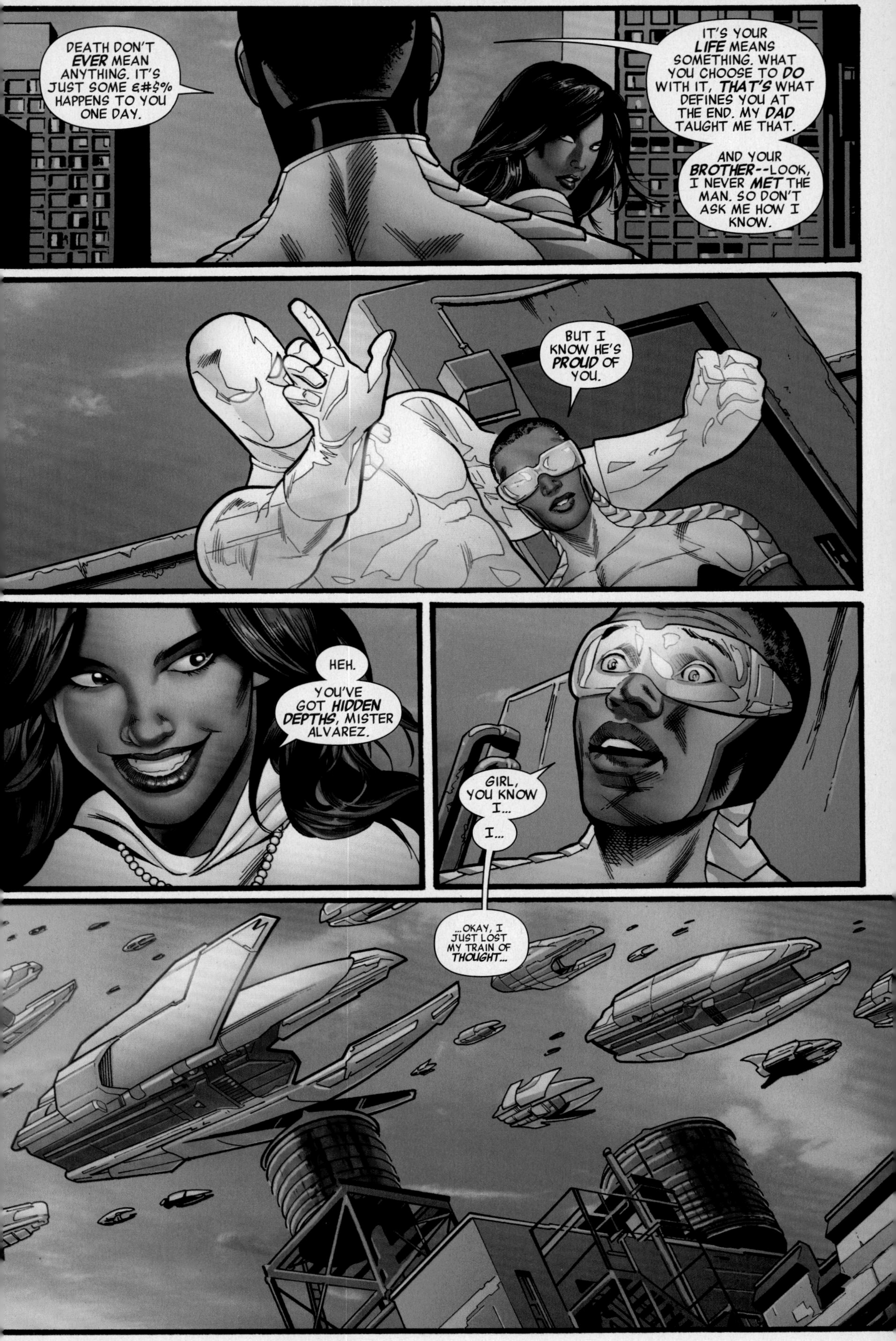
DEATH DON'T EVER MEAN ANYTHING. IT'S JUST SOME &#$% HAPPENS TO YOU ONE DAY.
IT'S YOUR LIFE MEANS SOMETHING. WHAT YOU CHOOSE TO DO WITH IT, THAT'S WHAT DEFINES YOU AT THE END. MY DAD TAUGHT ME THAT.
AND YOUR BROTHER--LOOK, I NEVER MET THE MAN. SO DON'T ASK ME HOW I KNOW.
BUT I KNOW HE'S PROUD OF YOU.
HEH.
YOU'VE GOT HIDDEN DEPTHS, MISTER ALVAREZ.
GIRL, YOU KNOW I...
I...
...OKAY, I JUST LOST MY TRAIN OF THOUGHT...

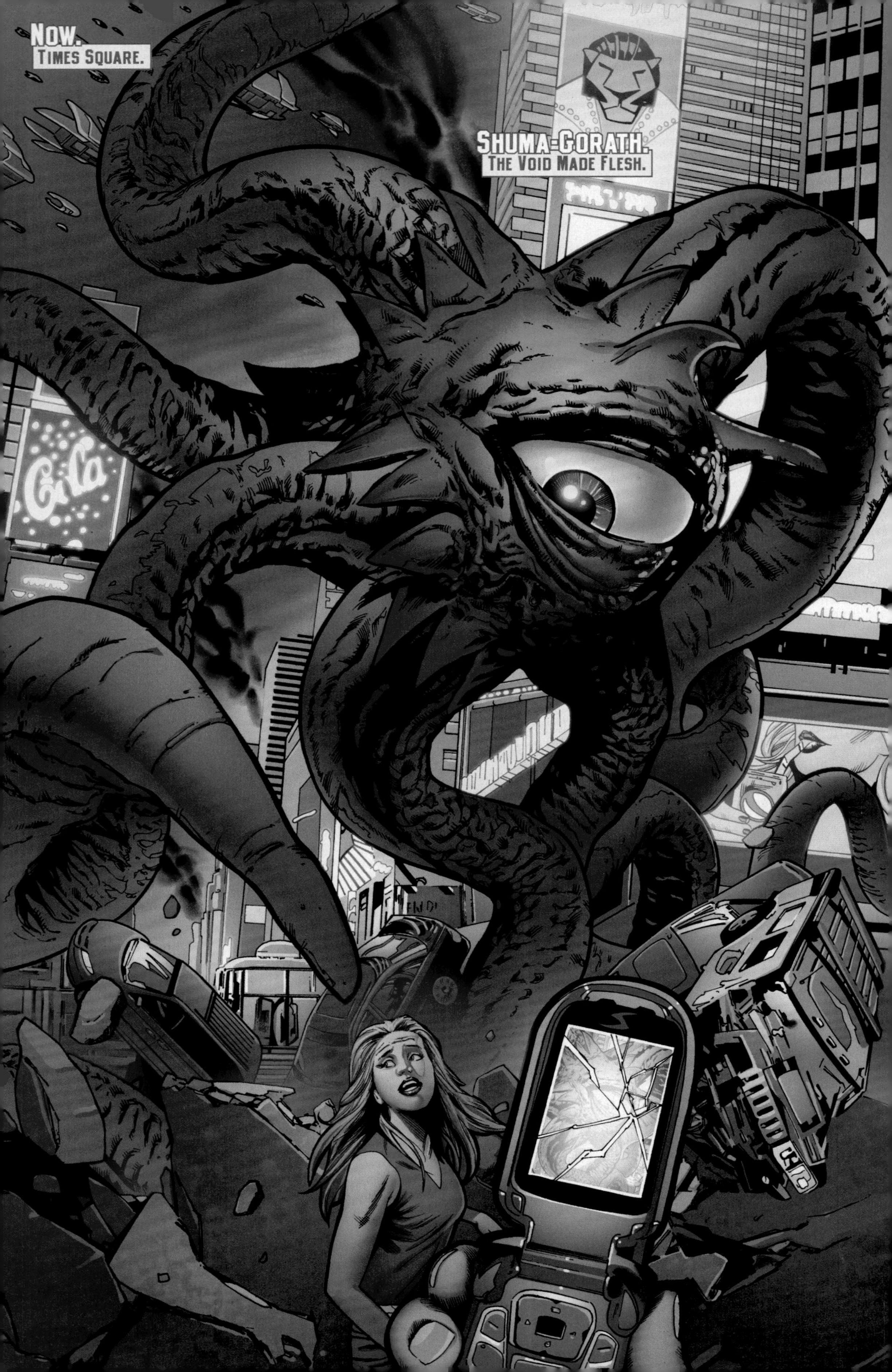
NOW.
TIMES SQUARE.
SHUMA-GORATH.
THE VOID MADE FLESH.

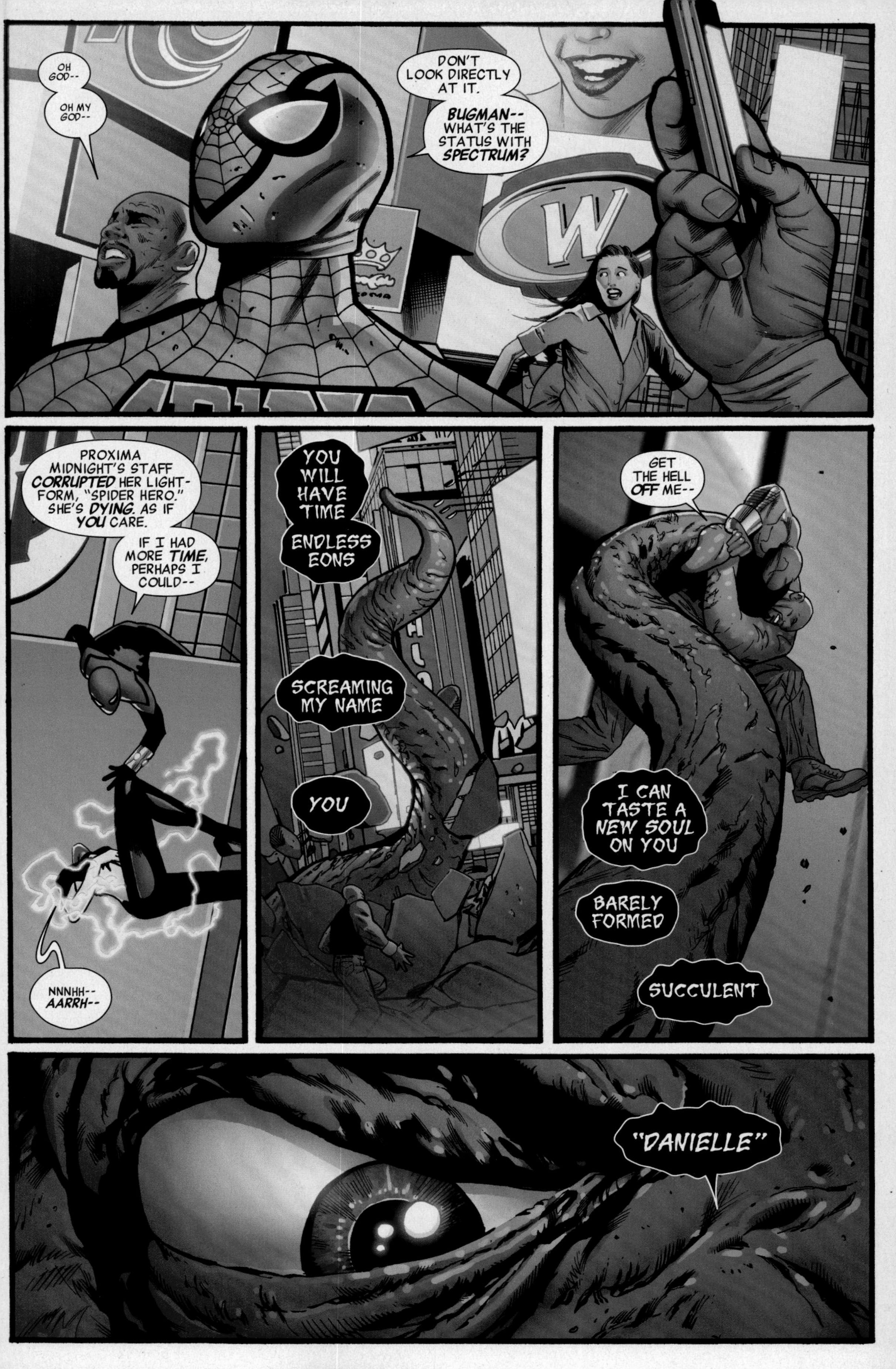
OH GOD--
OH MY GOD--
DON'T LOOK DIRECTLY AT IT.
BUGMAN-- WHAT'S THE STATUS WITH SPECTRUM?
PROXIMA MIDNIGHT'S STAFF CORRUPTED HER LIGHT-FORM, "SPIDER HERO." SHE'S DYING. AS IF YOU CARE.
IF I HAD MORE TIME, PERHAPS I COULD--
NNNHH-- AARRH--
YOU WILL HAVE TIME
ENDLESS EONS
SCREAMING MY NAME
YOU
GET THE HELL OFF ME--
I CAN TASTE A NEW SOUL ON YOU
BARELY FORMED
SUCCULENT
"DANIELLE"

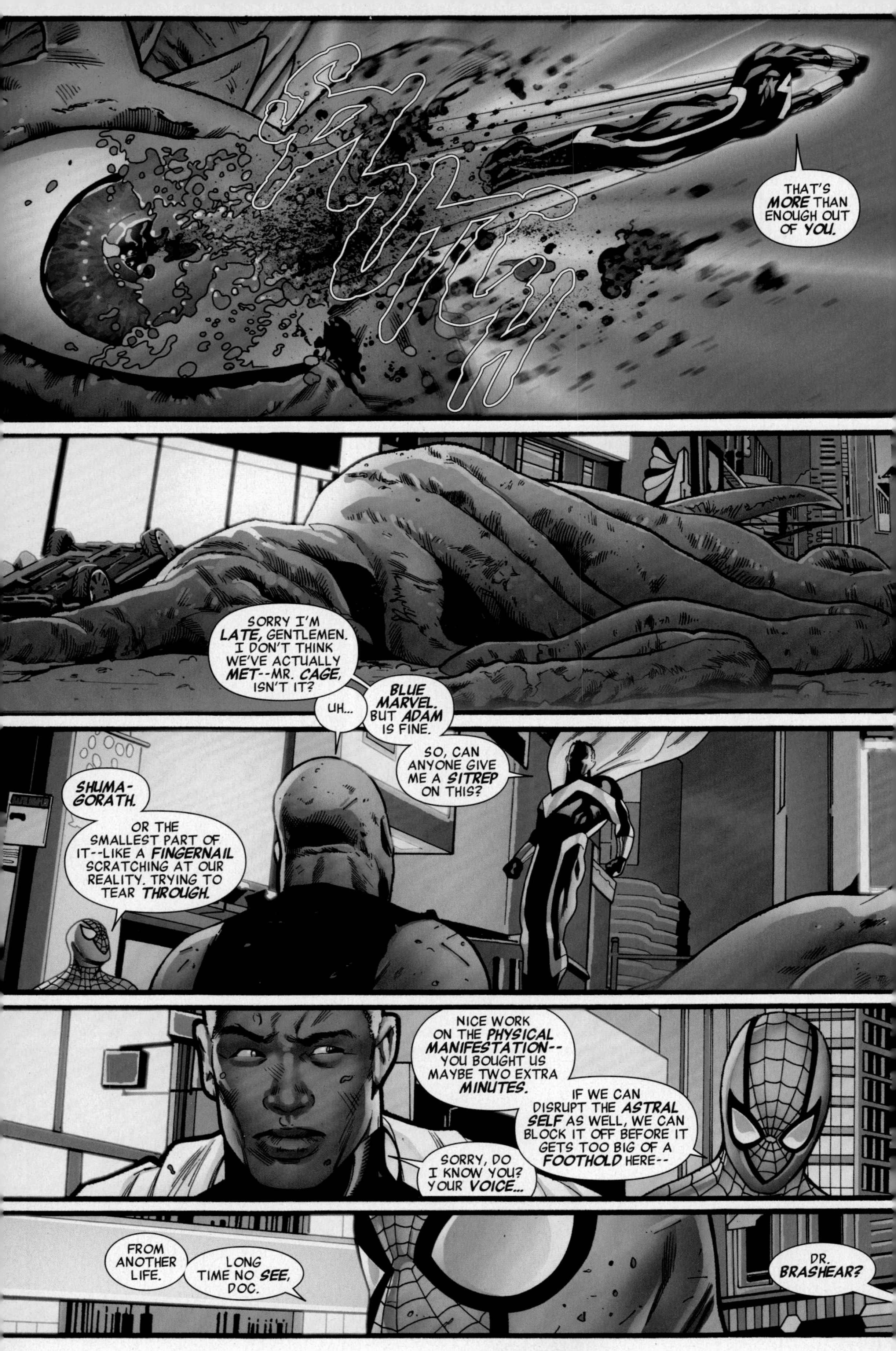

THAT'S MORE THAN ENOUGH OUT OF YOU.
SORRY I'M LATE, GENTLEMEN. I DON'T THINK WE'VE ACTUALLY MET--MR. CAGE, ISN'T IT?
UH...
BLUE MARVEL. BUT ADAM IS FINE.
SO, CAN ANYONE GIVE ME A SITREP ON THIS?
SHUMA-GORATH.
OR THE SMALLEST PART OF IT--LIKE A FINGERNAIL SCRATCHING AT OUR REALITY. TRYING TO TEAR THROUGH.
NICE WORK ON THE PHYSICAL MANIFESTATION--YOU BOUGHT US MAYBE TWO EXTRA MINUTES.
IF WE CAN DISRUPT THE ASTRAL SELF AS WELL, WE CAN BLOCK IT OFF BEFORE IT GETS TOO BIG OF A FOOTHOLD HERE--
SORRY, DO I KNOW YOU? YOUR VOICE...
DR. BRASHEAR?
FROM ANOTHER LIFE.
LONG TIME NO SEE, DOC.

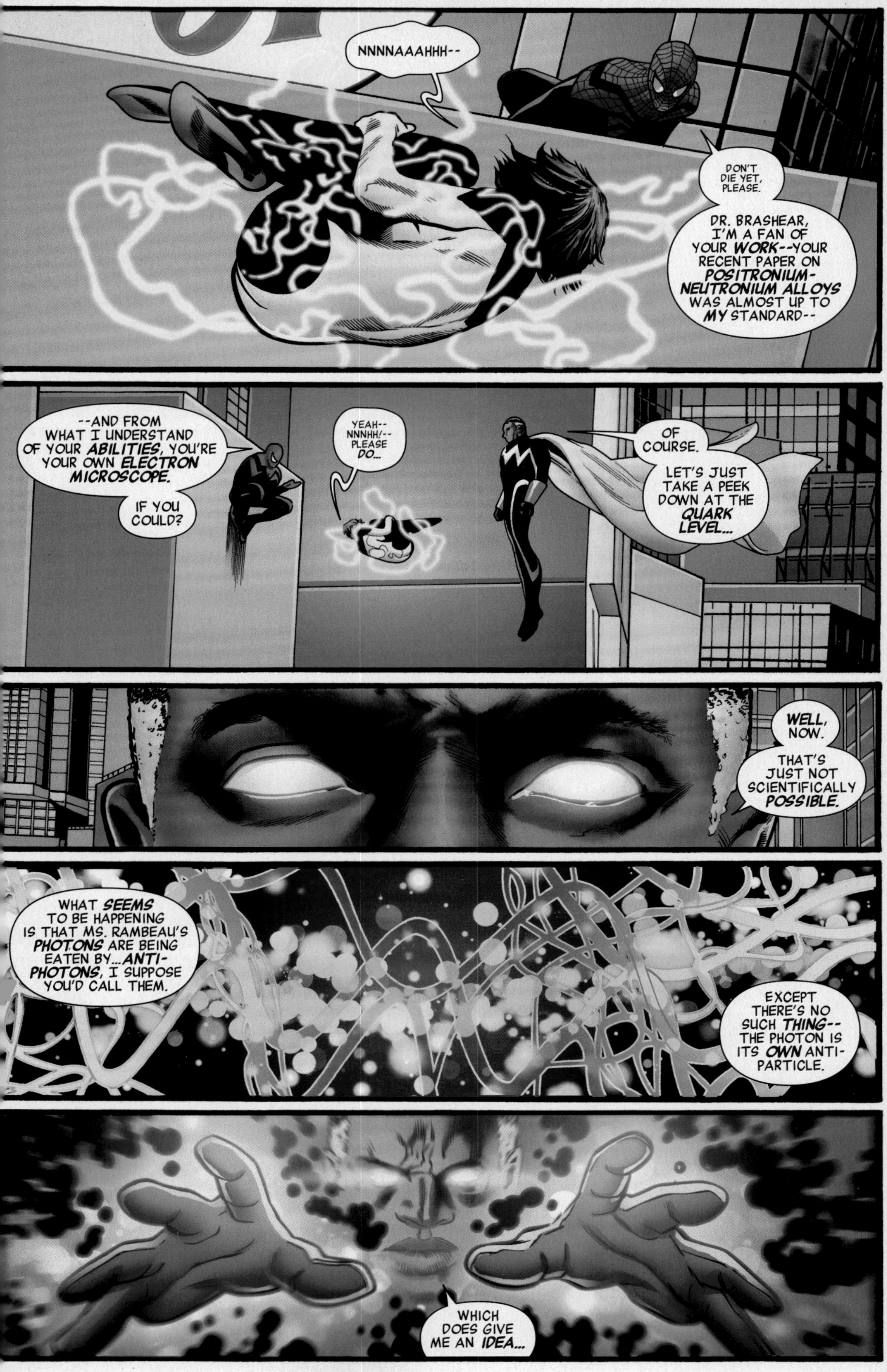
NNNNAAAHHH--
DON'T DIE YET, PLEASE.
DR. BRASHEAR, I'M A FAN OF YOUR WORK--YOUR RECENT PAPER ON POSITRONIUM-NEUTRONIUM ALLOYS WAS ALMOST UP TO MY STANDARD--
--AND FROM WHAT I UNDERSTAND OF YOUR ABILITIES, YOU'RE YOUR OWN ELECTRON MICROSCOPE.
IF YOU COULD?
YEAH--NNNHH!--PLEASE DO...
OF COURSE.
LET'S JUST TAKE A PEEK DOWN AT THE QUARK LEVEL...
WELL, NOW.
THAT'S JUST NOT SCIENTIFICALLY POSSIBLE.
WHAT SEEMS TO BE HAPPENING IS THAT MS. RAMBEAU'S PHOTONS ARE BEING EATEN BY...ANTI-PHOTONS, I SUPPOSE YOU'D CALL THEM.
EXCEPT THERE'S NO SUCH THING--THE PHOTON IS ITS OWN ANTI-PARTICLE.
WHICH DOES GIVE ME AN IDEA...

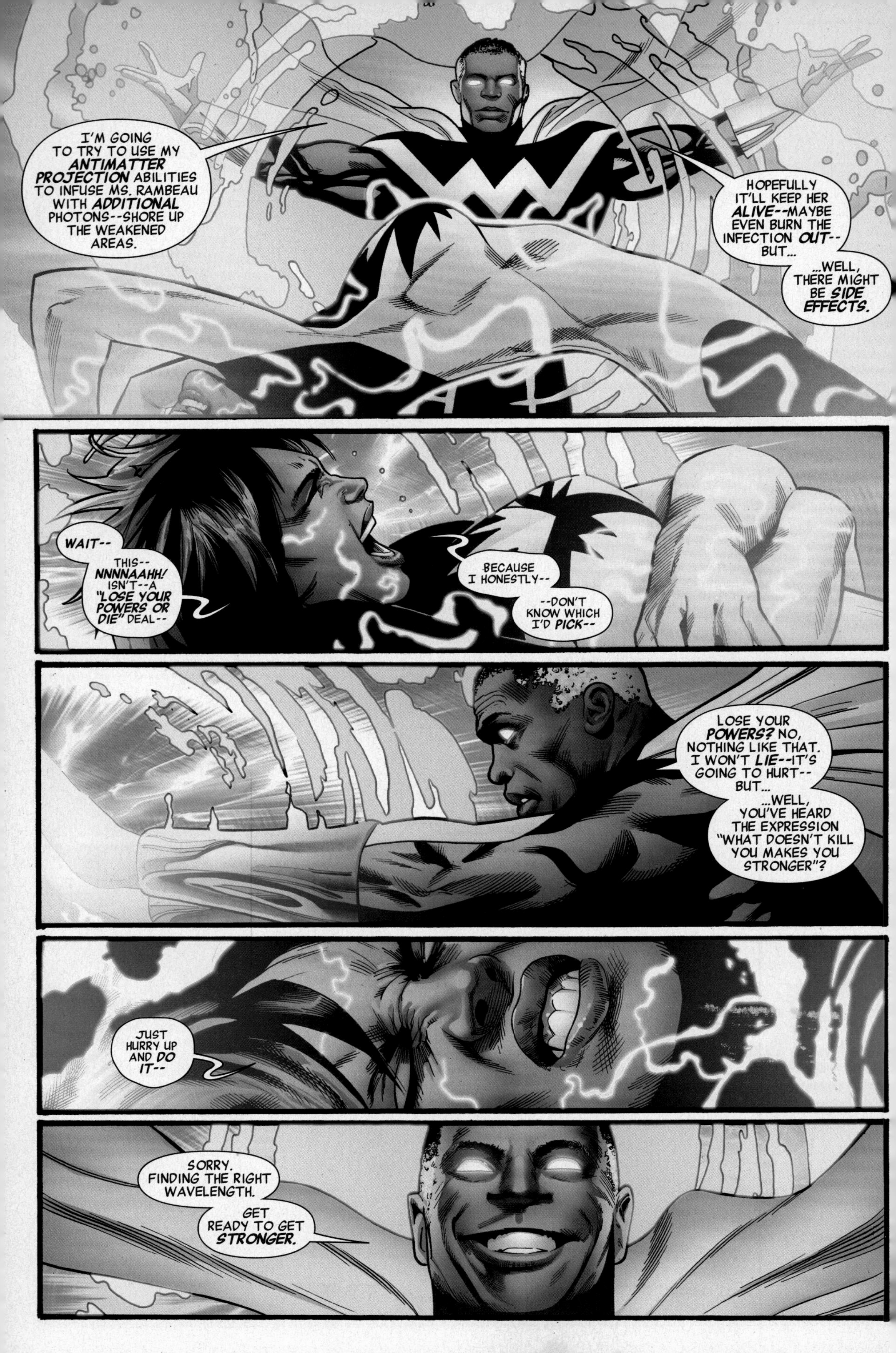
I'M GOING TO TRY TO USE MY ANTIMATTER PROJECTION ABILITIES TO INFUSE MS. RAMBEAU WITH ADDITIONAL PHOTONS--SHORE UP THE WEAKENED AREAS.
HOPEFULLY IT'LL KEEP HER ALIVE--MAYBE EVEN BURN THE INFECTION OUT--BUT...
...WELL, THERE MIGHT BE SIDE EFFECTS.
WAIT--
THIS--NNNNAAHH! ISN'T--A "LOSE YOUR POWERS OR DIE" DEAL--
BECAUSE I HONESTLY--
--DON'T KNOW WHICH I'D PICK--
LOSE YOUR POWERS? NO, NOTHING LIKE THAT. I WON'T LIE--IT'S GOING TO HURT--BUT...
...WELL, YOU'VE HEARD THE EXPRESSION "WHAT DOESN'T KILL YOU MAKES YOU STRONGER"?
JUST HURRY UP AND DO IT--
SORRY. FINDING THE RIGHT WAVELENGTH.
GET READY TO GET STRONGER.

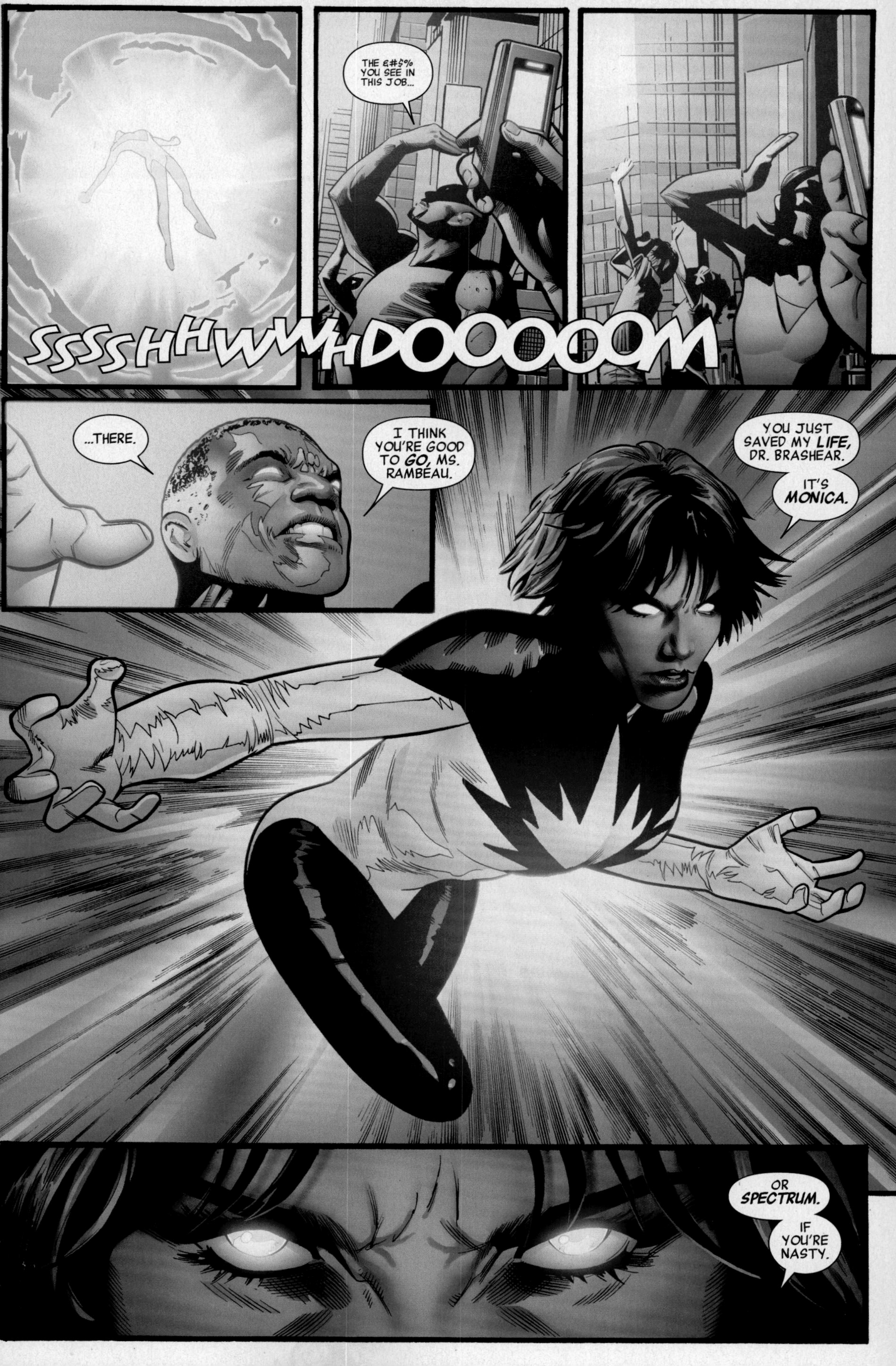
THE &#$% YOU SEE IN THIS JOB...
SSSSHHWWHDOOOOOOM
...THERE.
I THINK YOU'RE GOOD TO GO, MS. RAMBEAU.
YOU JUST SAVED MY LIFE, DR. BRASHEAR.
IT'S MONICA.
OR SPECTRUM.
IF YOU'RE NASTY.

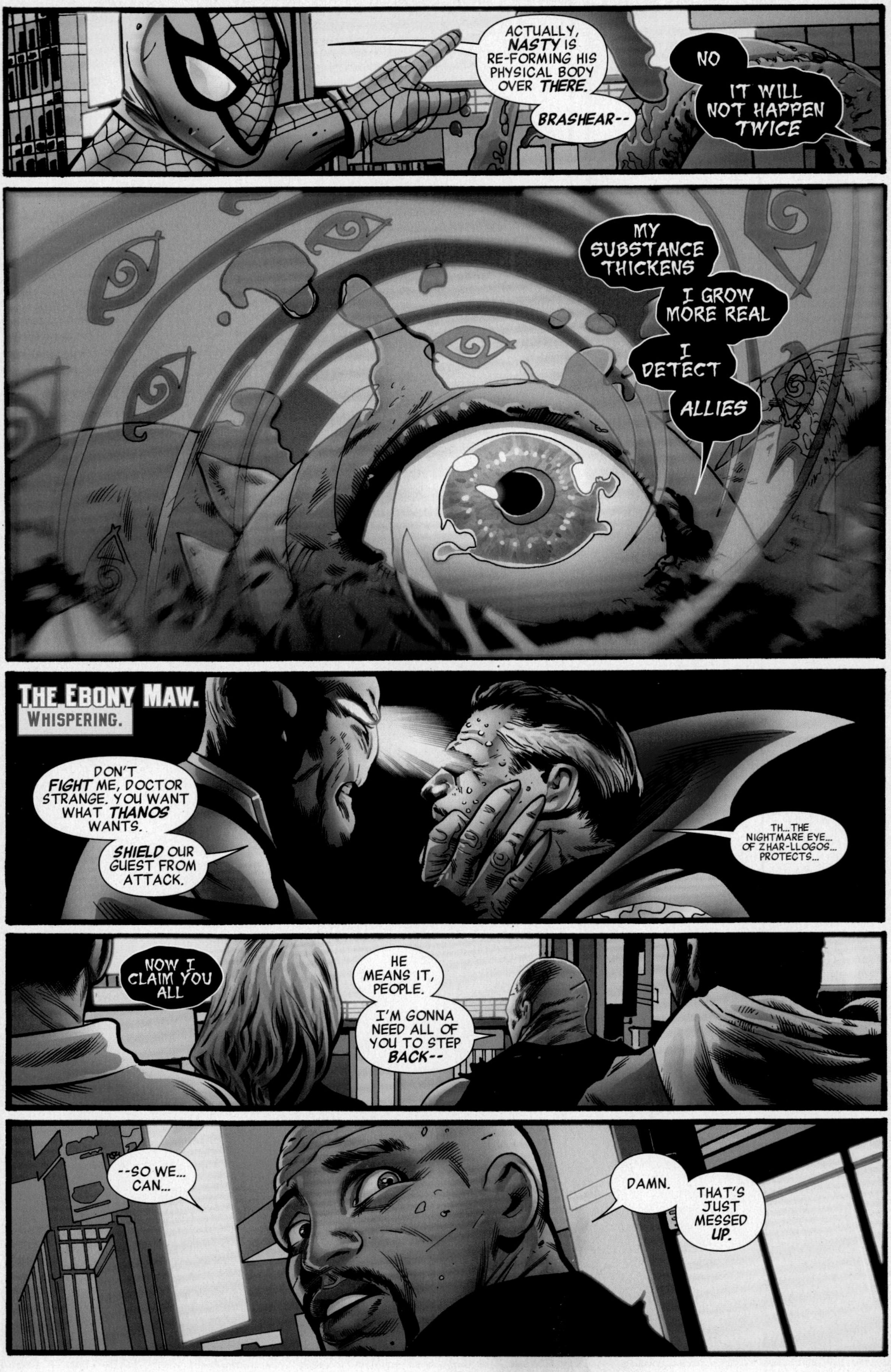
ACTUALLY, NASTY IS RE-FORMING HIS PHYSICAL BODY OVER THERE.
BRASHEAR--
NO
IT WILL NOT HAPPEN TWICE
MY SUBSTANCE THICKENS
I GROW MORE REAL
I DETECT
ALLIES
THE EBONY MAW.
WHISPERING.
DON'T FIGHT ME, DOCTOR STRANGE. YOU WANT WHAT THANOS WANTS.
SHIELD OUR GUEST FROM ATTACK.
TH...THE NIGHTMARE EYE... OF ZHAR-LLOGOS... PROTECTS...
NOW I CLAIM YOU ALL
HE MEANS IT, PEOPLE.
I'M GONNA NEED ALL OF YOU TO STEP BACK--
--SO WE... CAN...
DAMN.
THAT'S JUST MESSED UP.

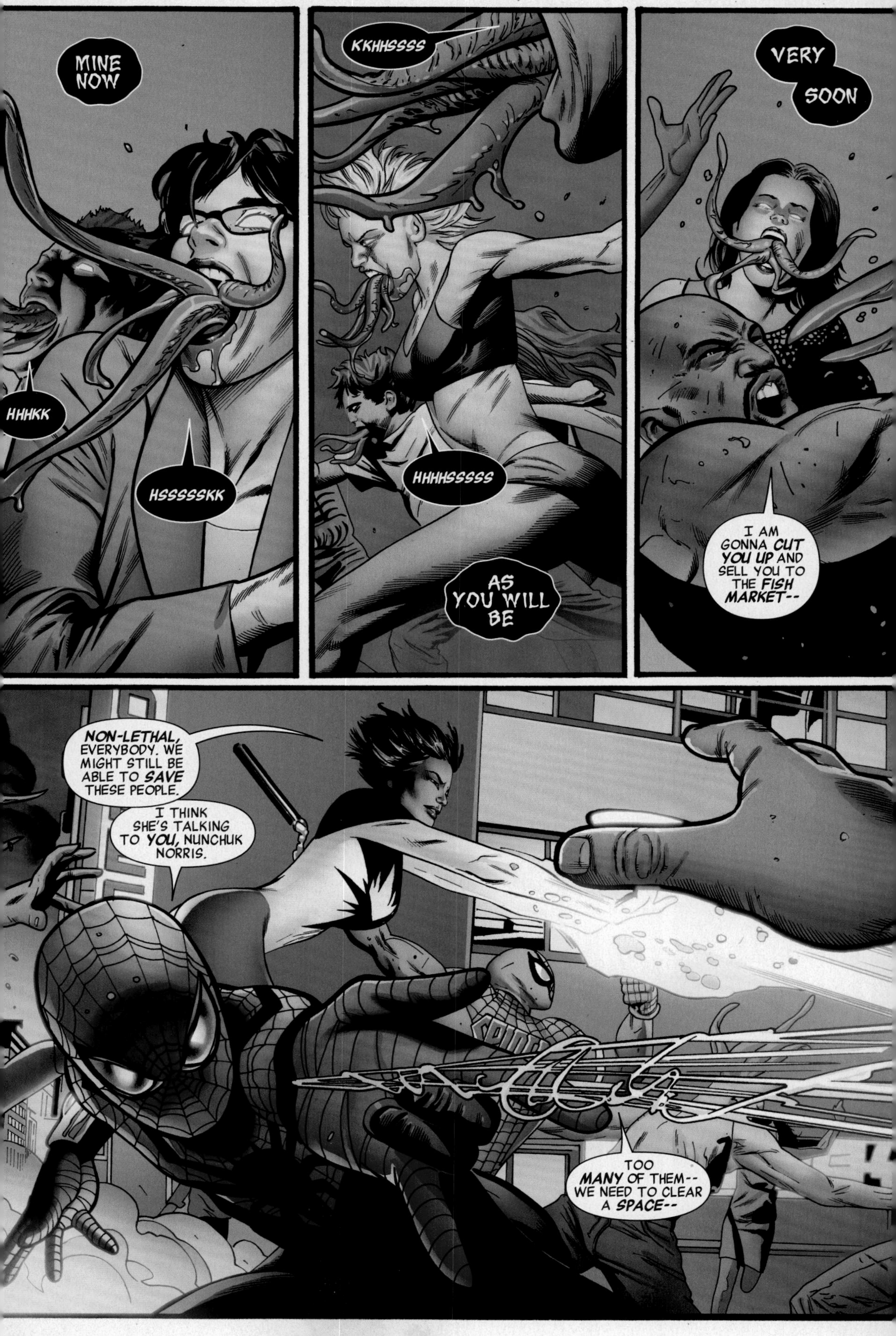
MINE NOW
HHHKK
HSSSSSKK
KKHHSSSS
HHHHSSSSS
AS YOU WILL BE
VERY
SOON
I AM GONNA CUT YOU UP AND SELL YOU TO THE FISH MARKET--
NON-LETHAL, EVERYBODY. WE MIGHT STILL BE ABLE TO SAVE THESE PEOPLE.
I THINK SHE'S TALKING TO YOU, NUNCHUK NORRIS.
TOO MANY OF THEM-- WE NEED TO CLEAR A SPACE--

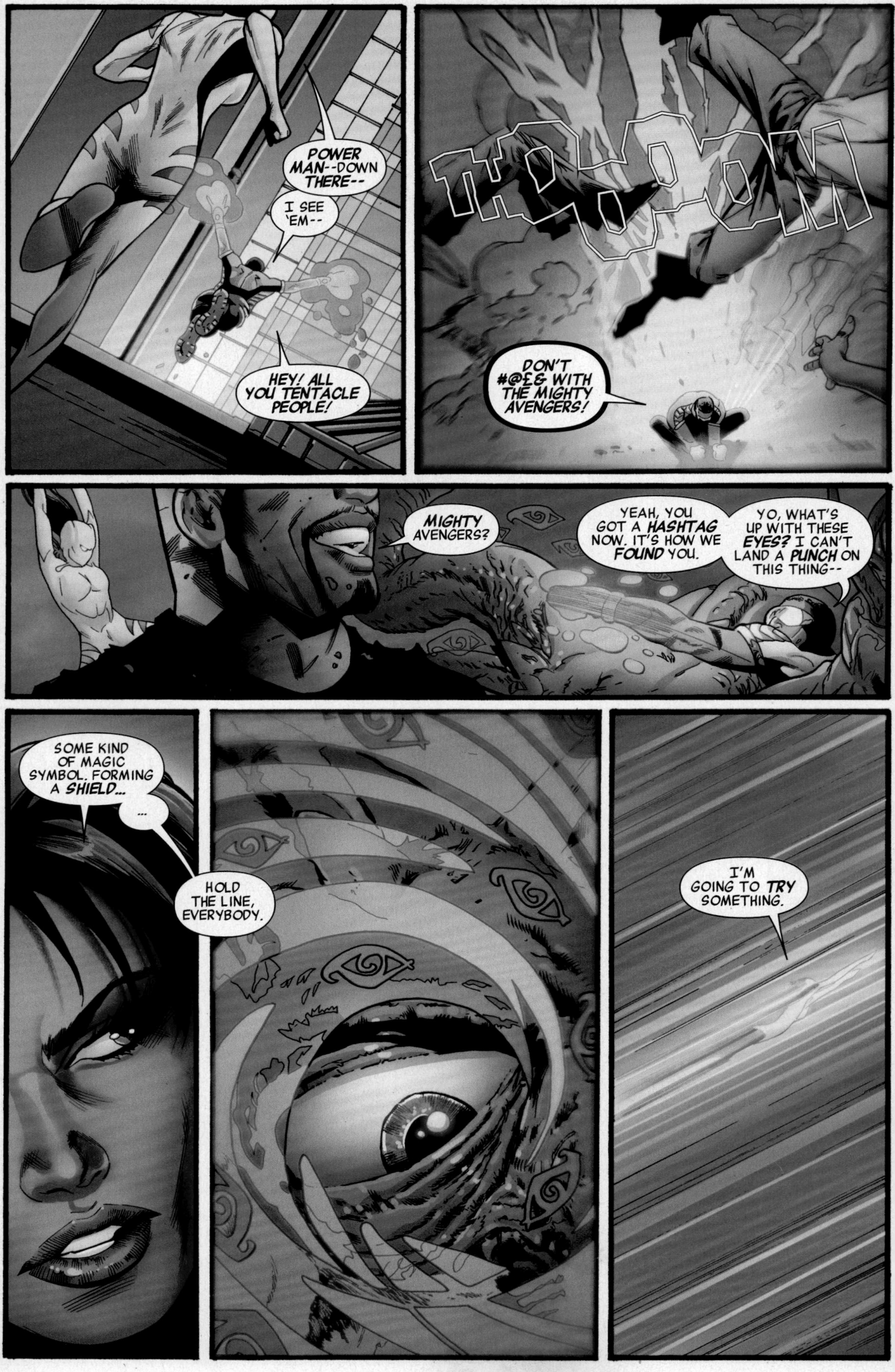
POWER MAN--DOWN THERE--
I SEE 'EM--
HEY! ALL YOU TENTACLE PEOPLE!
THOOOOOM
DON'T #@£& WITH THE MIGHTY AVENGERS!
MIGHTY AVENGERS?
YEAH, YOU GOT A HASHTAG NOW. IT'S HOW WE FOUND YOU.
YO, WHAT'S UP WITH THESE EYES? I CAN'T LAND A PUNCH ON THIS THING--
SOME KIND OF MAGIC SYMBOL. FORMING A SHIELD...
...
HOLD THE LINE, EVERYBODY.
I'M GOING TO TRY SOMETHING.

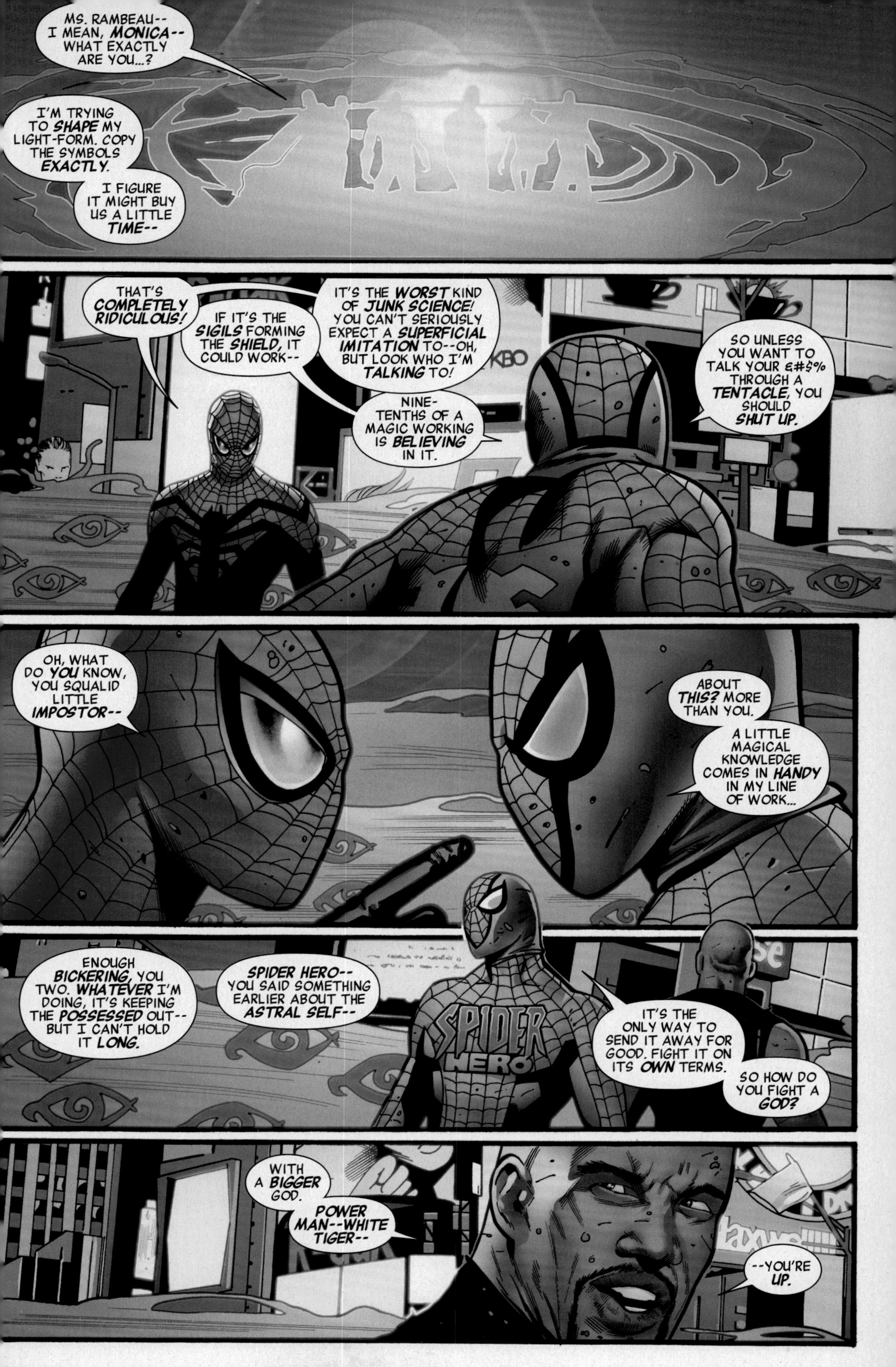
MS. RAMBEAU-- I MEAN, MONICA-- WHAT EXACTLY ARE YOU...?
I'M TRYING TO SHAPE MY LIGHT-FORM. COPY THE SYMBOLS EXACTLY.
I FIGURE IT MIGHT BUY US A LITTLE TIME--
THAT'S COMPLETELY RIDICULOUS!
IF IT'S THE SIGILS FORMING THE SHIELD, IT COULD WORK--
IT'S THE WORST KIND OF JUNK SCIENCE! YOU CAN'T SERIOUSLY EXPECT A SUPERFICIAL IMITATION TO--OH, BUT LOOK WHO I'M TALKING TO!
NINE-TENTHS OF A MAGIC WORKING IS BELIEVING IN IT.
SO UNLESS YOU WANT TO TALK YOUR &#$% THROUGH A TENTACLE, YOU SHOULD SHUT UP.
OH, WHAT DO YOU KNOW, YOU SQUALID LITTLE IMPOSTOR--
ABOUT THIS? MORE THAN YOU.
A LITTLE MAGICAL KNOWLEDGE COMES IN HANDY IN MY LINE OF WORK...
ENOUGH BICKERING, YOU TWO. WHATEVER I'M DOING, IT'S KEEPING THE POSSESSED OUT-- BUT I CAN'T HOLD IT LONG.
SPIDER HERO-- YOU SAID SOMETHING EARLIER ABOUT THE ASTRAL SELF--
SPIDER HERO
IT'S THE ONLY WAY TO SEND IT AWAY FOR GOOD. FIGHT IT ON ITS OWN TERMS.
SO HOW DO YOU FIGHT A GOD?
WITH A BIGGER GOD.
POWER MAN--WHITE TIGER--
--YOU'RE UP.

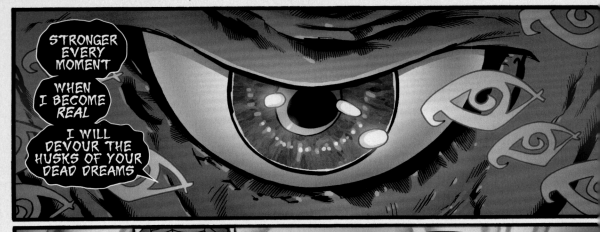

STRONGER EVERY MOMENT

WHEN I BECOME REAL

I WILL DEVOUR THE HUSKS OF YOUR DEAD DREAMS

CHARMING.

MONICA? I'M GOING TO TRY TO BROADCAST SOME MORE LIGHT ENERGY TO YOU--GIVE YOU A BOOST.

MUCH APPRECIATED, MARVEL.

ADAM. IT'S ADAM.

LISTEN, VIC--YOU HAVE DONE THIS BEFORE, RIGHT?

ONCE. IT WAS KIND OF UNFOCUSED, THOUGH--I MEAN, I NEVER CHANNELLED IT OR ANYTHING, I JUST--

DEEP BREATHS. CLEAR YOUR MIND.

MAN, I HOPE THIS WORKS--

RELAX, POWER MAN.

I'M THE ONE WITH THE HARD JOB.

CLEAR YOUR MIND.

NOW, FOCUS ON HOME. ON YOUR FAMILY. THE BUILDING YOU LIVE IN. EVERY BRICK, EVERY STONE. EVERY MEMORY.

MOVE OUT FROM THERE. STREETS AND LANDMARKS. KING STREET, SEDGWICK AVENUE, ZUCCOTTI PARK. PEOPLE AND HISTORY.

NEW YORK CITY.

IT ALL HAS CHI.

IT ALL HAS POWER.

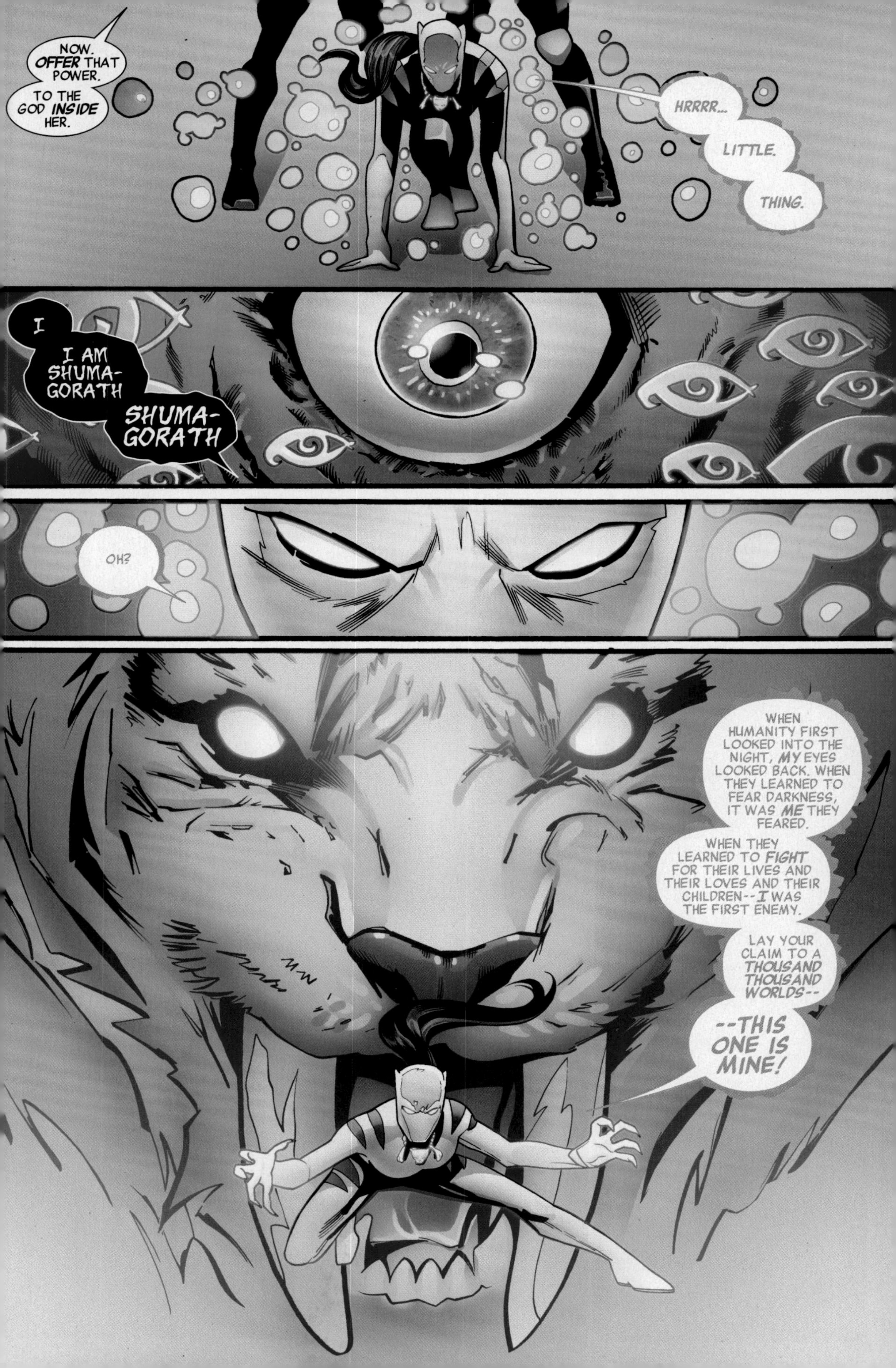
NOW. OFFER THAT POWER.
TO THE GOD INSIDE HER.
HRRRR...
LITTLE.
THING.
I
I AM SHUMA-GORATH
SHUMA-GORATH
OH?
WHEN HUMANITY FIRST LOOKED INTO THE NIGHT, MY EYES LOOKED BACK. WHEN THEY LEARNED TO FEAR DARKNESS, IT WAS ME THEY FEARED.
WHEN THEY LEARNED TO FIGHT FOR THEIR LIVES AND THEIR LOVES AND THEIR CHILDREN--I WAS THE FIRST ENEMY.
LAY YOUR CLAIM TO A THOUSAND THOUSAND WORLDS--
--THIS ONE IS MINE!

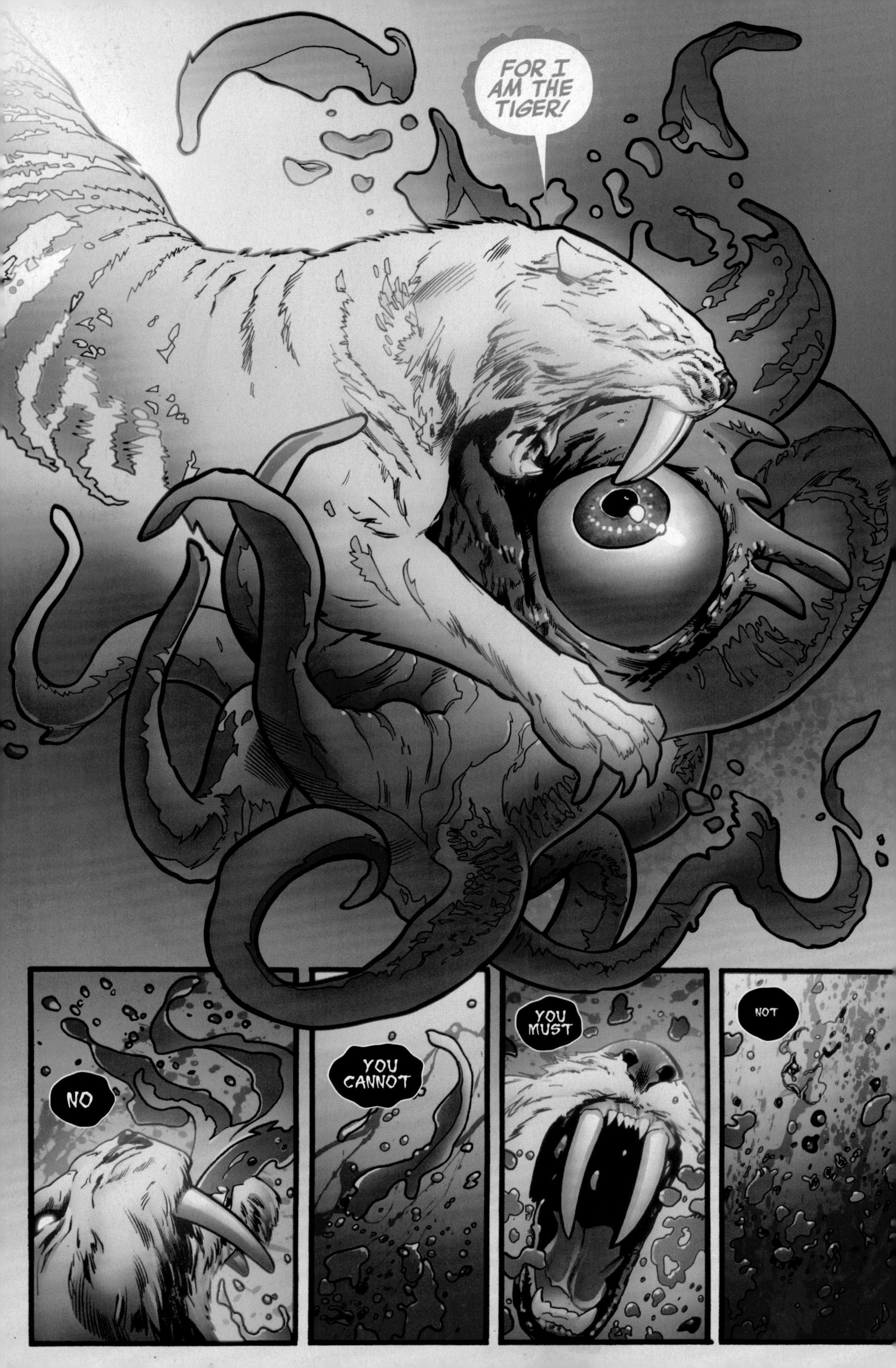
FOR I AM THE TIGER!
NO
YOU CANNOT
YOU MUST
NOT

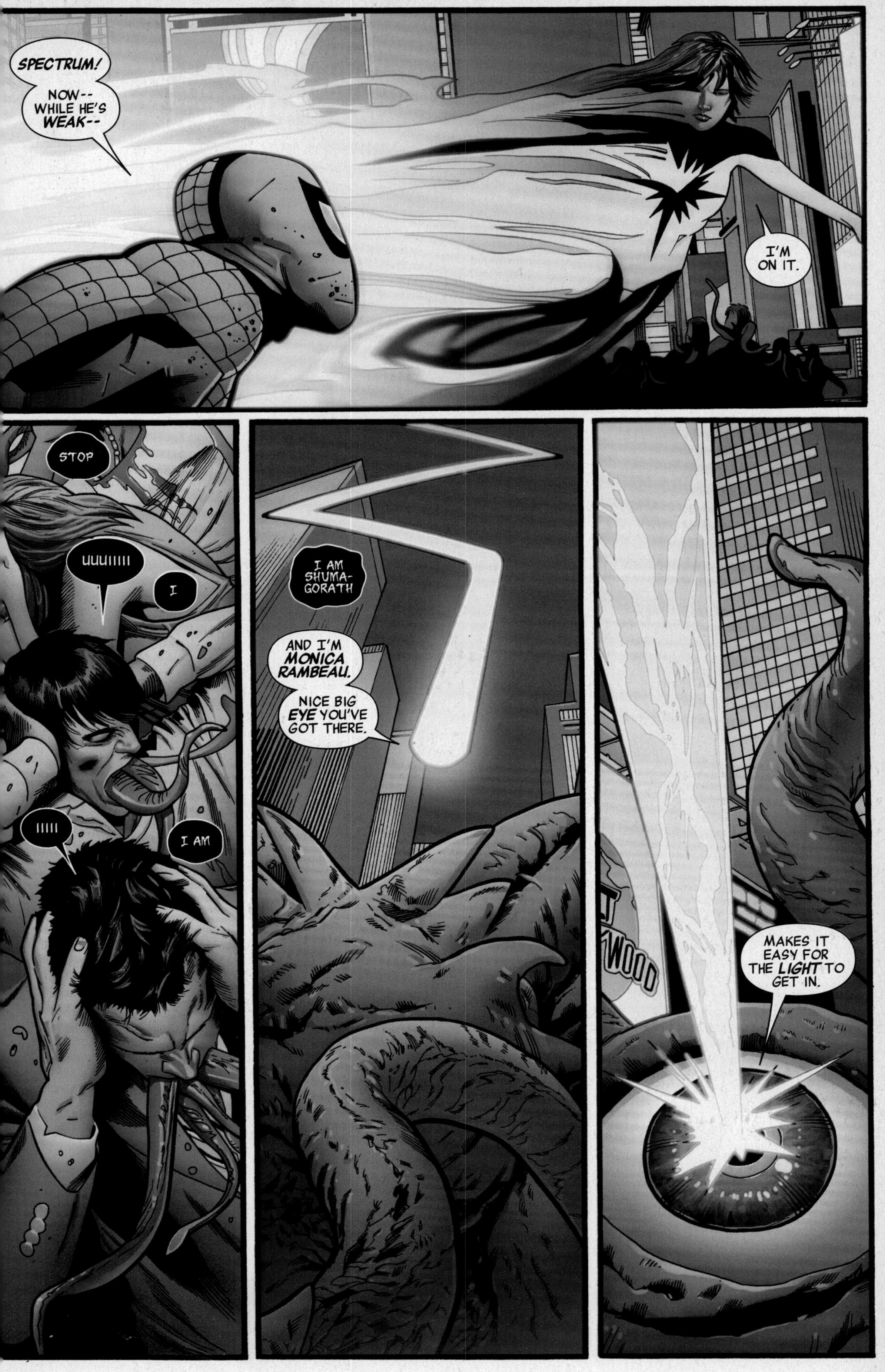
SPECTRUM!
NOW-- WHILE HE'S WEAK--
I'M ON IT.
STOP
UUUIIIII
I
IIIII
I AM
I AM SHUMA-GORATH
AND I'M MONICA RAMBEAU.
NICE BIG EYE YOU'VE GOT THERE.
MAKES IT EASY FOR THE LIGHT TO GET IN.

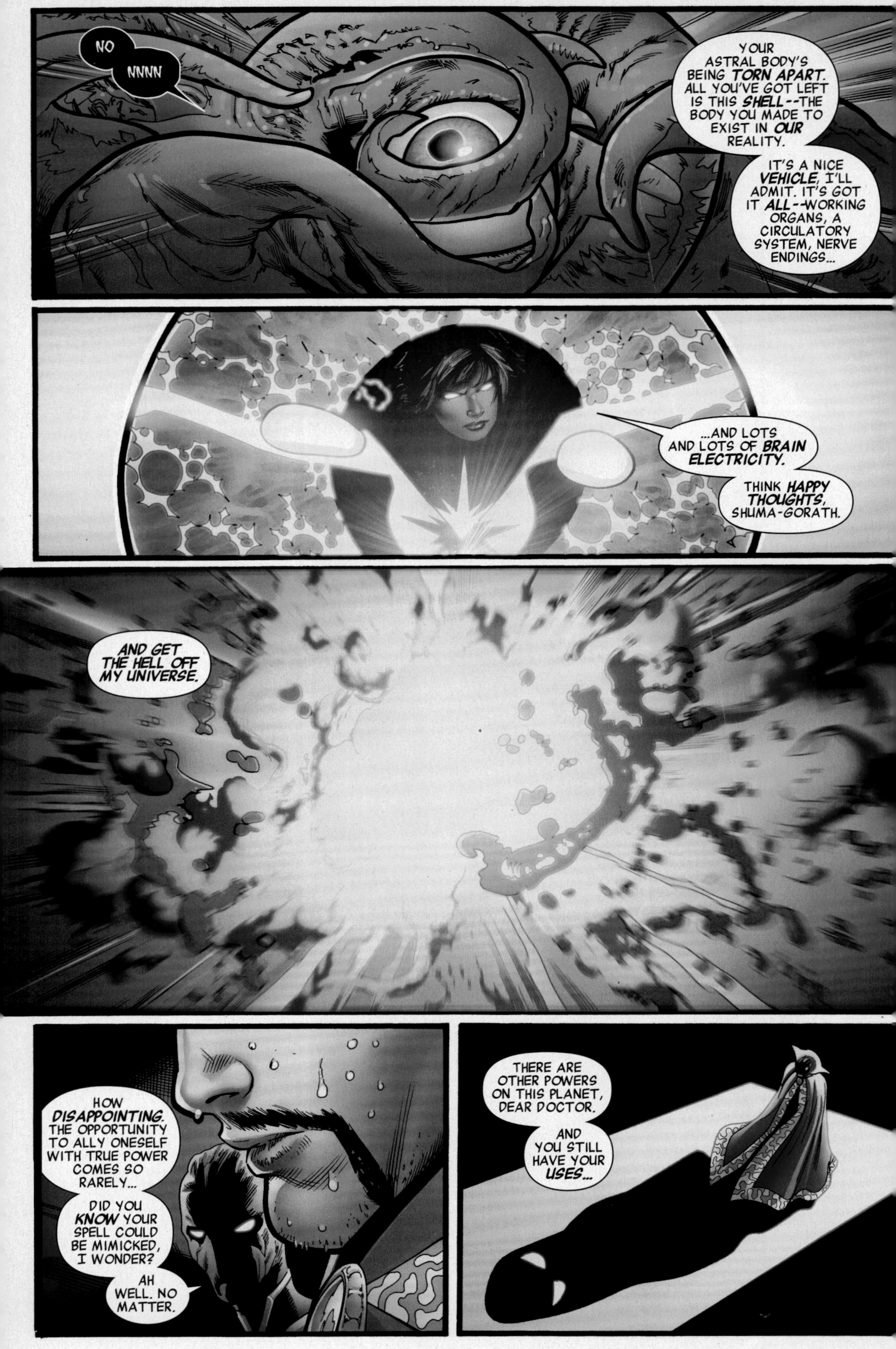
NO
NNNN
YOUR ASTRAL BODY'S BEING TORN APART. ALL YOU'VE GOT LEFT IS THIS SHELL--THE BODY YOU MADE TO EXIST IN OUR REALITY.
IT'S A NICE VEHICLE, I'LL ADMIT. IT'S GOT IT ALL--WORKING ORGANS, A CIRCULATORY SYSTEM, NERVE ENDINGS...
...AND LOTS AND LOTS OF BRAIN ELECTRICITY.
THINK HAPPY THOUGHTS, SHUMA-GORATH.
AND GET THE HELL OFF MY UNIVERSE.
HOW DISAPPOINTING. THE OPPORTUNITY TO ALLY ONESELF WITH TRUE POWER COMES SO RARELY...
DID YOU KNOW YOUR SPELL COULD BE MIMICKED, I WONDER?
AH WELL. NO MATTER.
THERE ARE OTHER POWERS ON THIS PLANET, DEAR DOCTOR.
AND YOU STILL HAVE YOUR USES...

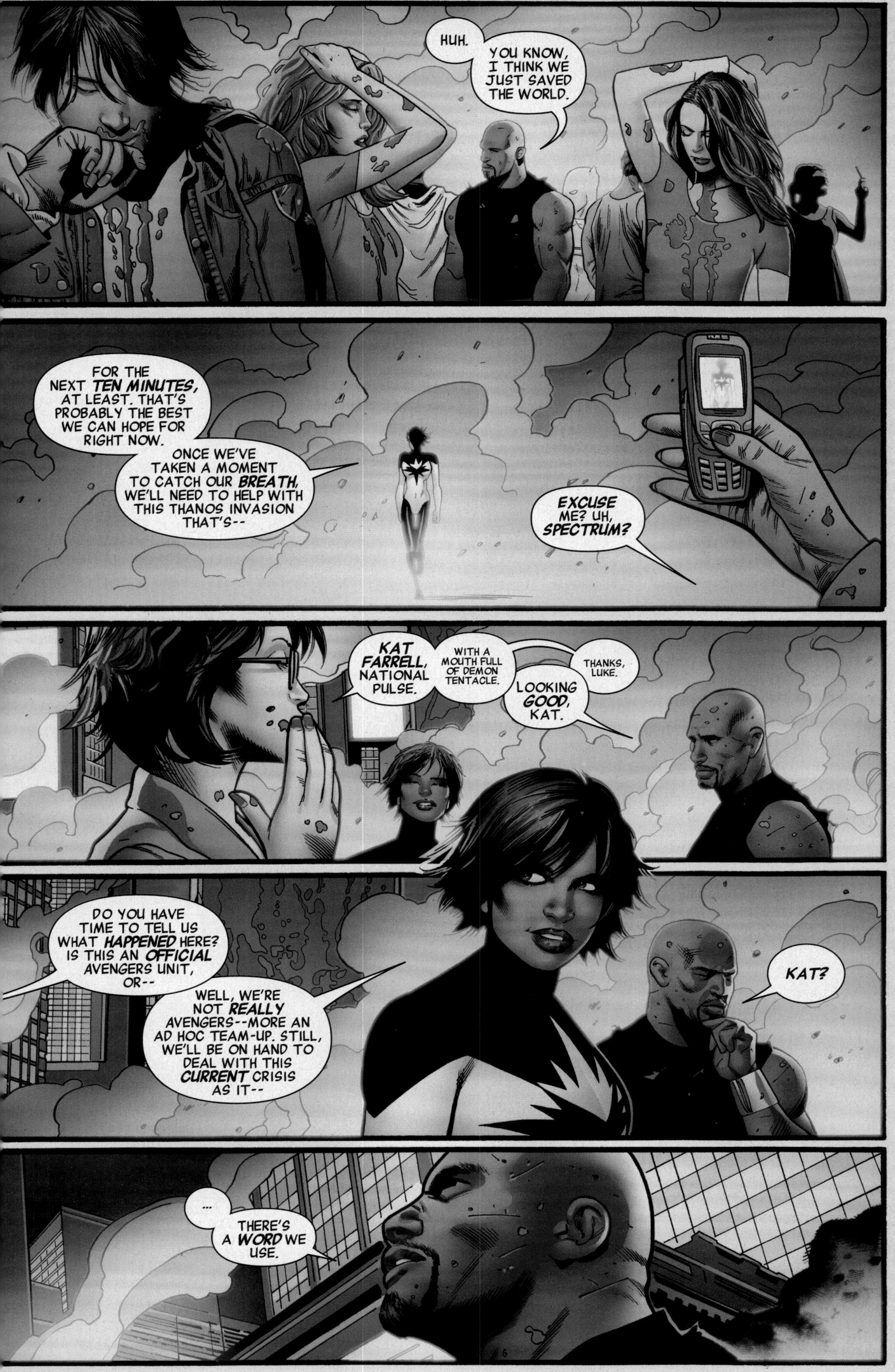
HUH.
YOU KNOW, I THINK WE JUST SAVED THE WORLD.
FOR THE NEXT TEN MINUTES, AT LEAST. THAT'S PROBABLY THE BEST WE CAN HOPE FOR RIGHT NOW.
ONCE WE'VE TAKEN A MOMENT TO CATCH OUR BREATH, WE'LL NEED TO HELP WITH THIS THANOS INVASION THAT'S--
EXCUSE ME? UH, SPECTRUM?
KAT FARRELL, NATIONAL PULSE.
WITH A MOUTH FULL OF DEMON TENTACLE.
THANKS, LUKE.
LOOKING GOOD, KAT.
DO YOU HAVE TIME TO TELL US WHAT HAPPENED HERE? IS THIS AN OFFICIAL AVENGERS UNIT, OR--
WELL, WE'RE NOT REALLY AVENGERS--MORE AN AD HOC TEAM-UP. STILL, WE'LL BE ON HAND TO DEAL WITH THIS CURRENT CRISIS AS IT--
KAT?
...
THERE'S A WORD WE USE.

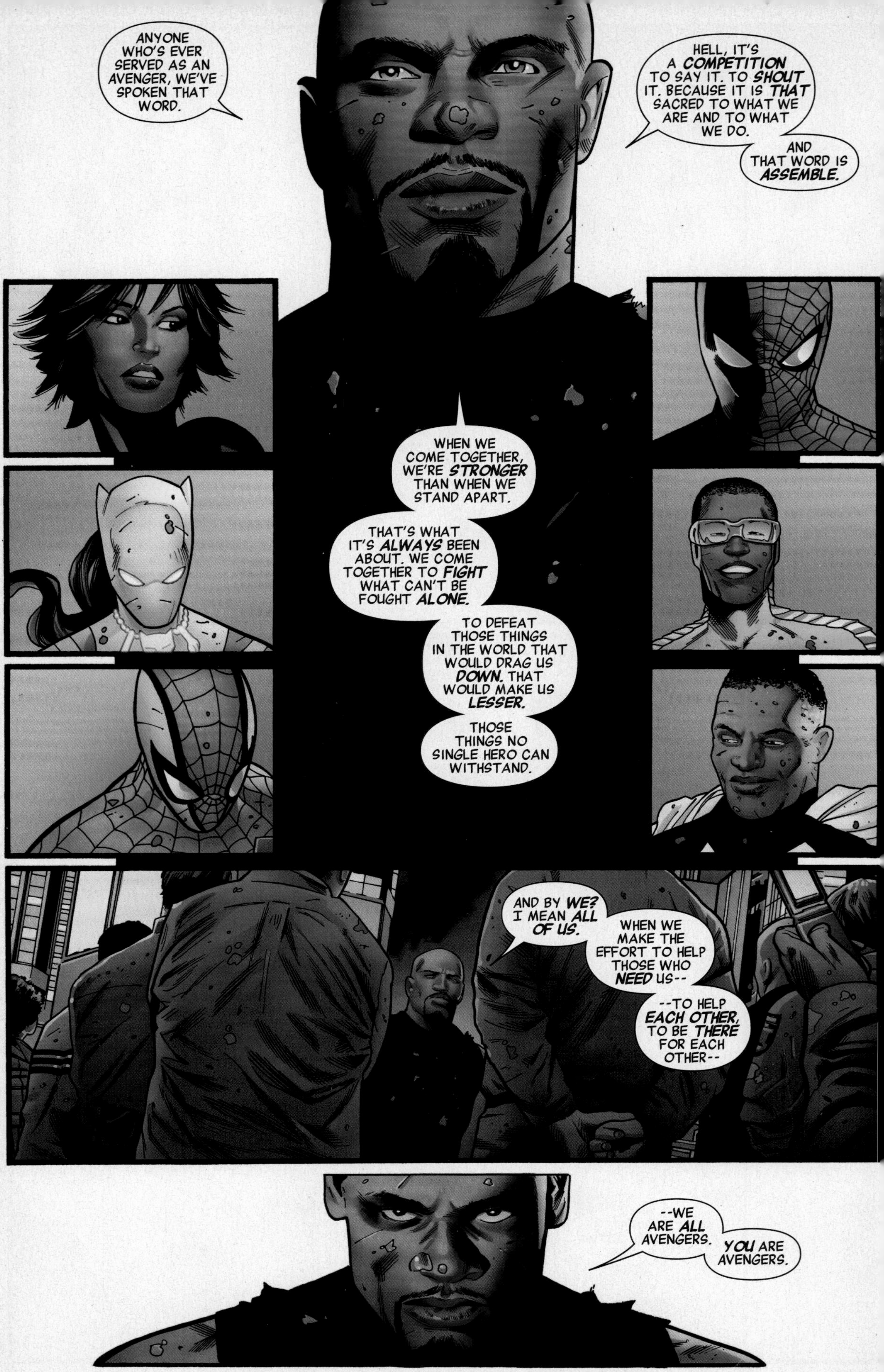
ANYONE WHO'S EVER SERVED AS AN AVENGER, WE'VE SPOKEN THAT WORD.
HELL, IT'S A COMPETITION TO SAY IT. TO SHOUT IT. BECAUSE IT IS THAT SACRED TO WHAT WE ARE AND TO WHAT WE DO.
AND THAT WORD IS ASSEMBLE.
WHEN WE COME TOGETHER, WE'RE STRONGER THAN WHEN WE STAND APART.
THAT'S WHAT IT'S ALWAYS BEEN ABOUT. WE COME TOGETHER TO FIGHT WHAT CAN'T BE FOUGHT ALONE.
TO DEFEAT THOSE THINGS IN THE WORLD THAT WOULD DRAG US DOWN. THAT WOULD MAKE US LESSER.
THOSE THINGS NO SINGLE HERO CAN WITHSTAND.
AND BY WE? I MEAN ALL OF US.
WHEN WE MAKE THE EFFORT TO HELP THOSE WHO NEED US--
--TO HELP EACH OTHER, TO BE THERE FOR EACH OTHER--
--WE ARE ALL AVENGERS.
YOU ARE AVENGERS.

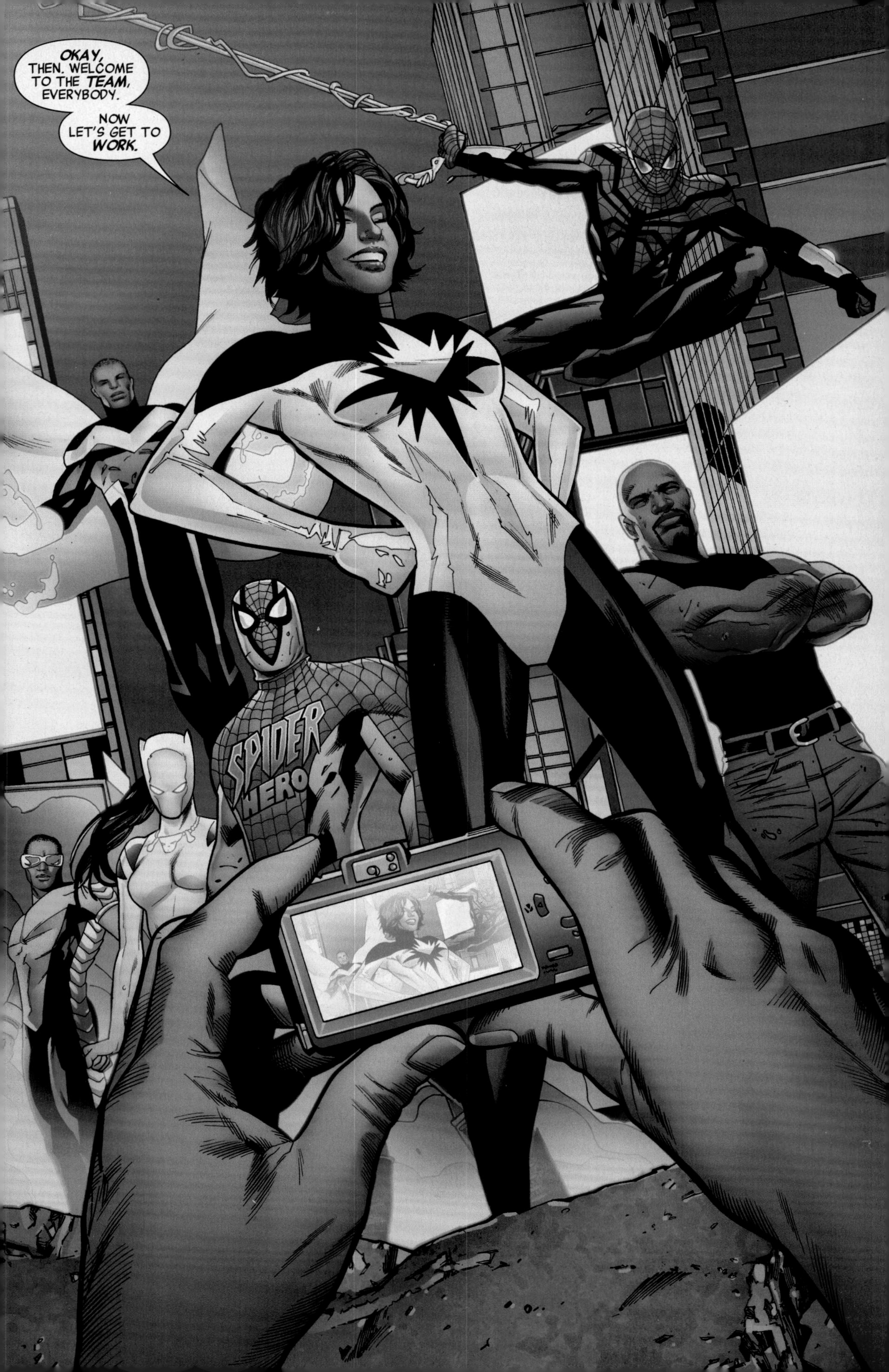

OKAY, THEN. WELCOME TO THE TEAM, EVERYBODY.
NOW LET'S GET TO WORK.
SPIDER HERO

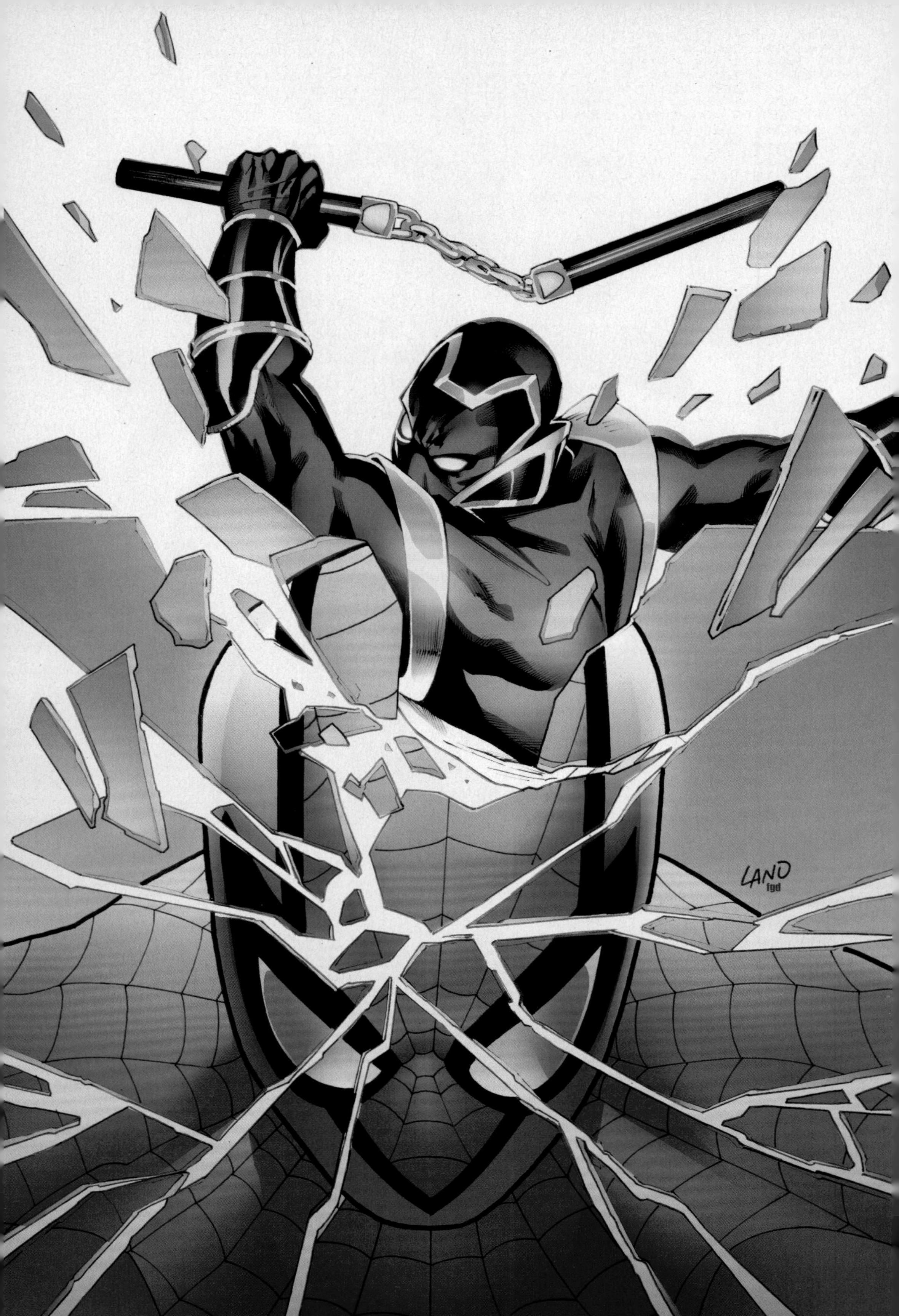
LAND
fgd

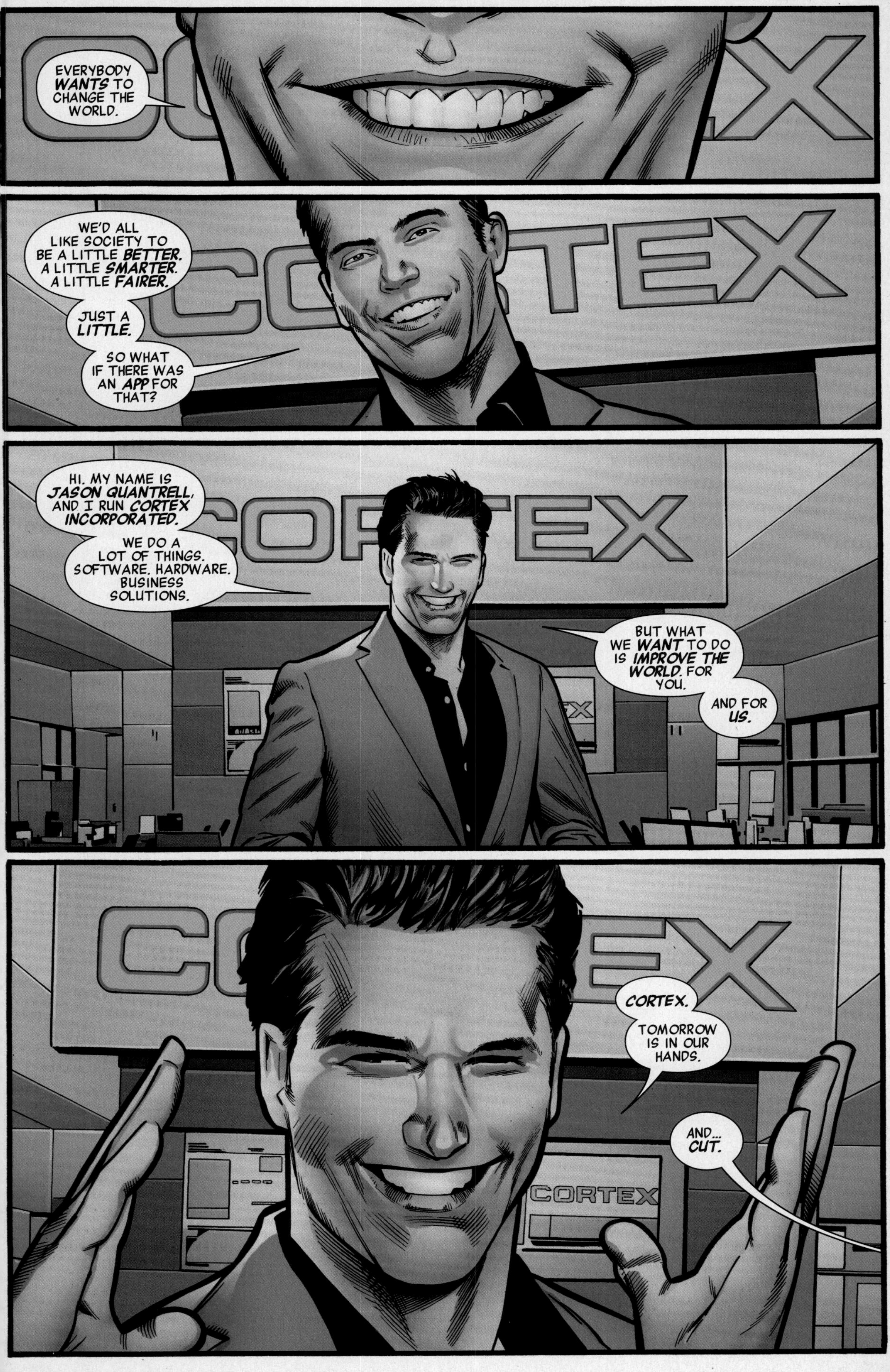
EVERYBODY WANTS TO CHANGE THE WORLD.
WE'D ALL LIKE SOCIETY TO BE A LITTLE BETTER. A LITTLE SMARTER. A LITTLE FAIRER.
JUST A LITTLE.
SO WHAT IF THERE WAS AN APP FOR THAT?
HI. MY NAME IS JASON QUANTRELL, AND I RUN CORTEX INCORPORATED.
WE DO A LOT OF THINGS. SOFTWARE. HARDWARE. BUSINESS SOLUTIONS.
CORTEX
BUT WHAT WE WANT TO DO IS IMPROVE THE WORLD. FOR YOU.
AND FOR US.
CORTEX
CORTEX.
TOMORROW IS IN OUR HANDS.
AND... CUT.

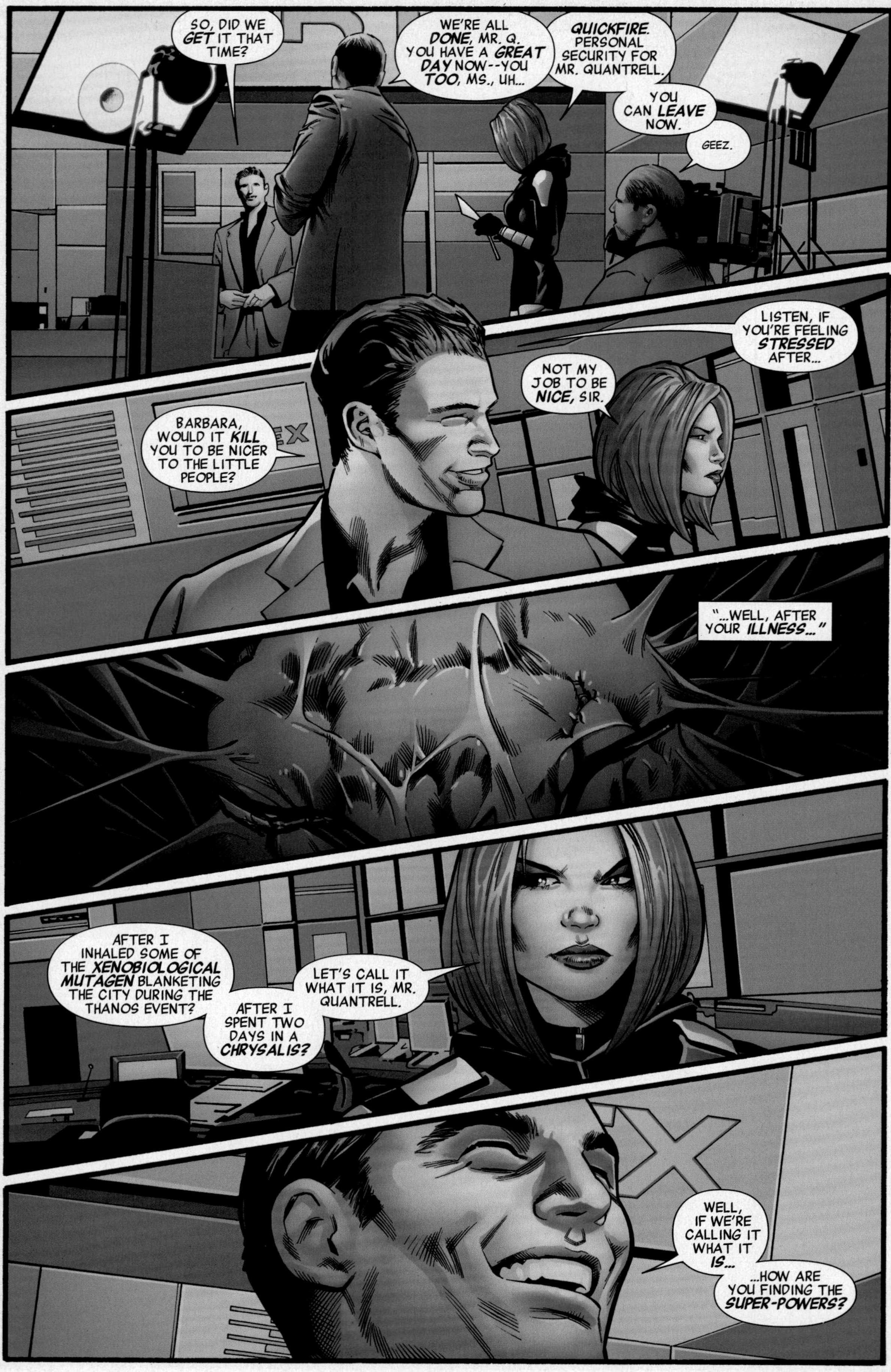

SO, DID WE GET IT THAT TIME?
WE'RE ALL DONE, MR. Q. YOU HAVE A GREAT DAY NOW--YOU TOO, MS., UH...
QUICKFIRE. PERSONAL SECURITY FOR MR. QUANTRELL.
YOU CAN LEAVE NOW.
GEEZ.
BARBARA, WOULD IT KILL YOU TO BE NICER TO THE LITTLE PEOPLE?
NOT MY JOB TO BE NICE, SIR.
LISTEN, IF YOU'RE FEELING STRESSED AFTER...
"...WELL, AFTER YOUR ILLNESS..."
LET'S CALL IT WHAT IT IS, MR. QUANTRELL.
AFTER I INHALED SOME OF THE XENOBIOLOGICAL MUTAGEN BLANKETING THE CITY DURING THE THANOS EVENT?
AFTER I SPENT TWO DAYS IN A CHRYSALIS?
WELL, IF WE'RE CALLING IT WHAT IT IS...
...HOW ARE YOU FINDING THE SUPER-POWERS?

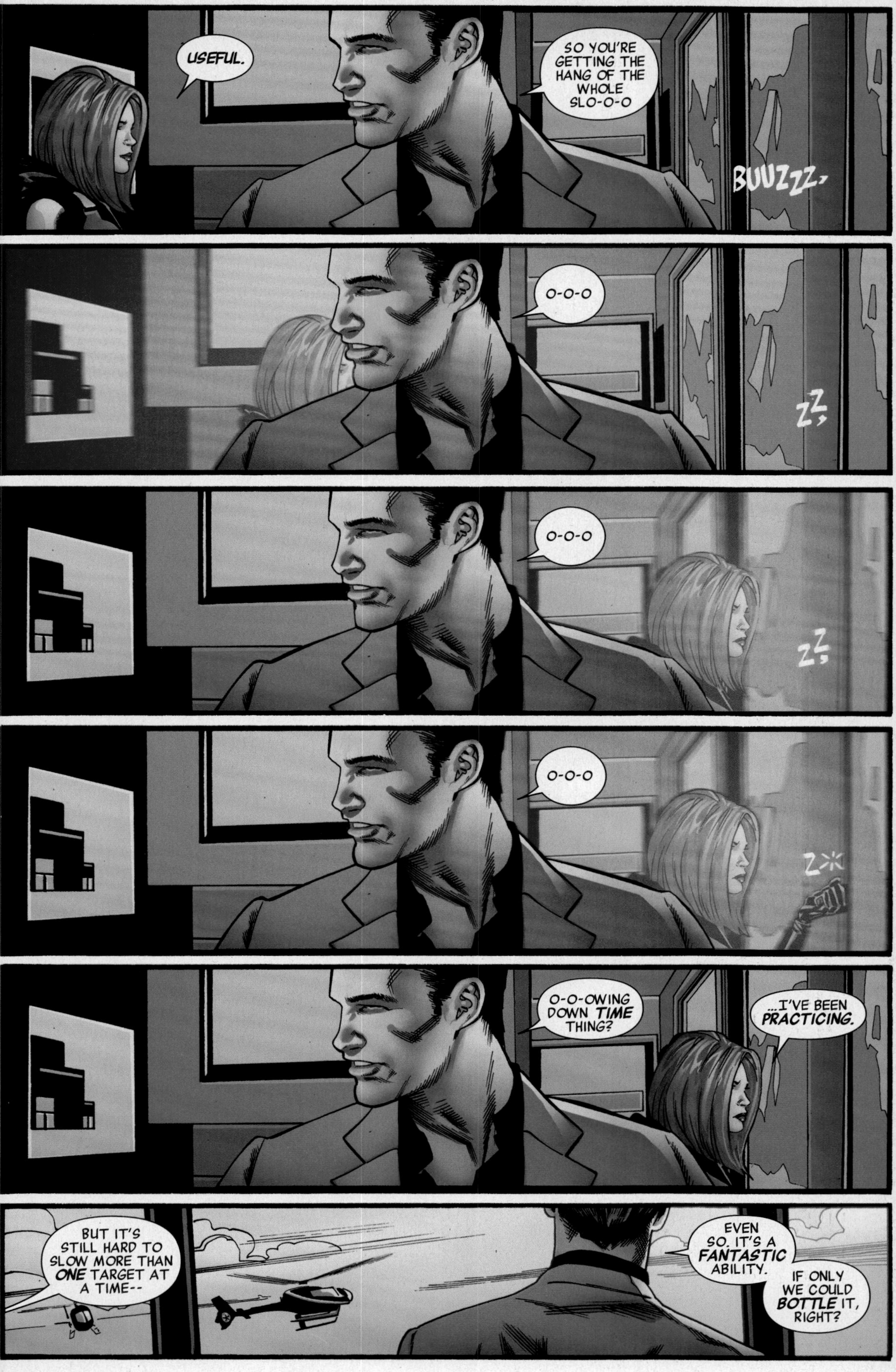
USEFUL.
SO YOU'RE GETTING THE HANG OF THE WHOLE SLO-O-O
BUUZZZ,
O-O-O
ZZ,
O-O-O
ZZ,
O-O-O
O-O-OWING DOWN TIME THING?
...I'VE BEEN PRACTICING.
BUT IT'S STILL HARD TO SLOW MORE THAN ONE TARGET AT A TIME--
EVEN SO. IT'S A FANTASTIC ABILITY.
IF ONLY WE COULD BOTTLE IT, RIGHT?

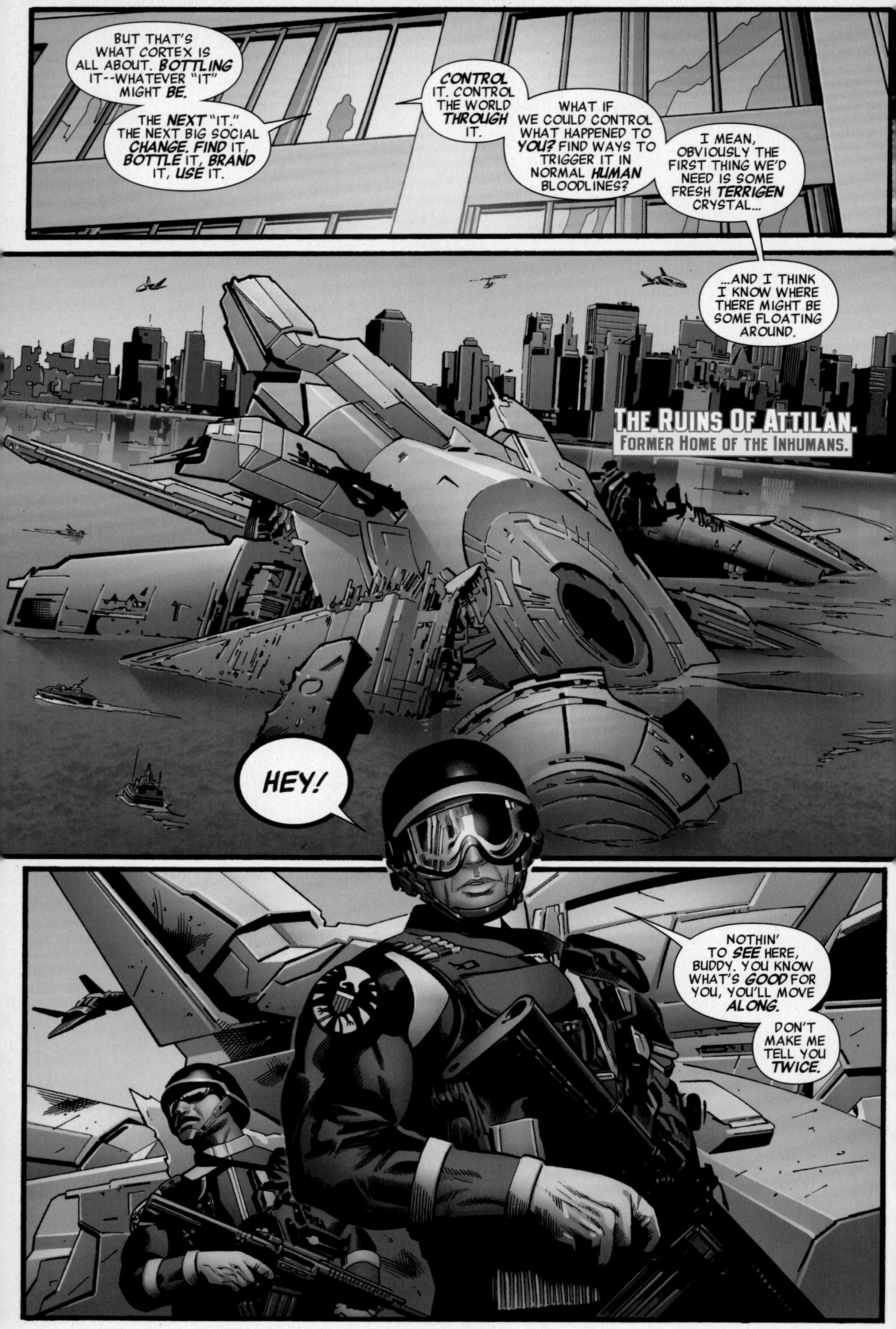

BUT THAT'S WHAT CORTEX IS ALL ABOUT. BOTTLING IT--WHATEVER "IT" MIGHT BE.
THE NEXT "IT." THE NEXT BIG SOCIAL CHANGE. FIND IT, BOTTLE IT, BRAND IT, USE IT.
CONTROL IT. CONTROL THE WORLD THROUGH IT.
WHAT IF WE COULD CONTROL WHAT HAPPENED TO YOU? FIND WAYS TO TRIGGER IT IN NORMAL HUMAN BLOODLINES?
I MEAN, OBVIOUSLY THE FIRST THING WE'D NEED IS SOME FRESH TERRIGEN CRYSTAL...
...AND I THINK I KNOW WHERE THERE MIGHT BE SOME FLOATING AROUND.
THE RUINS OF ATTILAN.
FORMER HOME OF THE INHUMANS.
HEY!
NOTHIN' TO SEE HERE, BUDDY. YOU KNOW WHAT'S GOOD FOR YOU, YOU'LL MOVE ALONG.
DON'T MAKE ME TELL YOU TWICE.

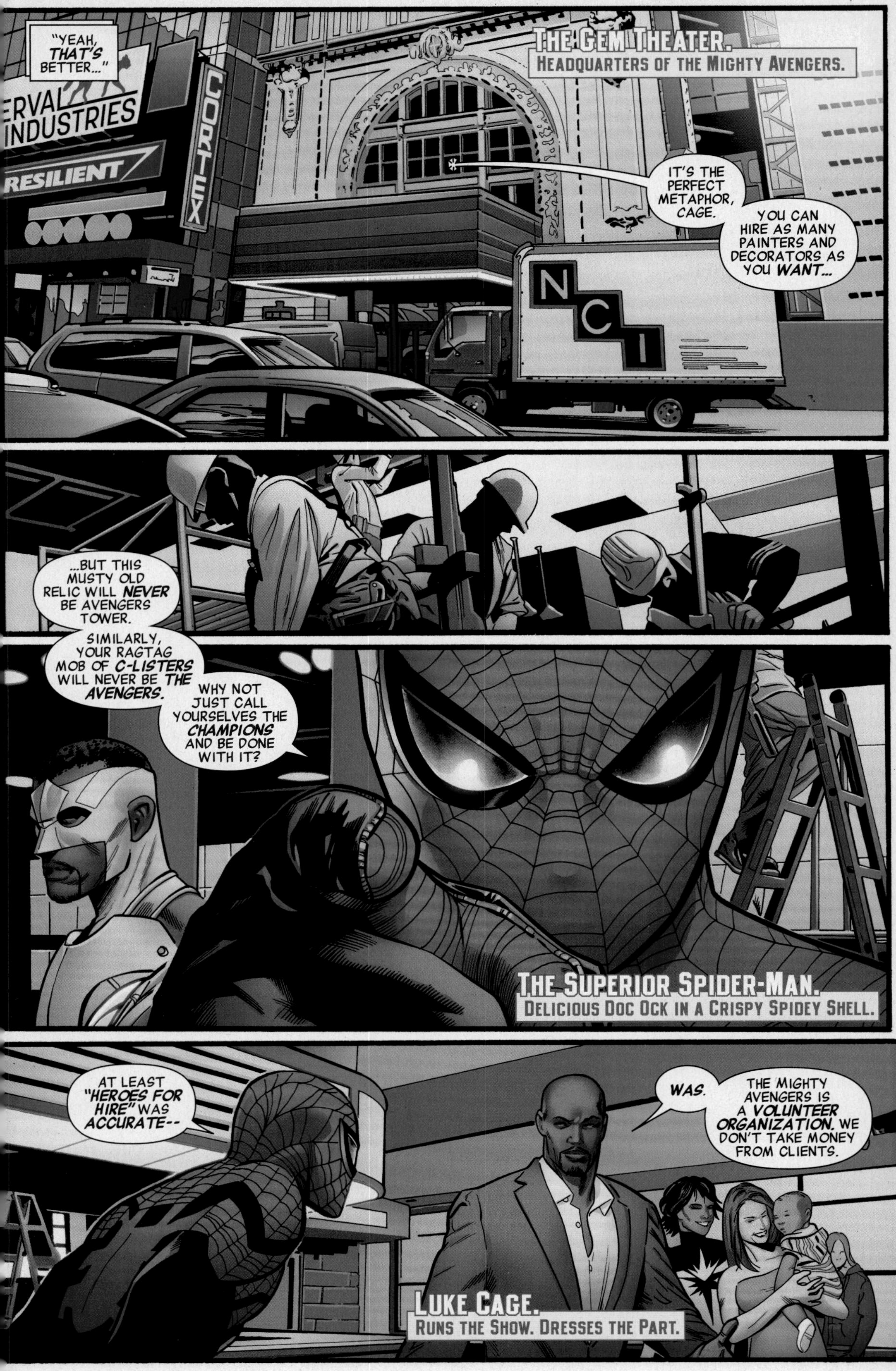
"YEAH, THAT'S BETTER..."
THE GEM THEATER.
HEADQUARTERS OF THE MIGHTY AVENGERS.
ERVAL INDUSTRIES
CORTEX
RESILIENT
NCI
IT'S THE PERFECT METAPHOR, CAGE.
YOU CAN HIRE AS MANY PAINTERS AND DECORATORS AS YOU WANT...
...BUT THIS MUSTY OLD RELIC WILL NEVER BE AVENGERS TOWER.
SIMILARLY, YOUR RAGTAG MOB OF C-LISTERS WILL NEVER BE THE AVENGERS.
WHY NOT JUST CALL YOURSELVES THE CHAMPIONS AND BE DONE WITH IT?
THE SUPERIOR SPIDER-MAN.
DELICIOUS DOC OCK IN A CRISPY SPIDEY SHELL.
AT LEAST "HEROES FOR HIRE" WAS ACCURATE--
WAS.
THE MIGHTY AVENGERS IS A VOLUNTEER ORGANIZATION. WE DON'T TAKE MONEY FROM CLIENTS.
LUKE CAGE.
RUNS THE SHOW. DRESSES THE PART.

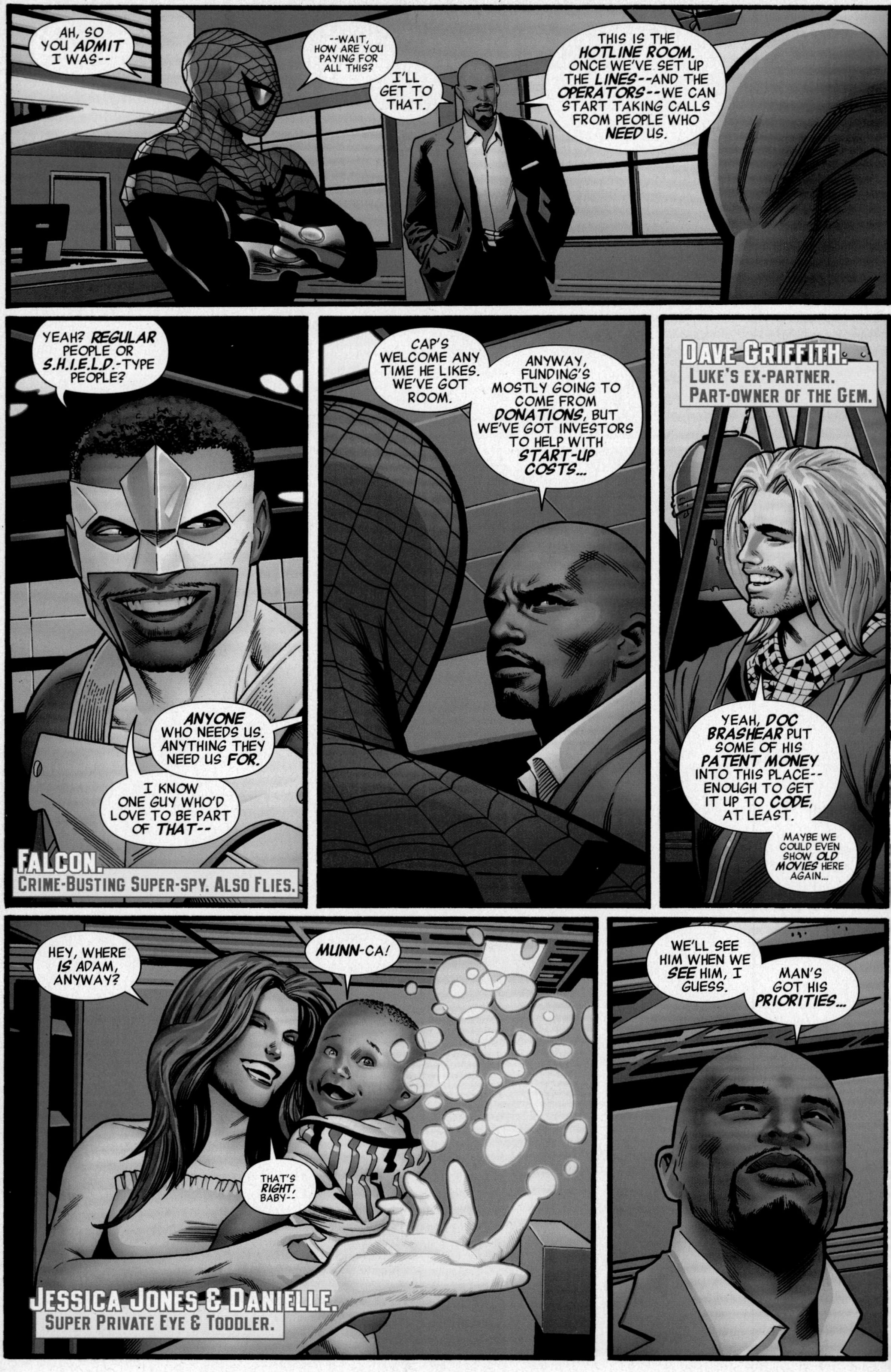
AH, SO YOU ADMIT I WAS--
--WAIT, HOW ARE YOU PAYING FOR ALL THIS?
I'LL GET TO THAT.
THIS IS THE HOTLINE ROOM. ONCE WE'VE SET UP THE LINES--AND THE OPERATORS--WE CAN START TAKING CALLS FROM PEOPLE WHO NEED US.
YEAH? REGULAR PEOPLE OR S.H.I.E.L.D.-TYPE PEOPLE?
ANYONE WHO NEEDS US. ANYTHING THEY NEED US FOR.
I KNOW ONE GUY WHO'D LOVE TO BE PART OF THAT--
FALCON.
CRIME-BUSTING SUPER-SPY. ALSO FLIES.
CAP'S WELCOME ANY TIME HE LIKES. WE'VE GOT ROOM.
ANYWAY, FUNDING'S MOSTLY GOING TO COME FROM DONATIONS, BUT WE'VE GOT INVESTORS TO HELP WITH START-UP COSTS...
DAVE GRIFFITH.
LUKE'S EX-PARTNER. PART-OWNER OF THE GEM.
YEAH, DOC BRASHEAR PUT SOME OF HIS PATENT MONEY INTO THIS PLACE--ENOUGH TO GET IT UP TO CODE, AT LEAST.
MAYBE WE COULD EVEN SHOW OLD MOVIES HERE AGAIN...
HEY, WHERE IS ADAM, ANYWAY?
MUNN-CA!
THAT'S RIGHT, BABY--
JESSICA JONES & DANIELLE.
SUPER PRIVATE EYE & TODDLER.
WE'LL SEE HIM WHEN WE SEE HIM, I GUESS.
MAN'S GOT HIS PRIORITIES...

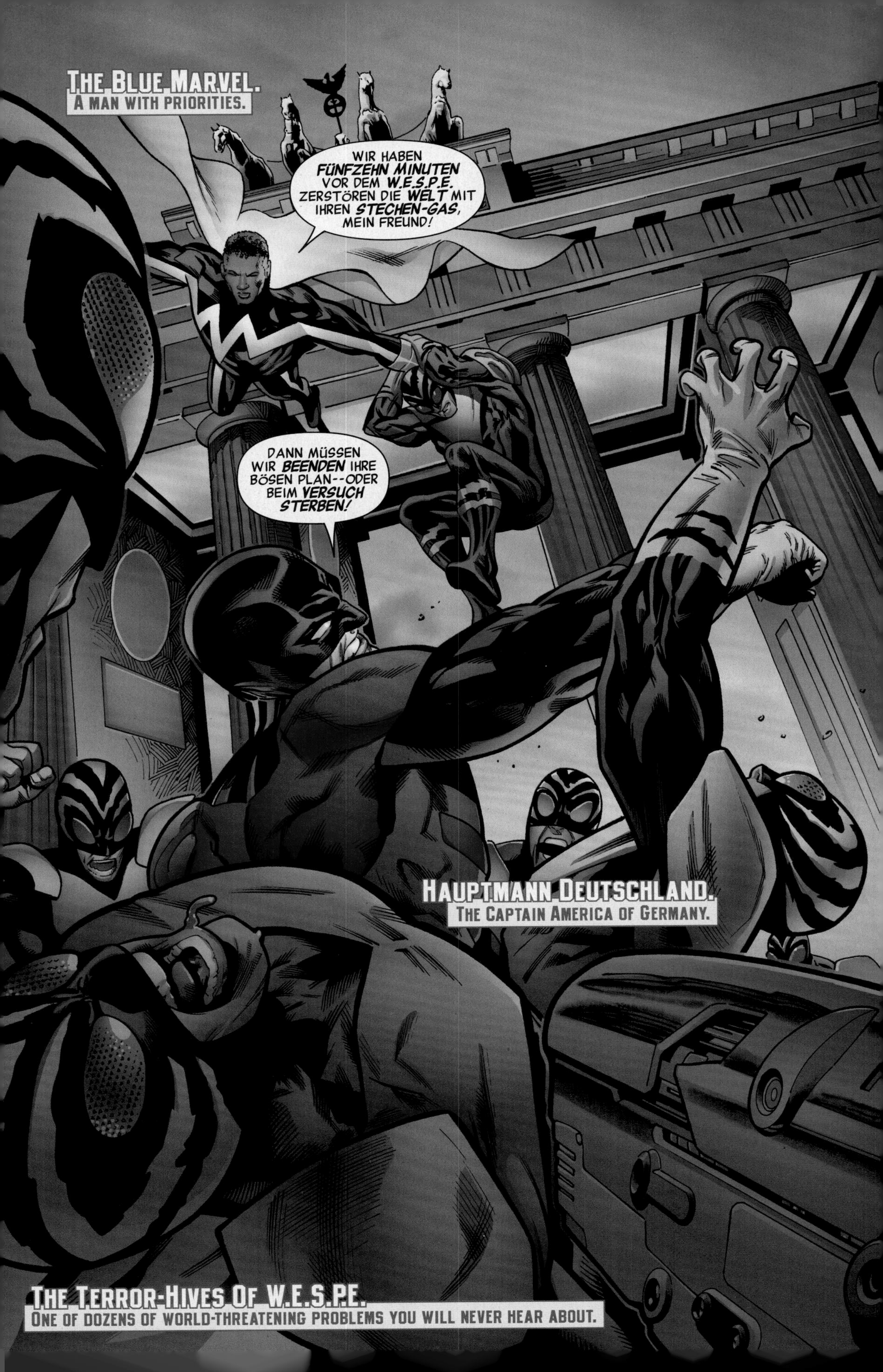
THE BLUE MARVEL.
A MAN WITH PRIORITIES.
WIR HABEN FÜNFZEHN MINUTEN VOR DEM W.E.S.P.E. ZERSTÖREN DIE WELT MIT IHREN STECHEN-GAS, MEIN FREUND!
DANN MÜSSEN WIR BEENDEN IHRE BÖSEN PLAN--ODER BEIM VERSUCH STERBEN!
HAUPTMANN DEUTSCHLAND.
THE CAPTAIN AMERICA OF GERMANY.
THE TERROR-HIVES OF W.E.S.PE.
ONE OF DOZENS OF WORLD-THREATENING PROBLEMS YOU WILL NEVER HEAR ABOUT.

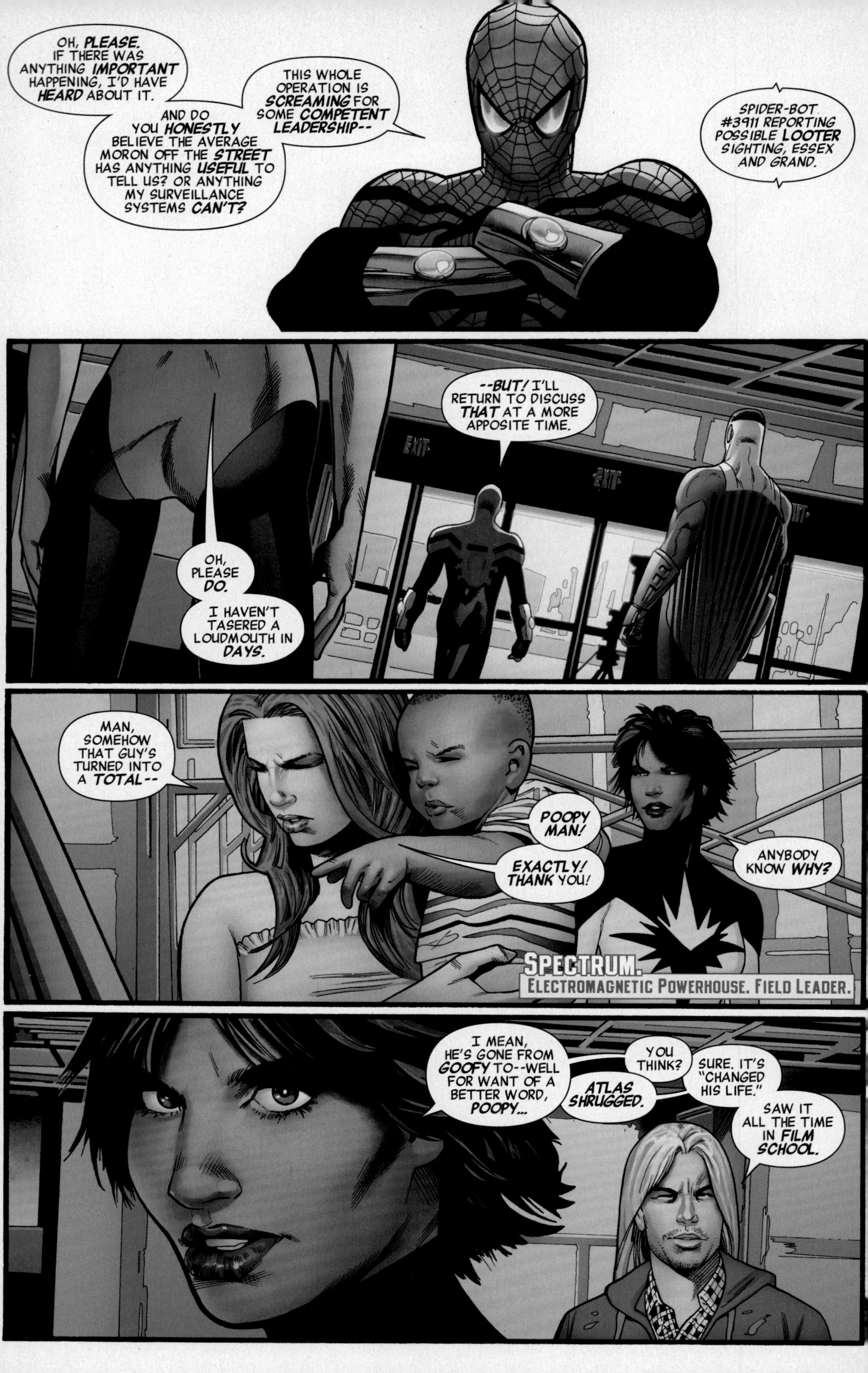
OH, PLEASE. IF THERE WAS ANYTHING IMPORTANT HAPPENING, I'D HAVE HEARD ABOUT IT.
AND DO YOU HONESTLY BELIEVE THE AVERAGE MORON OFF THE STREET HAS ANYTHING USEFUL TO TELL US? OR ANYTHING MY SURVEILLANCE SYSTEMS CAN'T?
THIS WHOLE OPERATION IS SCREAMING FOR SOME COMPETENT LEADERSHIP--
SPIDER-BOT #3911 REPORTING POSSIBLE LOOTER SIGHTING, ESSEX AND GRAND.
--BUT! I'LL RETURN TO DISCUSS THAT AT A MORE APPOSITE TIME.
EXIT
EXIT
OH, PLEASE DO.
I HAVEN'T TASERED A LOUDMOUTH IN DAYS.
MAN, SOMEHOW THAT GUY'S TURNED INTO A TOTAL--
POOPY MAN!
EXACTLY! THANK YOU!
ANYBODY KNOW WHY?
SPECTRUM.
ELECTROMAGNETIC POWERHOUSE. FIELD LEADER.
I MEAN, HE'S GONE FROM GOOFY TO--WELL FOR WANT OF A BETTER WORD, POOPY...
YOU THINK?
ATLAS SHRUGGED.
SURE. IT'S "CHANGED HIS LIFE."
SAW IT ALL THE TIME IN FILM SCHOOL.

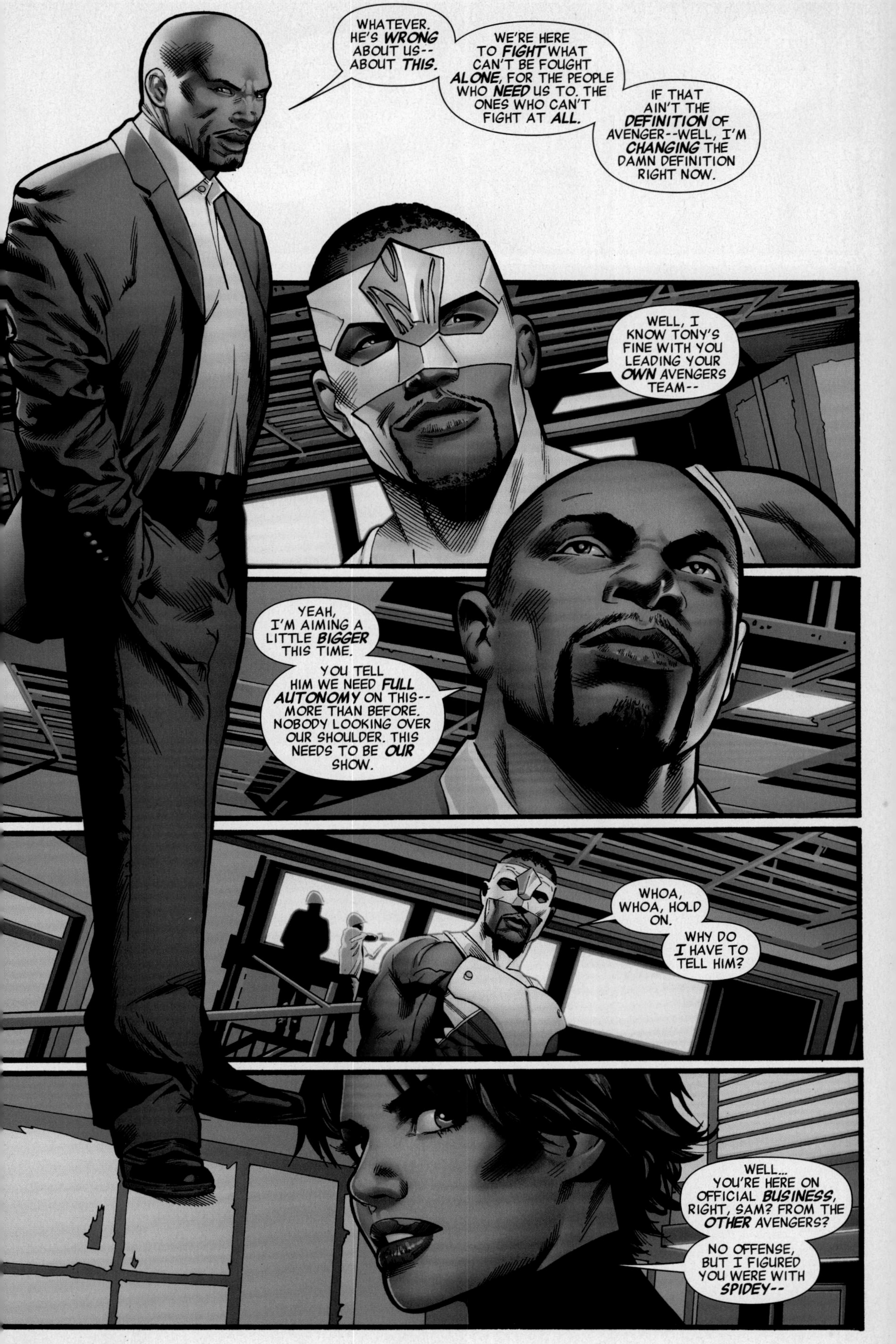
WHATEVER. HE'S WRONG ABOUT US-- ABOUT THIS.
WE'RE HERE TO FIGHT WHAT CAN'T BE FOUGHT ALONE, FOR THE PEOPLE WHO NEED US TO. THE ONES WHO CAN'T FIGHT AT ALL.
IF THAT AIN'T THE DEFINITION OF AVENGER--WELL, I'M CHANGING THE DAMN DEFINITION RIGHT NOW.
WELL, I KNOW TONY'S FINE WITH YOU LEADING YOUR OWN AVENGERS TEAM--
YEAH, I'M AIMING A LITTLE BIGGER THIS TIME.
YOU TELL HIM WE NEED FULL AUTONOMY ON THIS-- MORE THAN BEFORE. NOBODY LOOKING OVER OUR SHOULDER. THIS NEEDS TO BE OUR SHOW.
WHOA, WHOA, HOLD ON.
WHY DO I HAVE TO TELL HIM?
WELL... YOU'RE HERE ON OFFICIAL BUSINESS, RIGHT, SAM? FROM THE OTHER AVENGERS?
NO OFFENSE, BUT I FIGURED YOU WERE WITH SPIDEY--

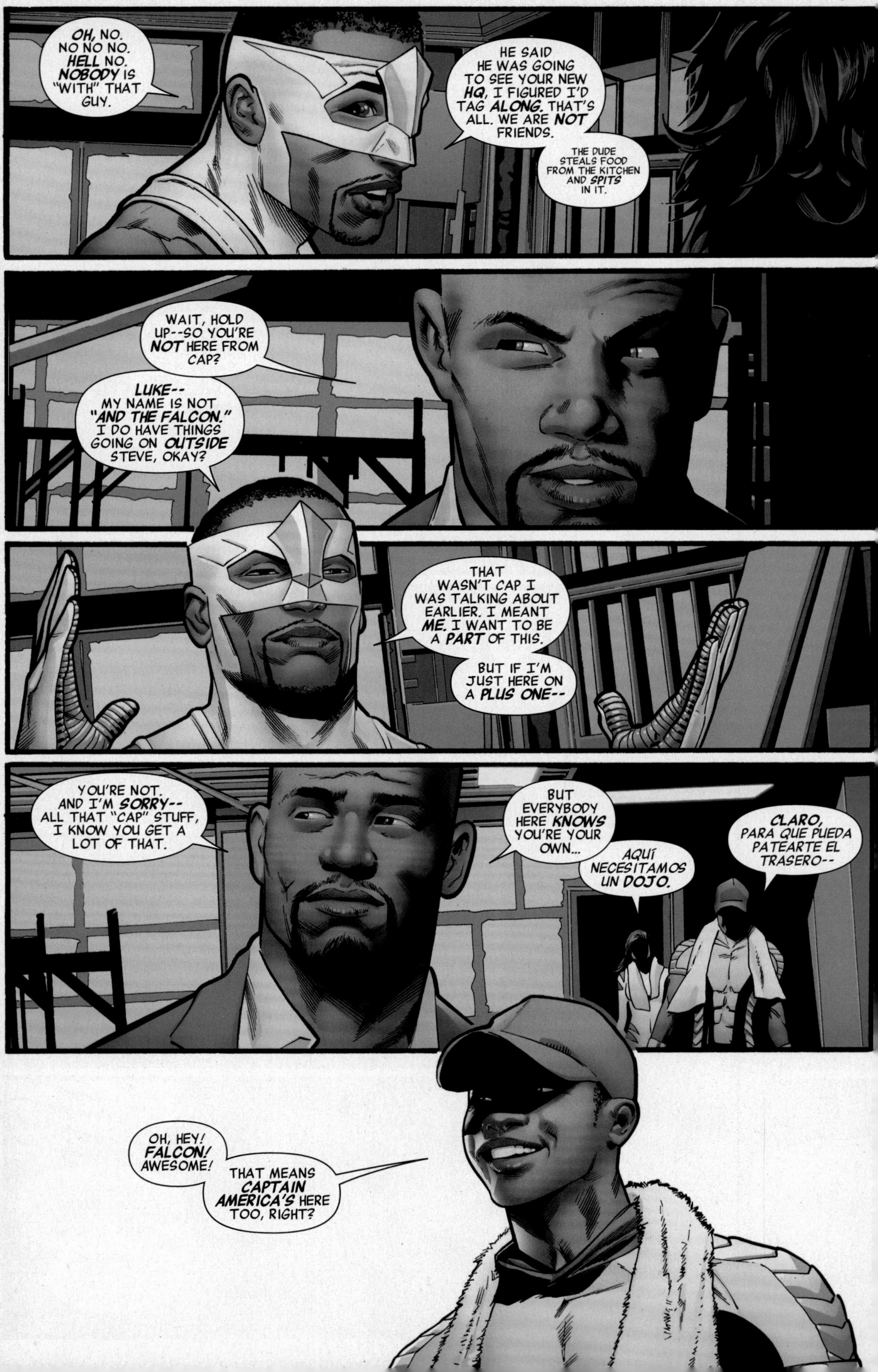
OH, NO. NO NO NO. HELL NO. NOBODY IS "WITH" THAT GUY.
HE SAID HE WAS GOING TO SEE YOUR NEW HQ, I FIGURED I'D TAG ALONG. THAT'S ALL. WE ARE NOT FRIENDS.
THE DUDE STEALS FOOD FROM THE KITCHEN AND SPITS IN IT.
WAIT, HOLD UP--SO YOU'RE NOT HERE FROM CAP?
LUKE-- MY NAME IS NOT "AND THE FALCON." I DO HAVE THINGS GOING ON OUTSIDE STEVE, OKAY?
THAT WASN'T CAP I WAS TALKING ABOUT EARLIER. I MEANT ME. I WANT TO BE A PART OF THIS.
BUT IF I'M JUST HERE ON A PLUS ONE--
YOU'RE NOT. AND I'M SORRY-- ALL THAT "CAP" STUFF, I KNOW YOU GET A LOT OF THAT.
BUT EVERYBODY HERE KNOWS YOU'RE YOUR OWN...
AQUÍ NECESITAMOS UN DOJO.
CLARO, PARA QUE PUEDA PATEARTE EL TRASERO--
OH, HEY! FALCON! AWESOME!
THAT MEANS CAPTAIN AMERICA'S HERE TOO, RIGHT?

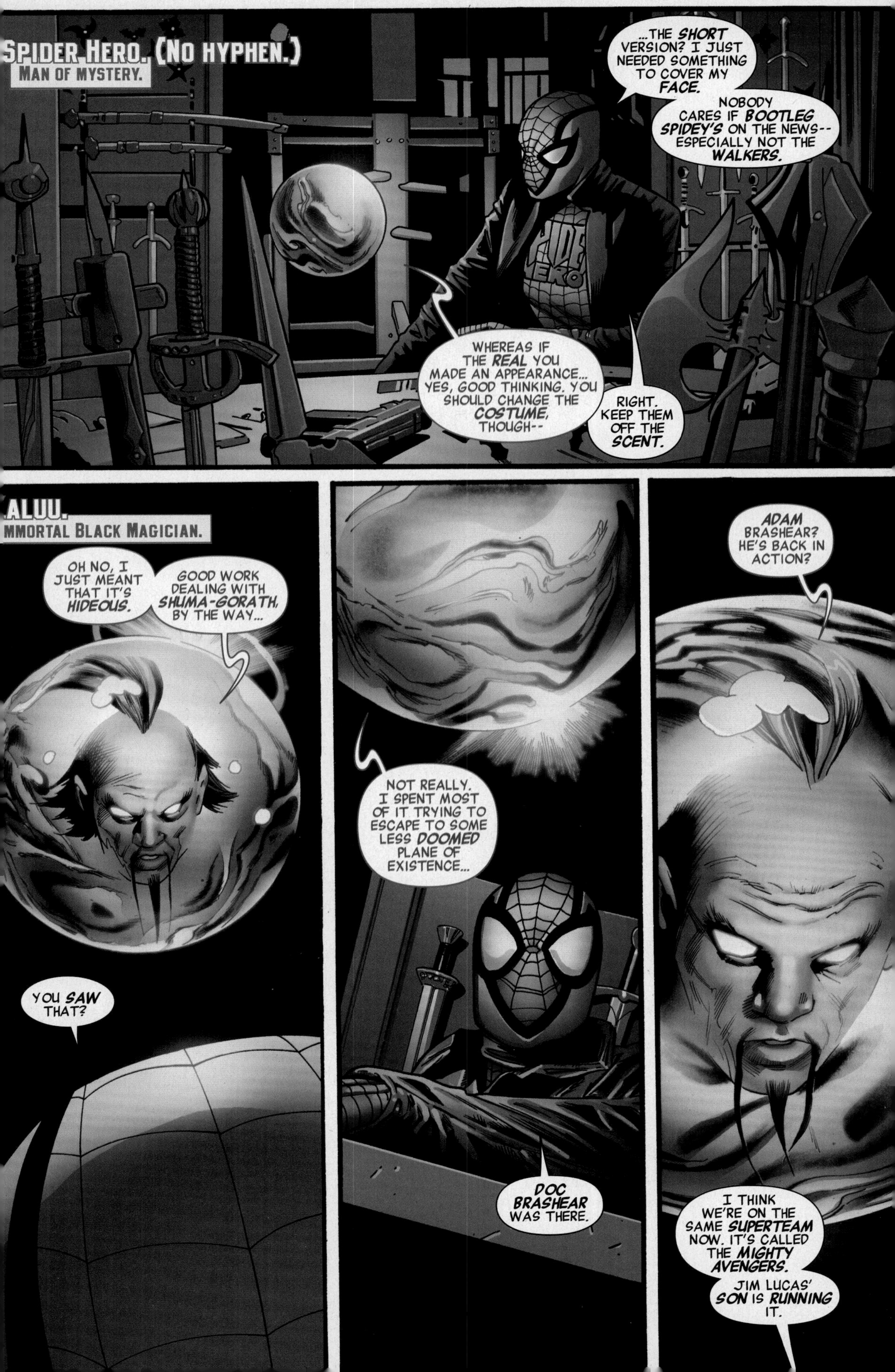
SPIDER HERO. (NO HYPHEN.)
MAN OF MYSTERY.
...THE SHORT VERSION? I JUST NEEDED SOMETHING TO COVER MY FACE.
NOBODY CARES IF BOOTLEG SPIDEY'S ON THE NEWS-- ESPECIALLY NOT THE WALKERS.
WHEREAS IF THE REAL YOU MADE AN APPEARANCE... YES, GOOD THINKING. YOU SHOULD CHANGE THE COSTUME, THOUGH--
RIGHT. KEEP THEM OFF THE SCENT.
ALUU.
MMORTAL BLACK MAGICIAN.
OH NO, I JUST MEANT THAT IT'S HIDEOUS.
GOOD WORK DEALING WITH SHUMA-GORATH, BY THE WAY...
YOU SAW THAT?
NOT REALLY. I SPENT MOST OF IT TRYING TO ESCAPE TO SOME LESS DOOMED PLANE OF EXISTENCE...
DOC BRASHEAR WAS THERE.
ADAM BRASHEAR? HE'S BACK IN ACTION?
I THINK WE'RE ON THE SAME SUPERTEAM NOW. IT'S CALLED THE MIGHTY AVENGERS.
JIM LUCAS' SON IS RUNNING IT.

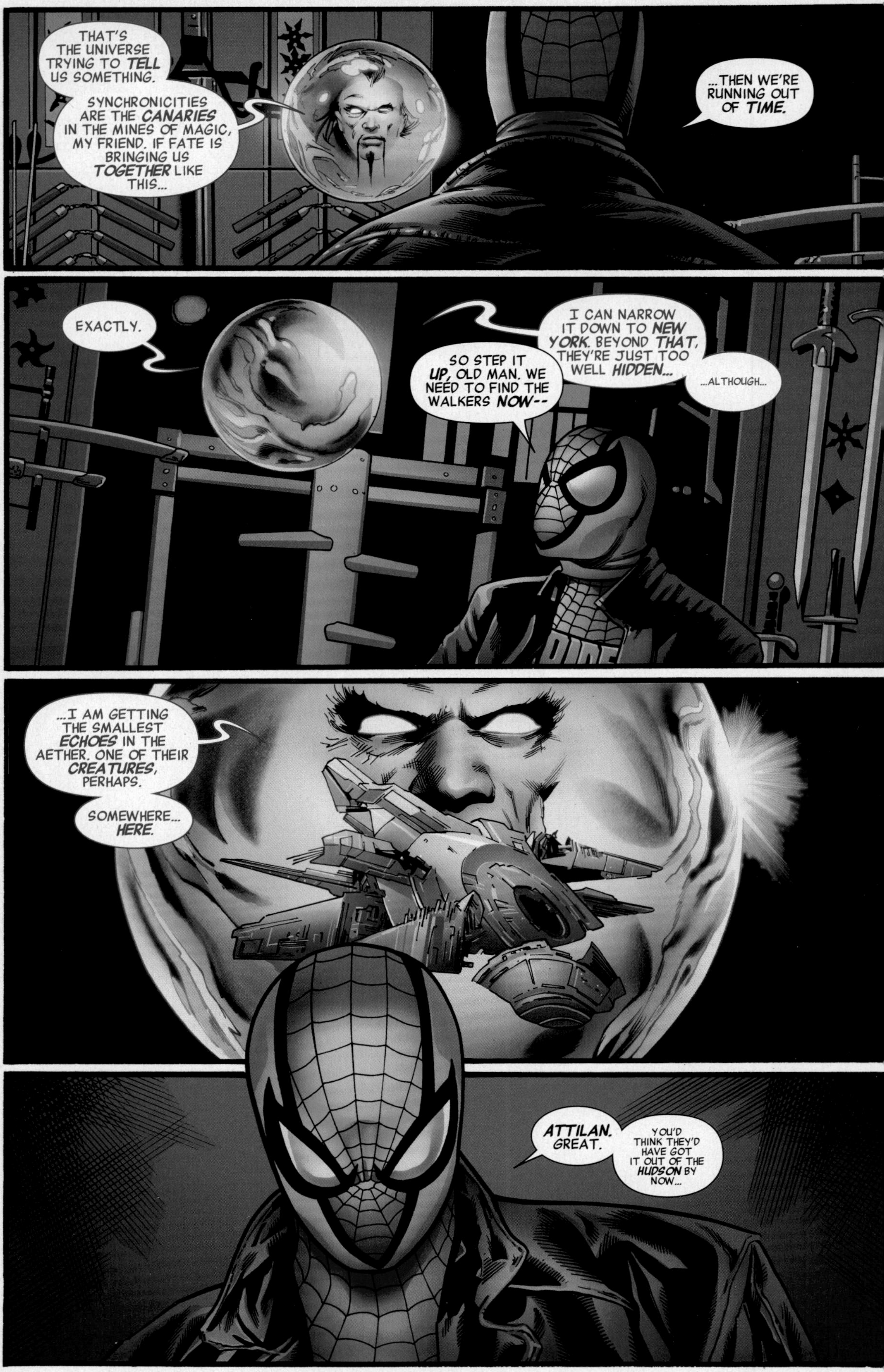
THAT'S THE UNIVERSE TRYING TO TELL US SOMETHING.
SYNCHRONICITIES ARE THE CANARIES IN THE MINES OF MAGIC, MY FRIEND. IF FATE IS BRINGING US TOGETHER LIKE THIS...
...THEN WE'RE RUNNING OUT OF TIME.
EXACTLY.
SO STEP IT UP, OLD MAN. WE NEED TO FIND THE WALKERS NOW--
I CAN NARROW IT DOWN TO NEW YORK. BEYOND THAT, THEY'RE JUST TOO WELL HIDDEN...
...ALTHOUGH...
...I AM GETTING THE SMALLEST ECHOES IN THE AETHER. ONE OF THEIR CREATURES, PERHAPS.
SOMEWHERE... HERE.
ATTILAN. GREAT.
YOU'D THINK THEY'D HAVE GOT IT OUT OF THE HUDSON BY NOW...

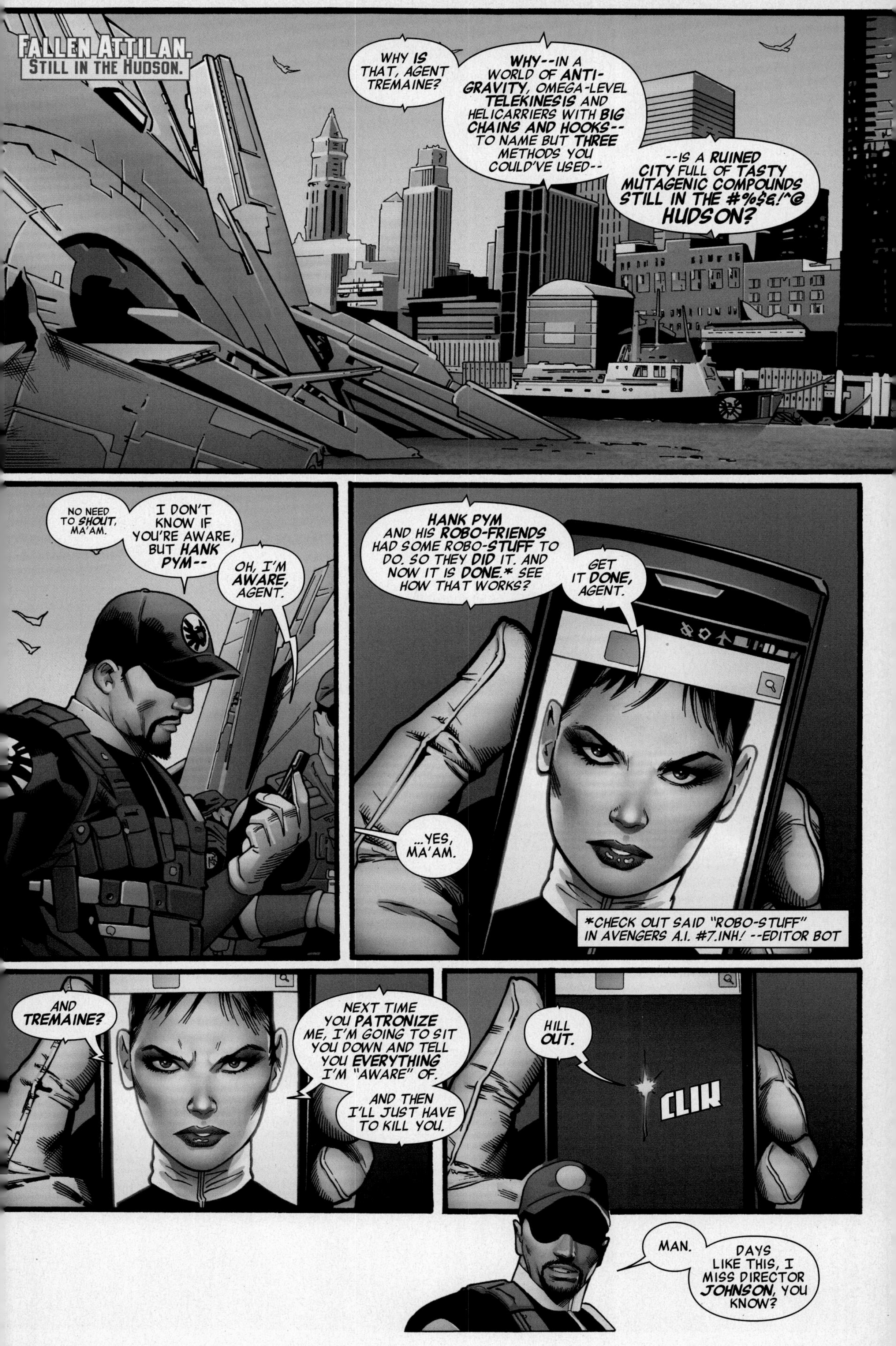
FALLEN ATTILAN.
STILL IN THE HUDSON.
WHY IS THAT, AGENT TREMAINE?
WHY--IN A WORLD OF ANTI-GRAVITY, OMEGA-LEVEL TELEKINESIS AND HELICARRIERS WITH BIG CHAINS AND HOOKS--TO NAME BUT THREE METHODS YOU COULD'VE USED--
--IS A RUINED CITY FULL OF TASTY MUTAGENIC COMPOUNDS STILL IN THE #%$&!^@ HUDSON?
NO NEED TO SHOUT, MA'AM.
I DON'T KNOW IF YOU'RE AWARE, BUT HANK PYM--
OH, I'M AWARE, AGENT.
HANK PYM AND HIS ROBO-FRIENDS HAD SOME ROBO-STUFF TO DO. SO THEY DID IT. AND NOW IT IS DONE.* SEE HOW THAT WORKS?
GET IT DONE, AGENT.
...YES, MA'AM.
*CHECK OUT SAID "ROBO-STUFF" IN AVENGERS A.I. #7.INH! --EDITOR BOT
AND TREMAINE?
NEXT TIME YOU PATRONIZE ME, I'M GOING TO SIT YOU DOWN AND TELL YOU EVERYTHING I'M "AWARE" OF.
AND THEN I'LL JUST HAVE TO KILL YOU.
HILL OUT.
CLIK
MAN.
DAYS LIKE THIS, I MISS DIRECTOR JOHNSON, YOU KNOW?

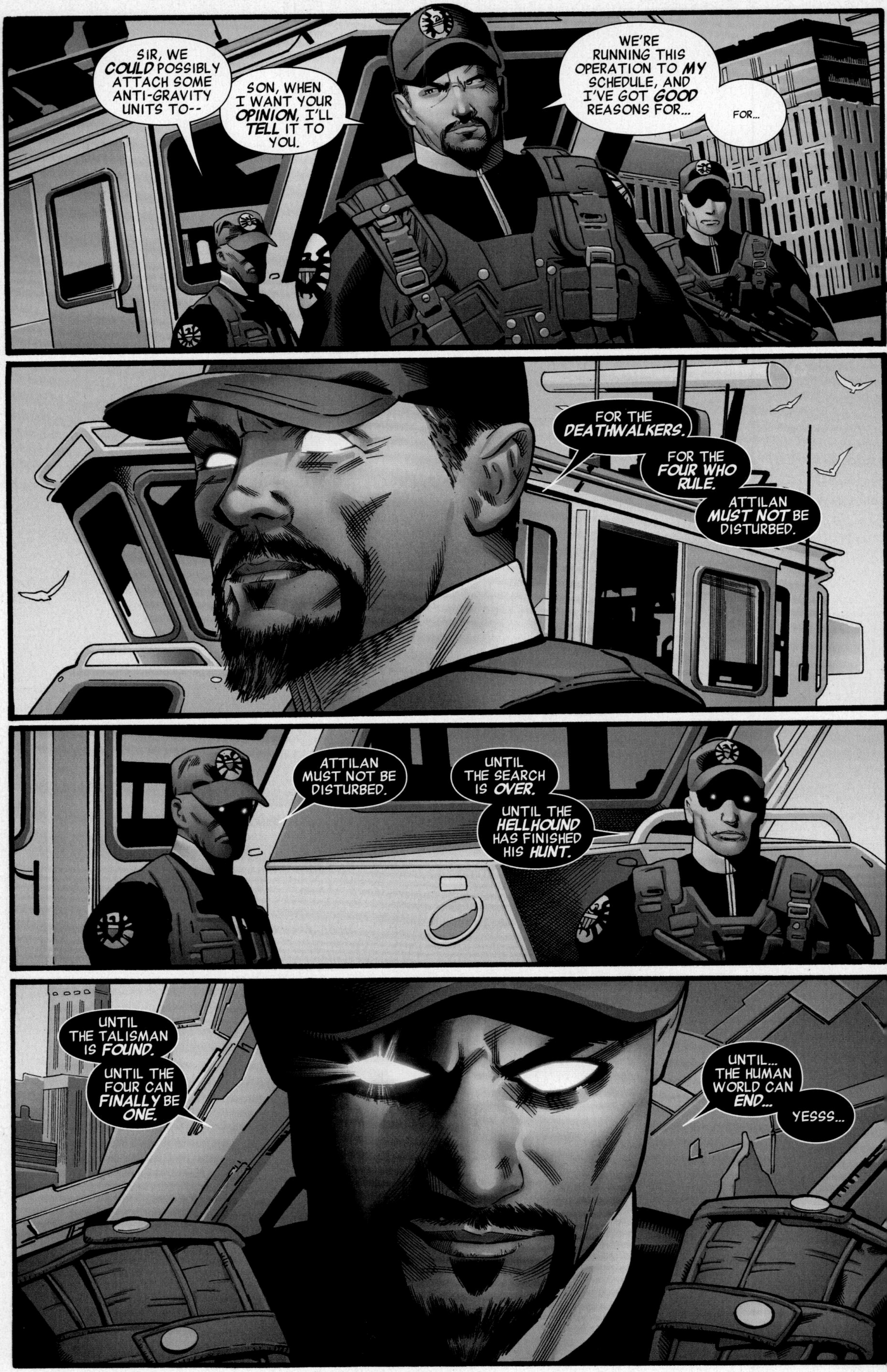
SIR, WE COULD POSSIBLY ATTACH SOME ANTI-GRAVITY UNITS TO--
SON, WHEN I WANT YOUR OPINION, I'LL TELL IT TO YOU.
WE'RE RUNNING THIS OPERATION TO MY SCHEDULE, AND I'VE GOT GOOD REASONS FOR...
FOR...
FOR THE DEATHWALKERS.
FOR THE FOUR WHO RULE.
ATTILAN MUST NOT BE DISTURBED.
ATTILAN MUST NOT BE DISTURBED.
UNTIL THE SEARCH IS OVER.
UNTIL THE HELLHOUND HAS FINISHED HIS HUNT.
UNTIL THE TALISMAN IS FOUND.
UNTIL THE FOUR CAN FINALLY BE ONE.
UNTIL... THE HUMAN WORLD CAN END...
YESSS...

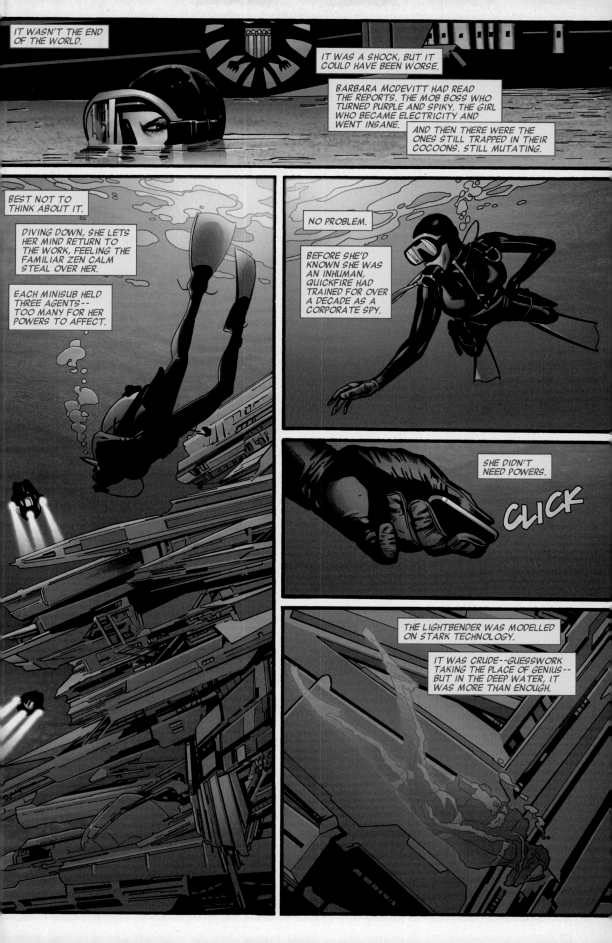

IT WASN'T THE END OF THE WORLD.

IT WAS A SHOCK, BUT IT COULD HAVE BEEN WORSE.

BARBARA MCDEVITT HAD READ THE REPORTS. THE MOB BOSS WHO TURNED PURPLE AND SPIKY. THE GIRL WHO BECAME ELECTRICITY AND WENT INSANE.

AND THEN THERE WERE THE ONES STILL TRAPPED IN THEIR COCOONS. STILL MUTATING.

BEST NOT TO THINK ABOUT IT.

DIVING DOWN, SHE LETS HER MIND RETURN TO THE WORK, FEELING THE FAMILIAR ZEN CALM STEAL OVER HER.

EACH MINISUB HELD THREE AGENTS-- TOO MANY FOR HER POWERS TO AFFECT.

NO PROBLEM.

BEFORE SHE'D KNOWN SHE WAS AN INHUMAN, QUICKFIRE HAD TRAINED FOR OVER A DECADE AS A CORPORATE SPY.

SHE DIDN'T NEED POWERS.

CLICK

THE LIGHTBENDER WAS MODELLED ON STARK TECHNOLOGY.

IT WAS CRUDE--GUESSWORK TAKING THE PLACE OF GENIUS-- BUT IN THE DEEP WATER, IT WAS MORE THAN ENOUGH.

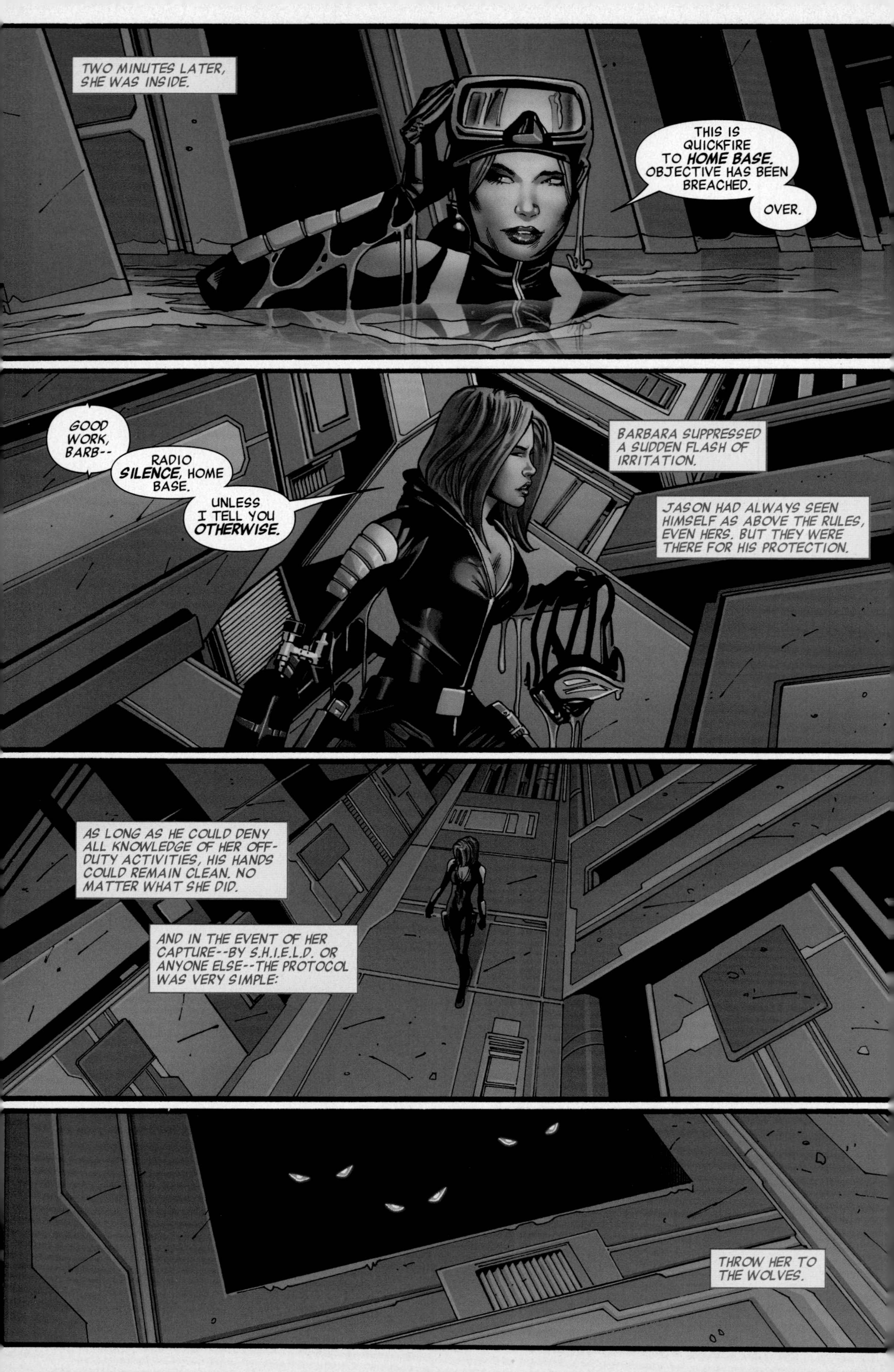
TWO MINUTES LATER, SHE WAS INSIDE.
THIS IS QUICKFIRE TO HOME BASE. OBJECTIVE HAS BEEN BREACHED.
OVER.
GOOD WORK, BARB--
RADIO SILENCE, HOME BASE.
UNLESS I TELL YOU OTHERWISE.
BARBARA SUPPRESSED A SUDDEN FLASH OF IRRITATION.
JASON HAD ALWAYS SEEN HIMSELF AS ABOVE THE RULES, EVEN HERS. BUT THEY WERE THERE FOR HIS PROTECTION.
AS LONG AS HE COULD DENY ALL KNOWLEDGE OF HER OFF-DUTY ACTIVITIES, HIS HANDS COULD REMAIN CLEAN. NO MATTER WHAT SHE DID.
AND IN THE EVENT OF HER CAPTURE--BY S.H.I.E.L.D. OR ANYONE ELSE--THE PROTOCOL WAS VERY SIMPLE:
THROW HER TO THE WOLVES.

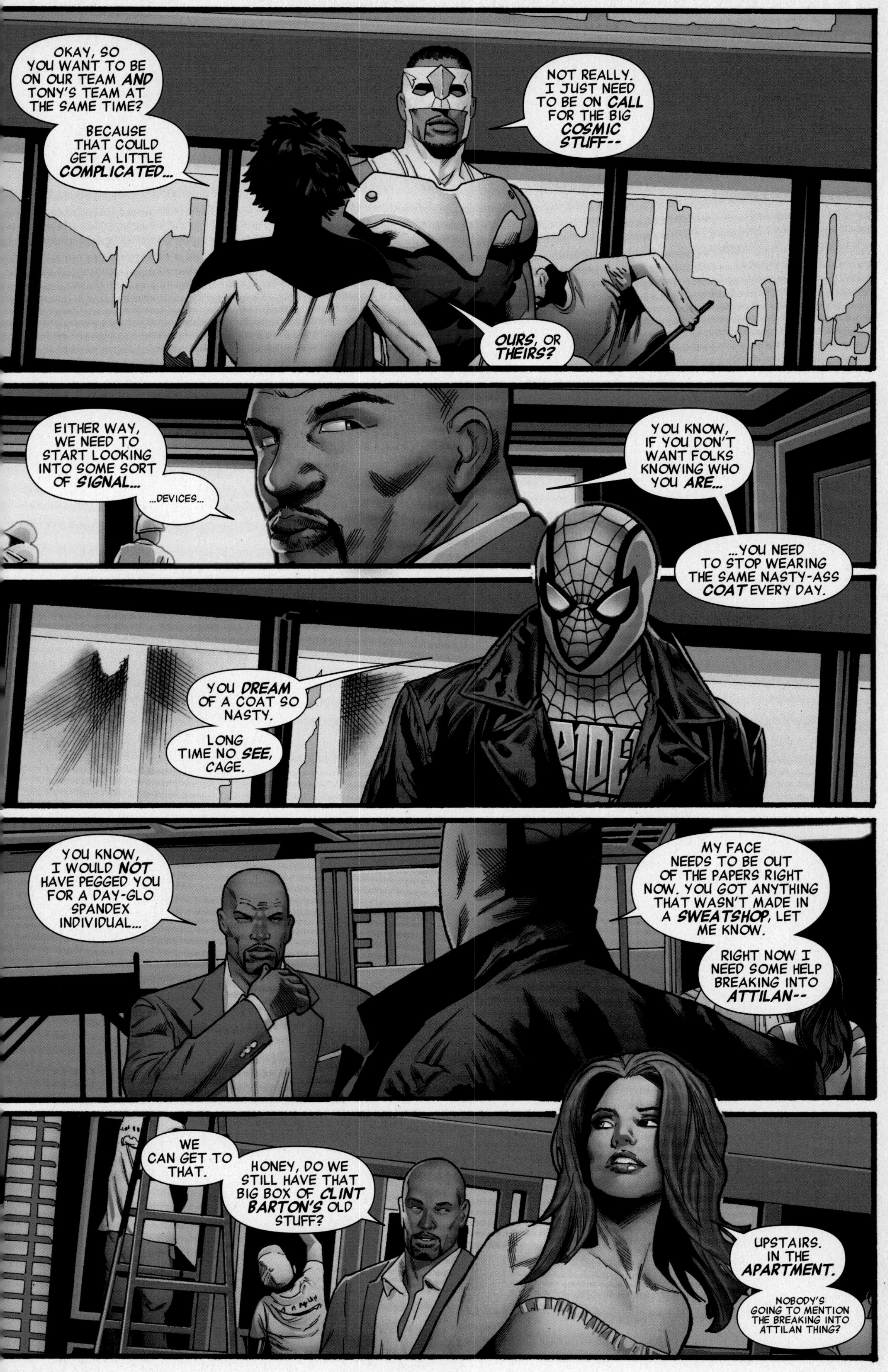
OKAY, SO YOU WANT TO BE ON OUR TEAM AND TONY'S TEAM AT THE SAME TIME?
BECAUSE THAT COULD GET A LITTLE COMPLICATED...
NOT REALLY. I JUST NEED TO BE ON CALL FOR THE BIG COSMIC STUFF--
OURS, OR THEIRS?
EITHER WAY, WE NEED TO START LOOKING INTO SOME SORT OF SIGNAL...
...DEVICES...
YOU KNOW, IF YOU DON'T WANT FOLKS KNOWING WHO YOU ARE...
...YOU NEED TO STOP WEARING THE SAME NASTY-ASS COAT EVERY DAY.
YOU DREAM OF A COAT SO NASTY.
LONG TIME NO SEE, CAGE.
YOU KNOW, I WOULD NOT HAVE PEGGED YOU FOR A DAY-GLO SPANDEX INDIVIDUAL...
MY FACE NEEDS TO BE OUT OF THE PAPERS RIGHT NOW. YOU GOT ANYTHING THAT WASN'T MADE IN A SWEATSHOP, LET ME KNOW.
RIGHT NOW I NEED SOME HELP BREAKING INTO ATTILAN--
WE CAN GET TO THAT.
HONEY, DO WE STILL HAVE THAT BIG BOX OF CLINT BARTON'S OLD STUFF?
UPSTAIRS. IN THE APARTMENT.
NOBODY'S GOING TO MENTION THE BREAKING INTO ATTILAN THING?

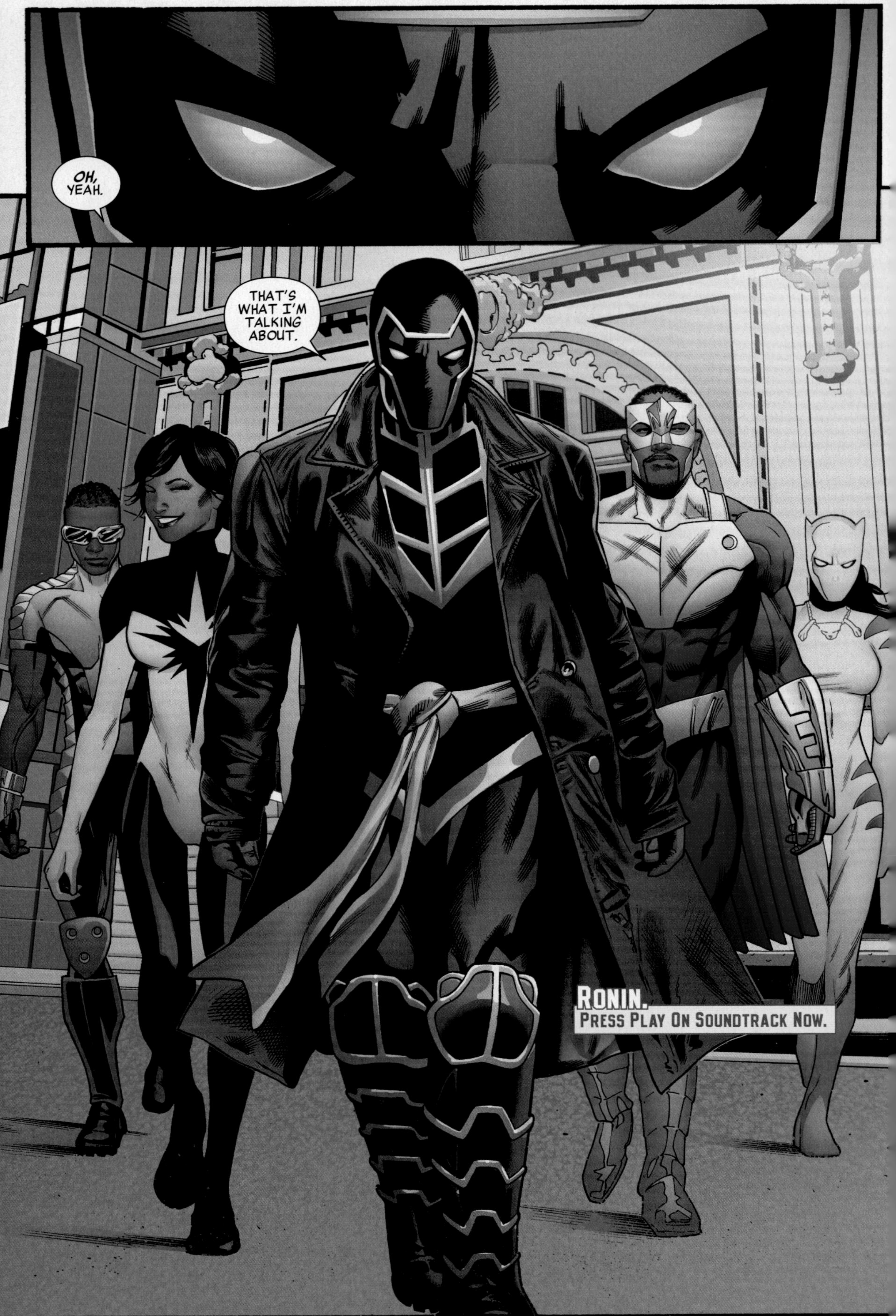
OH, YEAH.
THAT'S WHAT I'M TALKING ABOUT.
RONIN.
PRESS PLAY ON SOUNDTRACK NOW.

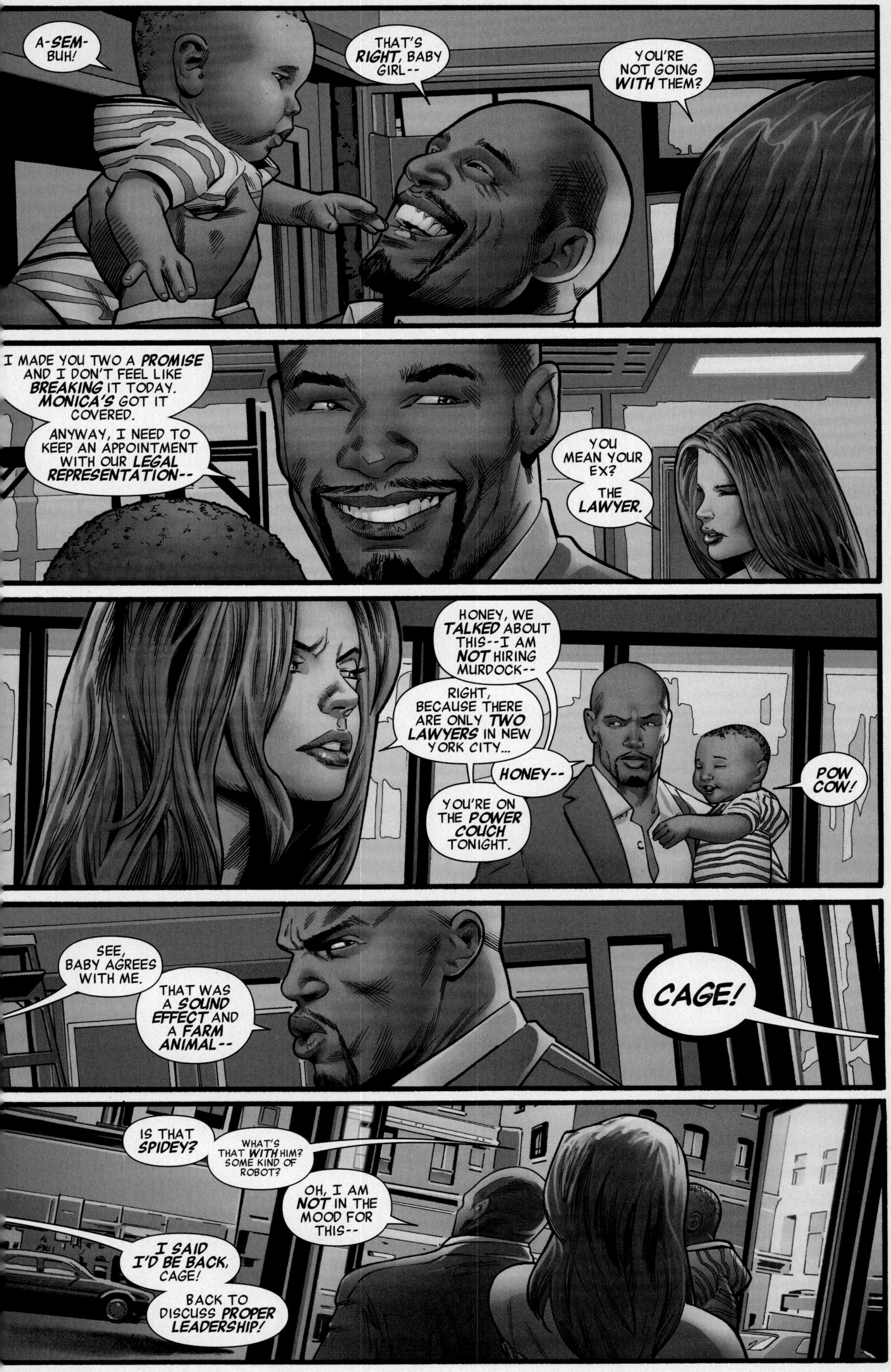

A-SEM-BUH!
THAT'S RIGHT, BABY GIRL--
YOU'RE NOT GOING WITH THEM?
I MADE YOU TWO A PROMISE AND I DON'T FEEL LIKE BREAKING IT TODAY. MONICA'S GOT IT COVERED.
ANYWAY, I NEED TO KEEP AN APPOINTMENT WITH OUR LEGAL REPRESENTATION--
YOU MEAN YOUR EX?
THE LAWYER.
HONEY, WE TALKED ABOUT THIS--I AM NOT HIRING MURDOCK--
RIGHT, BECAUSE THERE ARE ONLY TWO LAWYERS IN NEW YORK CITY...
HONEY--
YOU'RE ON THE POWER COUCH TONIGHT.
POW COW!
SEE, BABY AGREES WITH ME.
THAT WAS A SOUND EFFECT AND A FARM ANIMAL--
CAGE!
IS THAT SPIDEY?
WHAT'S THAT WITH HIM? SOME KIND OF ROBOT?
OH, I AM NOT IN THE MOOD FOR THIS--
I SAID I'D BE BACK, CAGE!
BACK TO DISCUSS PROPER LEADERSHIP!

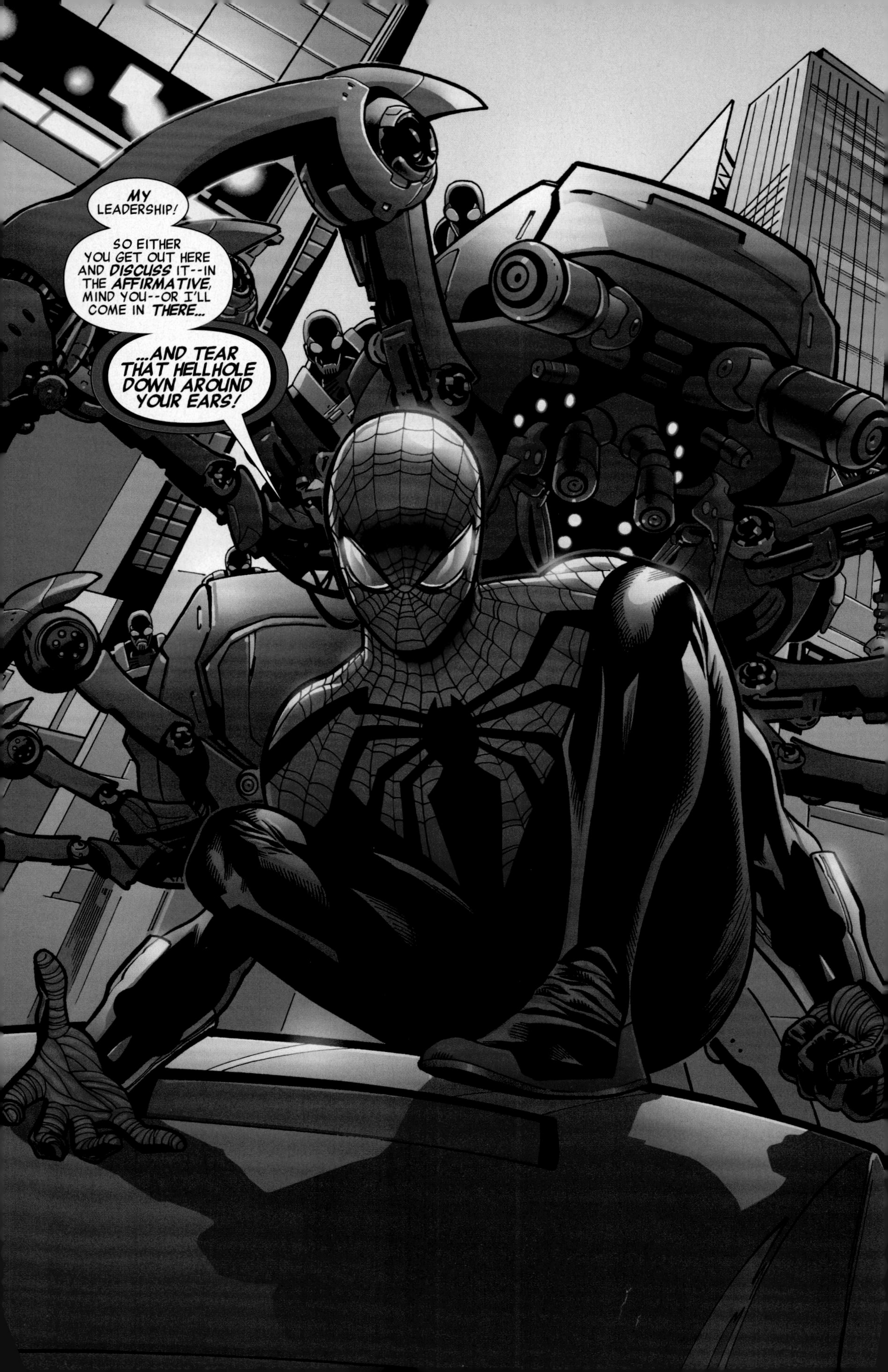
MY LEADERSHIP!
SO EITHER YOU GET OUT HERE AND DISCUSS IT--IN THE AFFIRMATIVE, MIND YOU--OR I'LL COME IN THERE...
...AND TEAR THAT HELLHOLE DOWN AROUND YOUR EARS!

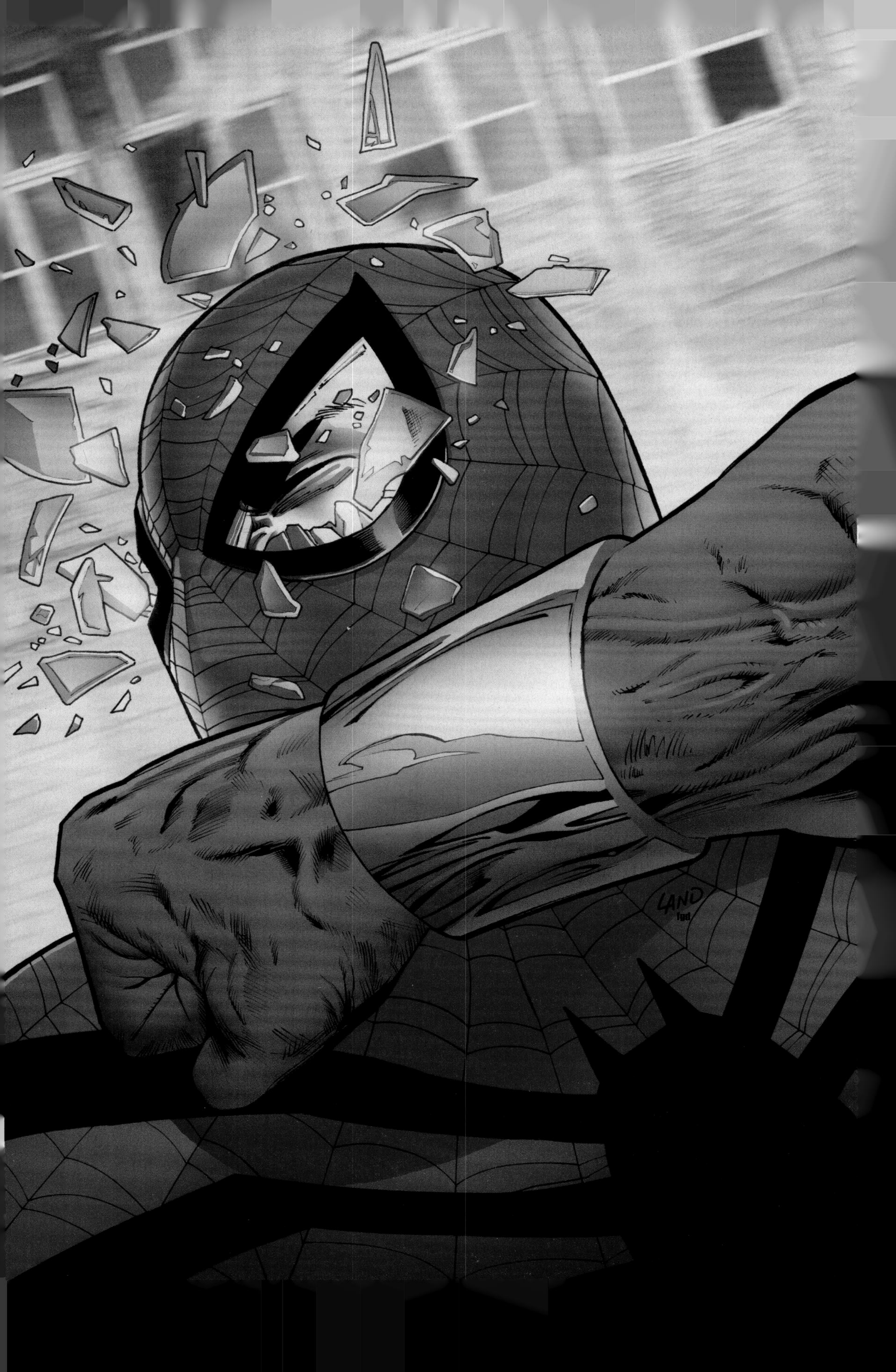

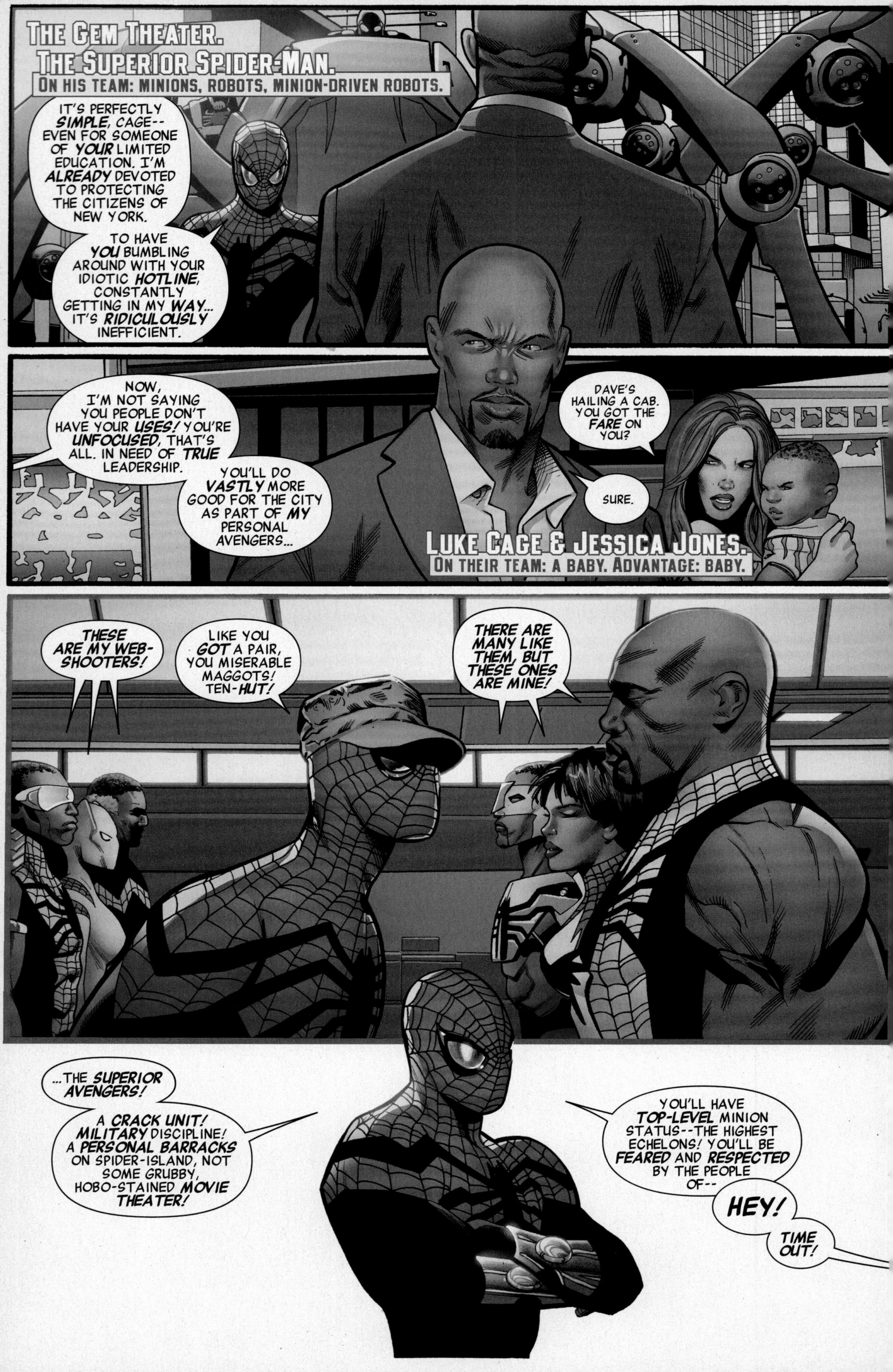
THE GEM THEATER.
THE SUPERIOR SPIDER-MAN.
ON HIS TEAM: MINIONS, ROBOTS, MINION-DRIVEN ROBOTS.
IT'S PERFECTLY SIMPLE, CAGE-- EVEN FOR SOMEONE OF YOUR LIMITED EDUCATION. I'M ALREADY DEVOTED TO PROTECTING THE CITIZENS OF NEW YORK.
TO HAVE YOU BUMBLING AROUND WITH YOUR IDIOTIC HOTLINE, CONSTANTLY GETTING IN MY WAY... IT'S RIDICULOUSLY INEFFICIENT.
NOW, I'M NOT SAYING YOU PEOPLE DON'T HAVE YOUR USES! YOU'RE UNFOCUSED, THAT'S ALL. IN NEED OF TRUE LEADERSHIP.
YOU'LL DO VASTLY MORE GOOD FOR THE CITY AS PART OF MY PERSONAL AVENGERS...
DAVE'S HAILING A CAB. YOU GOT THE FARE ON YOU?
SURE.
LUKE CAGE & JESSICA JONES.
ON THEIR TEAM: A BABY. ADVANTAGE: BABY.
THESE ARE MY WEB-SHOOTERS!
LIKE YOU GOT A PAIR, YOU MISERABLE MAGGOTS! TEN-HUT!
THERE ARE MANY LIKE THEM, BUT THESE ONES ARE MINE!
...THE SUPERIOR AVENGERS!
A CRACK UNIT! MILITARY DISCIPLINE! A PERSONAL BARRACKS ON SPIDER-ISLAND, NOT SOME GRUBBY, HOBO-STAINED MOVIE THEATER!
YOU'LL HAVE TOP-LEVEL MINION STATUS--THE HIGHEST ECHELONS! YOU'LL BE FEARED AND RESPECTED BY THE PEOPLE OF--
HEY!
TIME OUT!

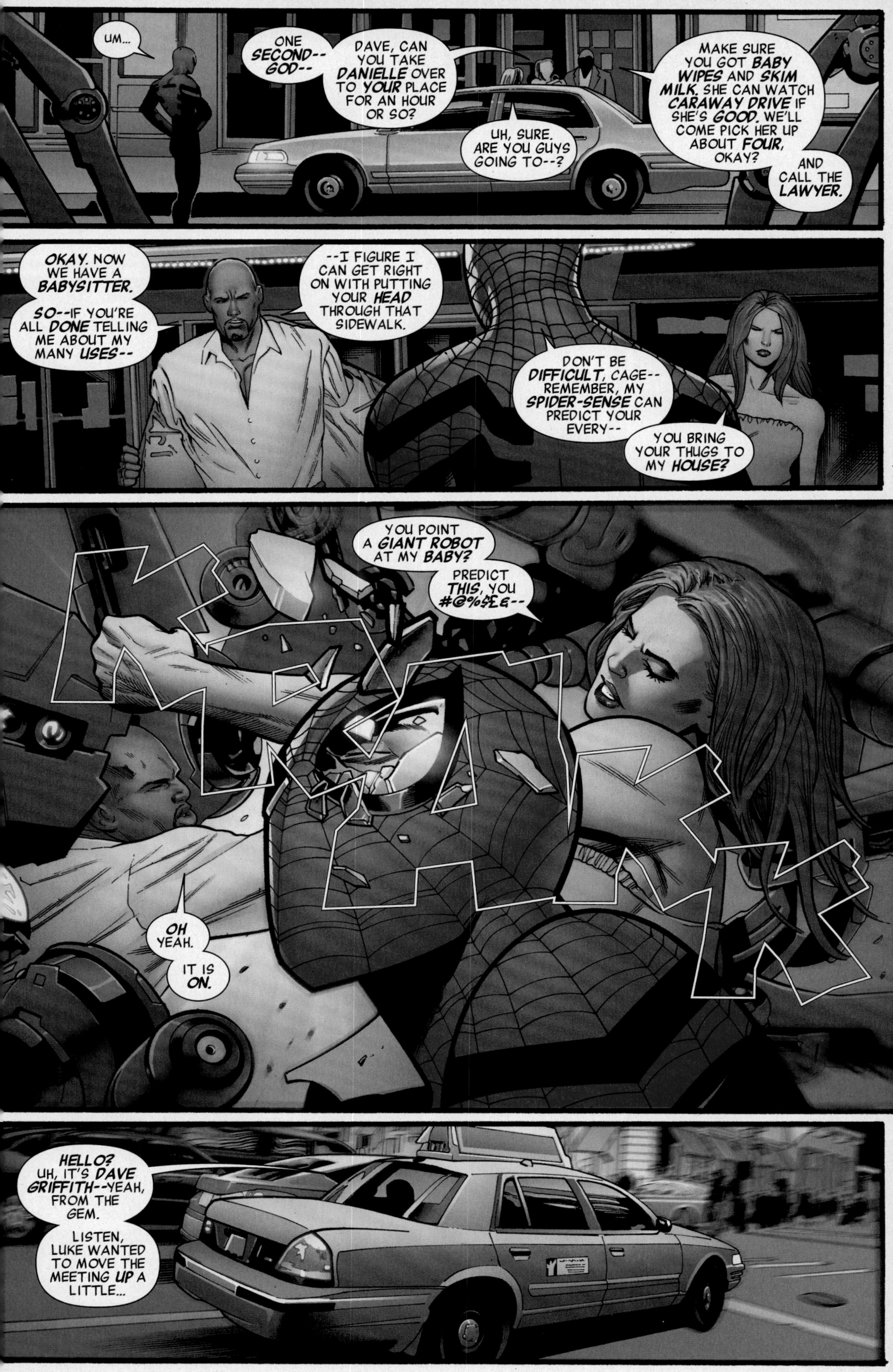
UM...
ONE SECOND-- GOD--
DAVE, CAN YOU TAKE DANIELLE OVER TO YOUR PLACE FOR AN HOUR OR SO?
UH, SURE. ARE YOU GUYS GOING TO--?
MAKE SURE YOU GOT BABY WIPES AND SKIM MILK. SHE CAN WATCH CARAWAY DRIVE IF SHE'S GOOD. WE'LL COME PICK HER UP ABOUT FOUR, OKAY?
AND CALL THE LAWYER.
OKAY. NOW WE HAVE A BABYSITTER.
SO--IF YOU'RE ALL DONE TELLING ME ABOUT MY MANY USES--
--I FIGURE I CAN GET RIGHT ON WITH PUTTING YOUR HEAD THROUGH THAT SIDEWALK.
DON'T BE DIFFICULT, CAGE-- REMEMBER, MY SPIDER-SENSE CAN PREDICT YOUR EVERY--
YOU BRING YOUR THUGS TO MY HOUSE?
YOU POINT A GIANT ROBOT AT MY BABY?
PREDICT THIS, YOU #@%$£€--
OH YEAH.
IT IS ON.
HELLO? UH, IT'S DAVE GRIFFITH--YEAH, FROM THE GEM.
LISTEN, LUKE WANTED TO MOVE THE MEETING UP A LITTLE...

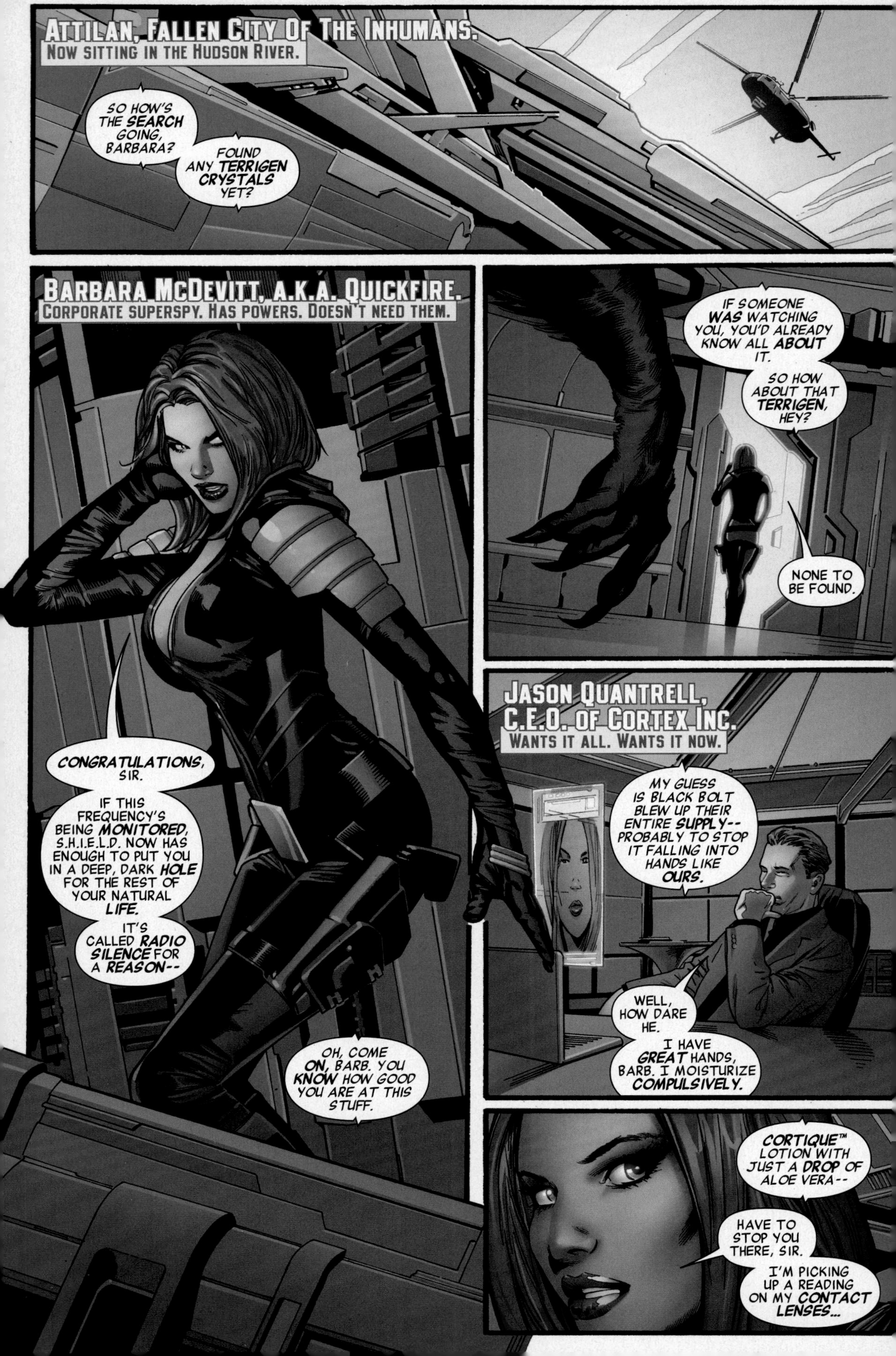
ATTILAN, FALLEN CITY OF THE INHUMANS.
NOW SITTING IN THE HUDSON RIVER.
SO HOW'S THE SEARCH GOING, BARBARA?
FOUND ANY TERRIGEN CRYSTALS YET?
BARBARA McDEVITT, A.K.A. QUICKFIRE.
CORPORATE SUPERSPY. HAS POWERS. DOESN'T NEED THEM.
CONGRATULATIONS, SIR.
IF THIS FREQUENCY'S BEING MONITORED, S.H.I.E.L.D. NOW HAS ENOUGH TO PUT YOU IN A DEEP, DARK HOLE FOR THE REST OF YOUR NATURAL LIFE.
IT'S CALLED RADIO SILENCE FOR A REASON--
OH, COME ON, BARB. YOU KNOW HOW GOOD YOU ARE AT THIS STUFF.
IF SOMEONE WAS WATCHING YOU, YOU'D ALREADY KNOW ALL ABOUT IT.
SO HOW ABOUT THAT TERRIGEN, HEY?
NONE TO BE FOUND.
JASON QUANTRELL, C.E.O. OF CORTEX INC.
WANTS IT ALL. WANTS IT NOW.
MY GUESS IS BLACK BOLT BLEW UP THEIR ENTIRE SUPPLY-- PROBABLY TO STOP IT FALLING INTO HANDS LIKE OURS.
WELL, HOW DARE HE.
I HAVE GREAT HANDS, BARB. I MOISTURIZE COMPULSIVELY.
CORTIQUE™ LOTION WITH JUST A DROP OF ALOE VERA--
HAVE TO STOP YOU THERE, SIR.
I'M PICKING UP A READING ON MY CONTACT LENSES...

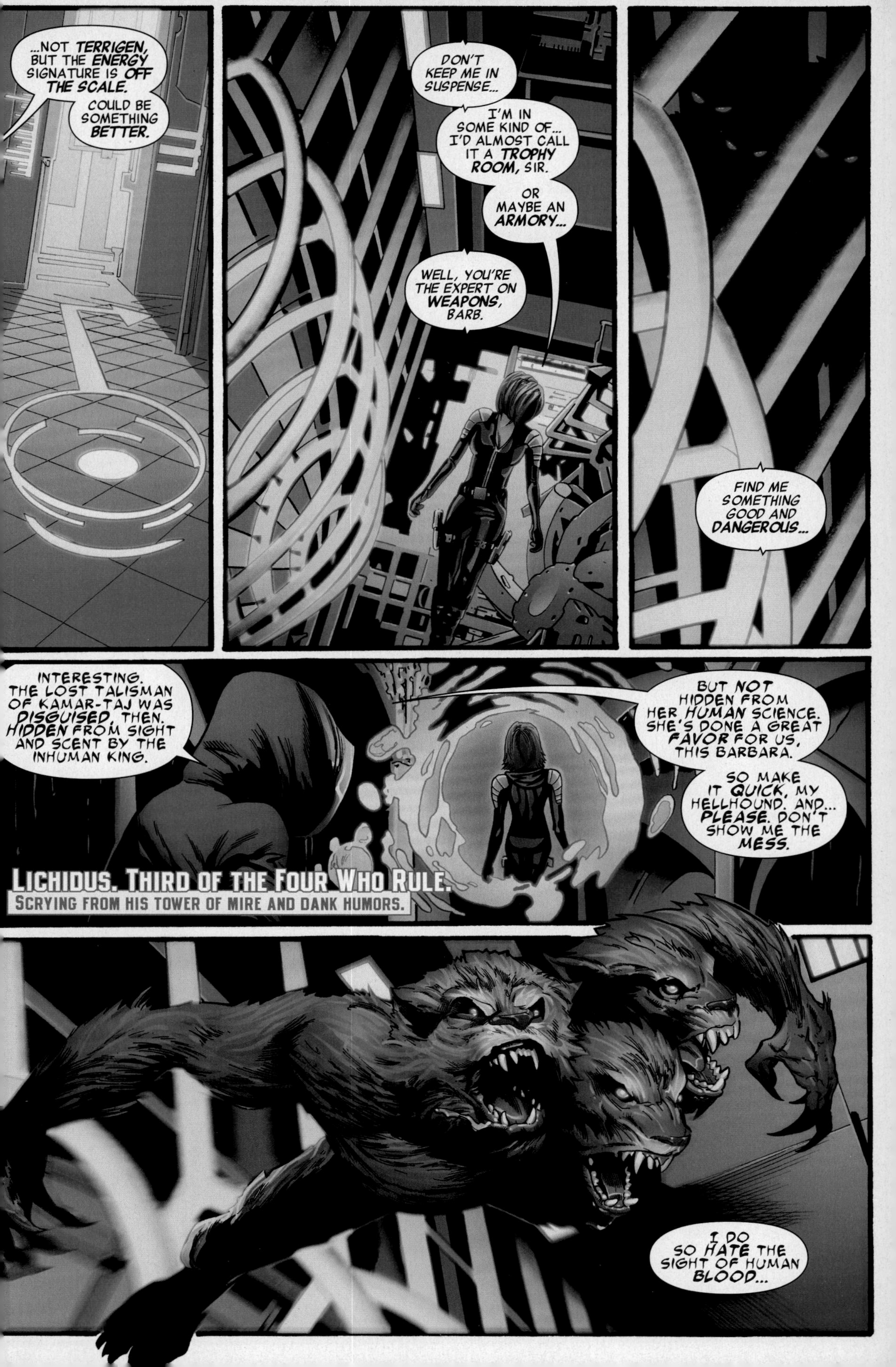
...NOT TERRIGEN, BUT THE ENERGY SIGNATURE IS OFF THE SCALE.
COULD BE SOMETHING BETTER.
DON'T KEEP ME IN SUSPENSE...
I'M IN SOME KIND OF... I'D ALMOST CALL IT A TROPHY ROOM, SIR.
OR MAYBE AN ARMORY...
WELL, YOU'RE THE EXPERT ON WEAPONS, BARB.
FIND ME SOMETHING GOOD AND DANGEROUS...
INTERESTING. THE LOST TALISMAN OF KAMAR-TAJ WAS DISGUISED, THEN. HIDDEN FROM SIGHT AND SCENT BY THE INHUMAN KING.
BUT NOT HIDDEN FROM HER HUMAN SCIENCE. SHE'S DONE A GREAT FAVOR FOR US, THIS BARBARA.
SO MAKE IT QUICK, MY HELLHOUND, AND... PLEASE. DON'T SHOW ME THE MESS.
LICHIDUS. THIRD OF THE FOUR WHO RULE.
SCRYING FROM HIS TOWER OF MIRE AND DANK HUMORS.
I DO SO HATE THE SIGHT OF HUMAN BLOOD...

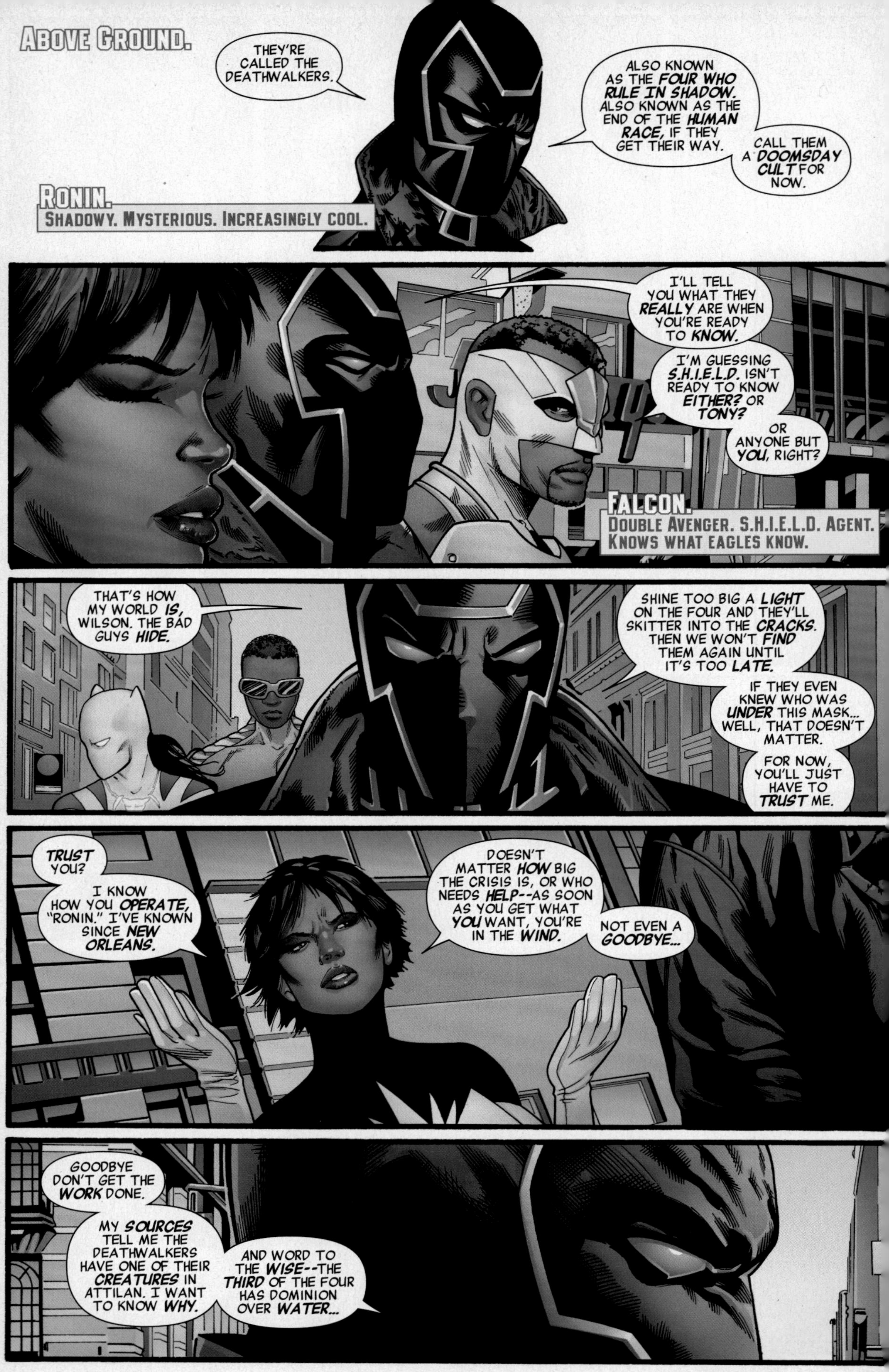
ABOVE GROUND.
THEY'RE CALLED THE DEATHWALKERS.
ALSO KNOWN AS THE FOUR WHO RULE IN SHADOW. ALSO KNOWN AS THE END OF THE HUMAN RACE, IF THEY GET THEIR WAY.
CALL THEM A DOOMSDAY CULT FOR NOW.
RONIN.
SHADOWY. MYSTERIOUS. INCREASINGLY COOL.
I'LL TELL YOU WHAT THEY REALLY ARE WHEN YOU'RE READY TO KNOW.
I'M GUESSING S.H.I.E.L.D. ISN'T READY TO KNOW EITHER? OR TONY?
OR ANYONE BUT YOU, RIGHT?
FALCON.
DOUBLE AVENGER. S.H.I.E.L.D. AGENT. KNOWS WHAT EAGLES KNOW.
THAT'S HOW MY WORLD IS, WILSON. THE BAD GUYS HIDE.
SHINE TOO BIG A LIGHT ON THE FOUR AND THEY'LL SKITTER INTO THE CRACKS. THEN WE WON'T FIND THEM AGAIN UNTIL IT'S TOO LATE.
IF THEY EVEN KNEW WHO WAS UNDER THIS MASK... WELL, THAT DOESN'T MATTER.
FOR NOW, YOU'LL JUST HAVE TO TRUST ME.
TRUST YOU?
I KNOW HOW YOU OPERATE, "RONIN." I'VE KNOWN SINCE NEW ORLEANS.
DOESN'T MATTER HOW BIG THE CRISIS IS, OR WHO NEEDS HELP--AS SOON AS YOU GET WHAT YOU WANT, YOU'RE IN THE WIND.
NOT EVEN A GOODBYE...
GOODBYE DON'T GET THE WORK DONE.
MY SOURCES TELL ME THE DEATHWALKERS HAVE ONE OF THEIR CREATURES IN ATTILAN. I WANT TO KNOW WHY.
AND WORD TO THE WISE--THE THIRD OF THE FOUR HAS DOMINION OVER WATER...

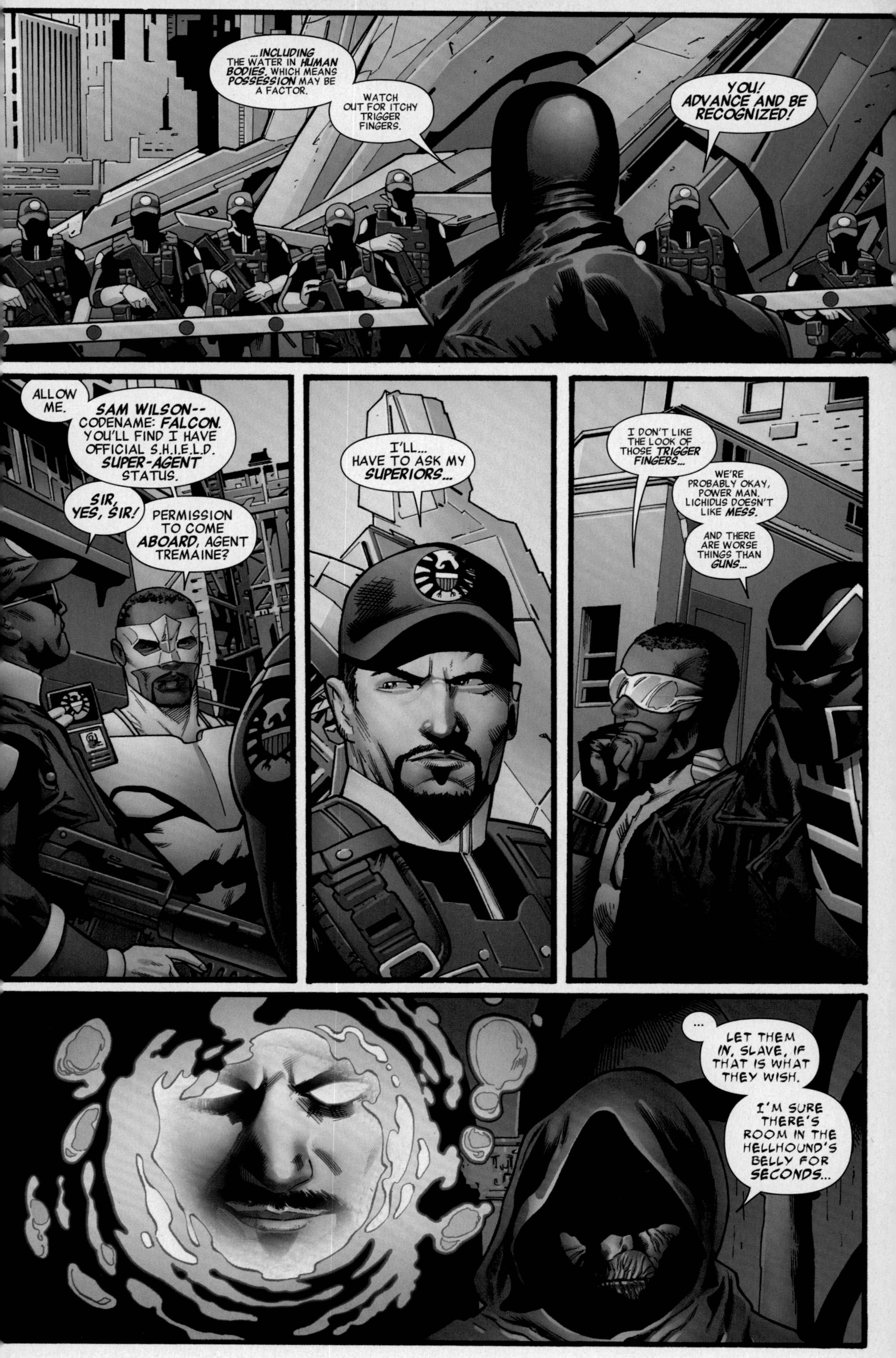
...INCLUDING THE WATER IN HUMAN BODIES. WHICH MEANS POSSESSION MAY BE A FACTOR.
WATCH OUT FOR ITCHY TRIGGER FINGERS.
YOU! ADVANCE AND BE RECOGNIZED!
ALLOW ME.
SAM WILSON-- CODENAME: FALCON. YOU'LL FIND I HAVE OFFICIAL S.H.I.E.L.D. SUPER-AGENT STATUS.
SIR, YES, SIR!
PERMISSION TO COME ABOARD, AGENT TREMAINE?
I'LL... HAVE TO ASK MY SUPERIORS...
I DON'T LIKE THE LOOK OF THOSE TRIGGER FINGERS...
WE'RE PROBABLY OKAY, POWER MAN. LICHIDUS DOESN'T LIKE MESS.
AND THERE ARE WORSE THINGS THAN GUNS...
...
LET THEM IN, SLAVE, IF THAT IS WHAT THEY WISH.
I'M SURE THERE'S ROOM IN THE HELLHOUND'S BELLY FOR SECONDS...

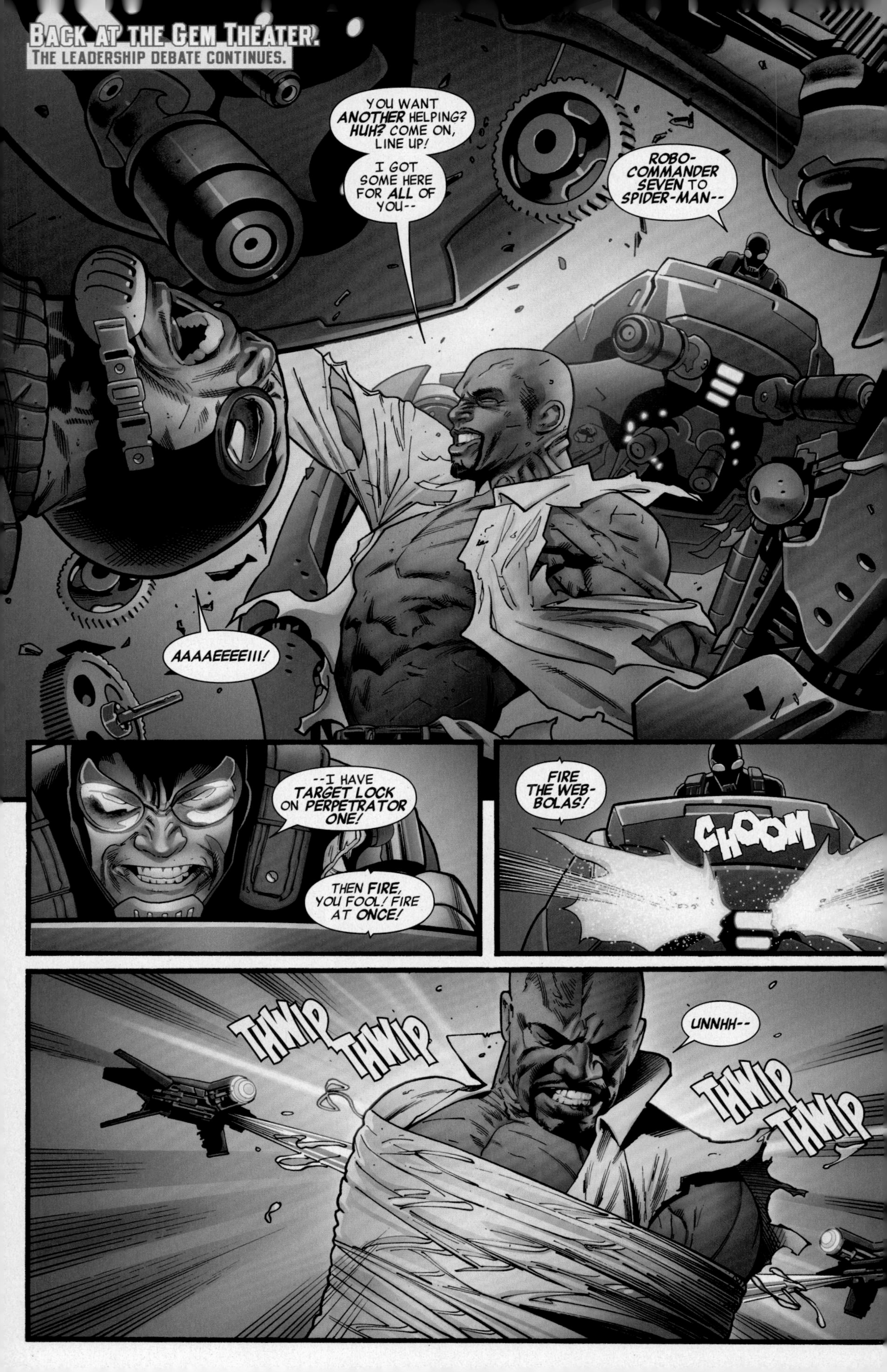
BACK AT THE GEM THEATER.
THE LEADERSHIP DEBATE CONTINUES.
YOU WANT ANOTHER HELPING? HUH? COME ON, LINE UP!
I GOT SOME HERE FOR ALL OF YOU--
ROBO-COMMANDER SEVEN TO SPIDER-MAN--
AAAAEEEEIII!
--I HAVE TARGET LOCK ON PERPETRATOR ONE!
THEN FIRE, YOU FOOL! FIRE AT ONCE!
FIRE THE WEB-BOLAS!
CHOOM
THWIP THWIP
UNNHH--
THWIP THWIP

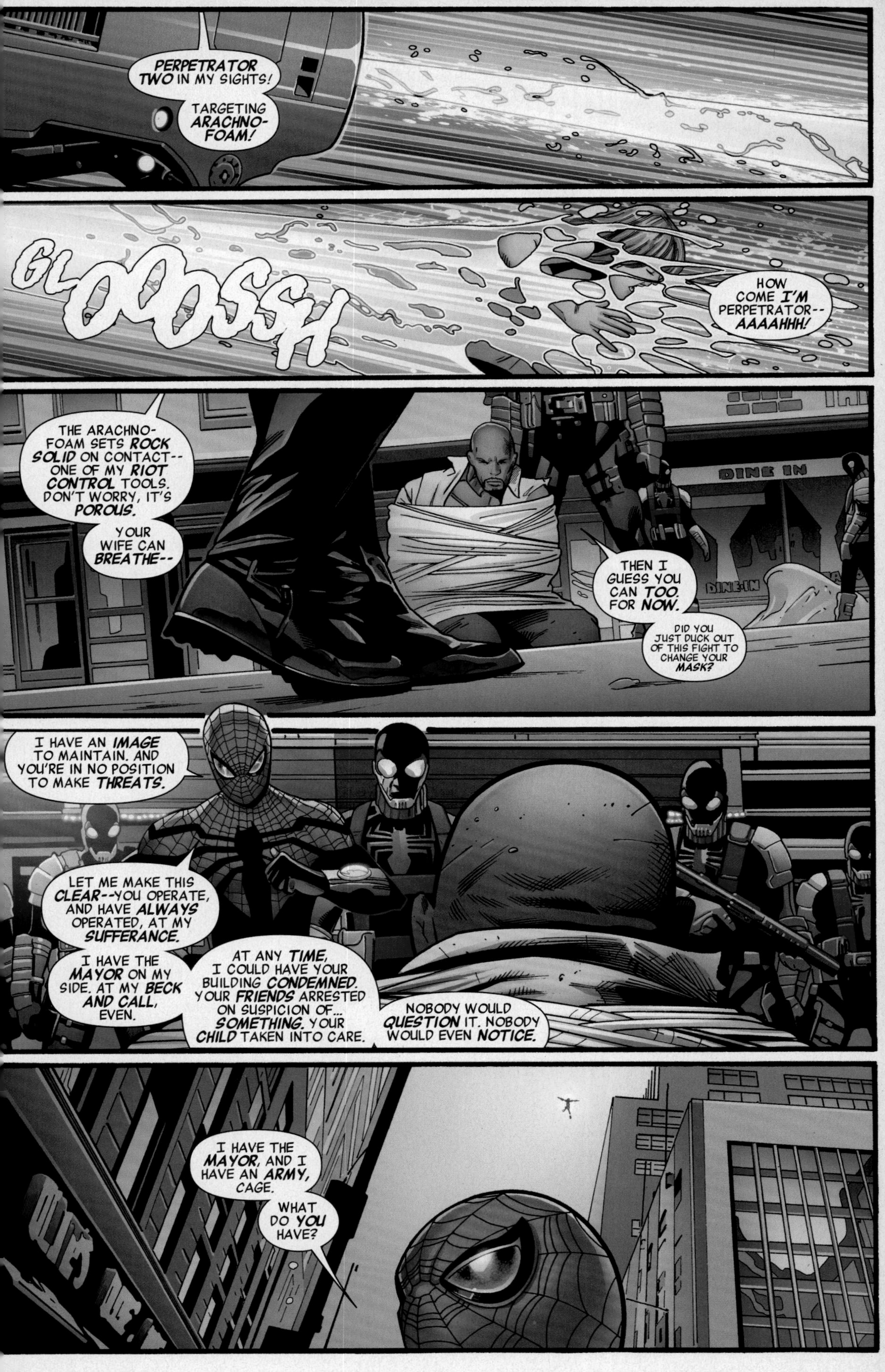
PERPETRATOR TWO IN MY SIGHTS!
TARGETING ARACHNO-FOAM!
GLOOOSSH
HOW COME I'M PERPETRATOR-- AAAAHHH!
THE ARACHNO-FOAM SETS ROCK SOLID ON CONTACT-- ONE OF MY RIOT CONTROL TOOLS. DON'T WORRY, IT'S POROUS.
YOUR WIFE CAN BREATHE--
DINE IN
THEN I GUESS YOU CAN TOO. FOR NOW.
DID YOU JUST DUCK OUT OF THIS FIGHT TO CHANGE YOUR MASK?
I HAVE AN IMAGE TO MAINTAIN. AND YOU'RE IN NO POSITION TO MAKE THREATS.
LET ME MAKE THIS CLEAR--YOU OPERATE, AND HAVE ALWAYS OPERATED, AT MY SUFFERANCE.
I HAVE THE MAYOR ON MY SIDE. AT MY BECK AND CALL, EVEN.
AT ANY TIME, I COULD HAVE YOUR BUILDING CONDEMNED. YOUR FRIENDS ARRESTED ON SUSPICION OF... SOMETHING. YOUR CHILD TAKEN INTO CARE.
NOBODY WOULD QUESTION IT. NOBODY WOULD EVEN NOTICE.
I HAVE THE MAYOR, AND I HAVE AN ARMY, CAGE.
WHAT DO YOU HAVE?

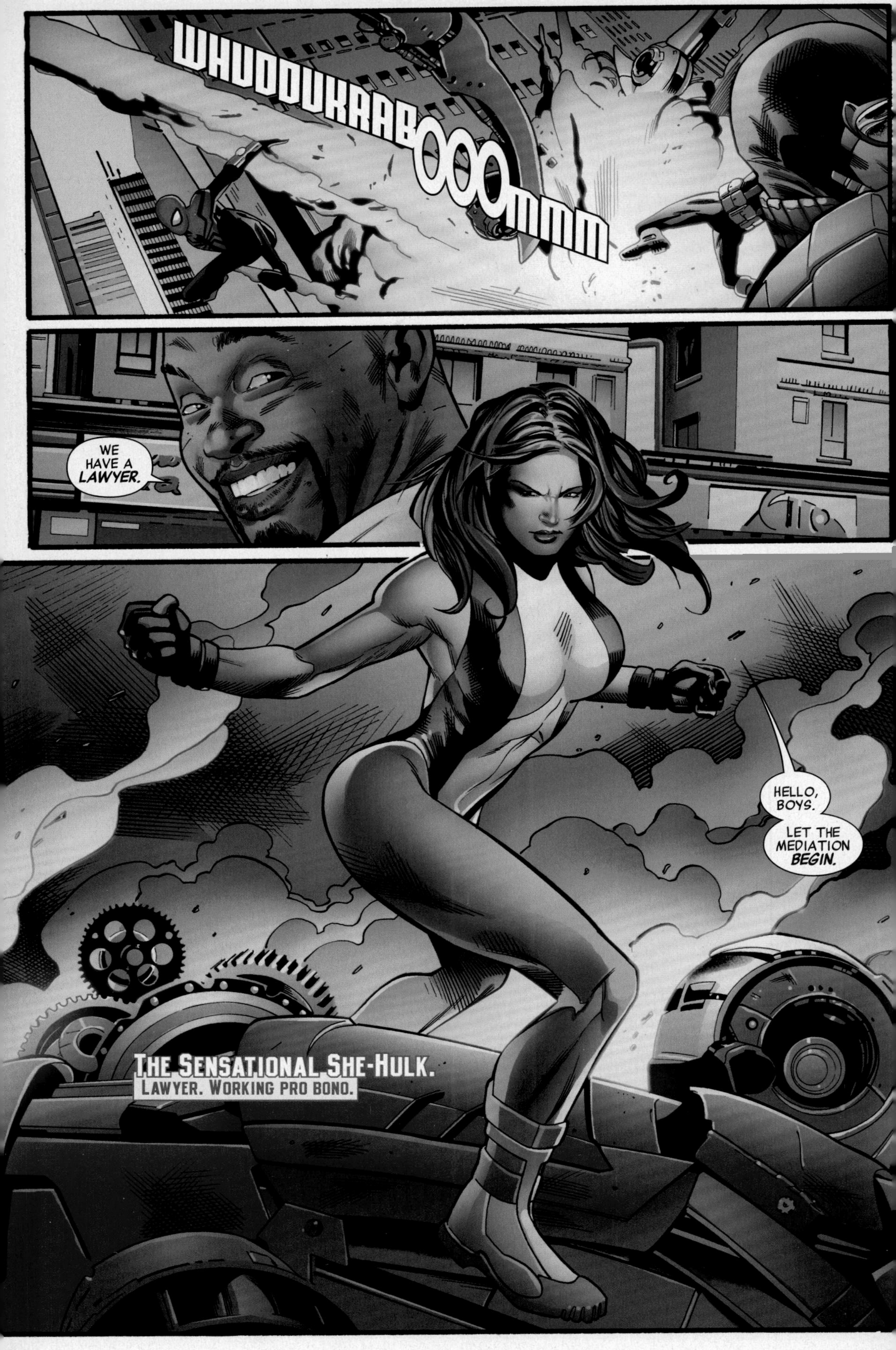
WHUDDUKRABOOOMMM
WE HAVE A LAWYER.
HELLO, BOYS.
LET THE MEDIATION BEGIN.
THE SENSATIONAL SHE-HULK.
LAWYER. WORKING PRO BONO.

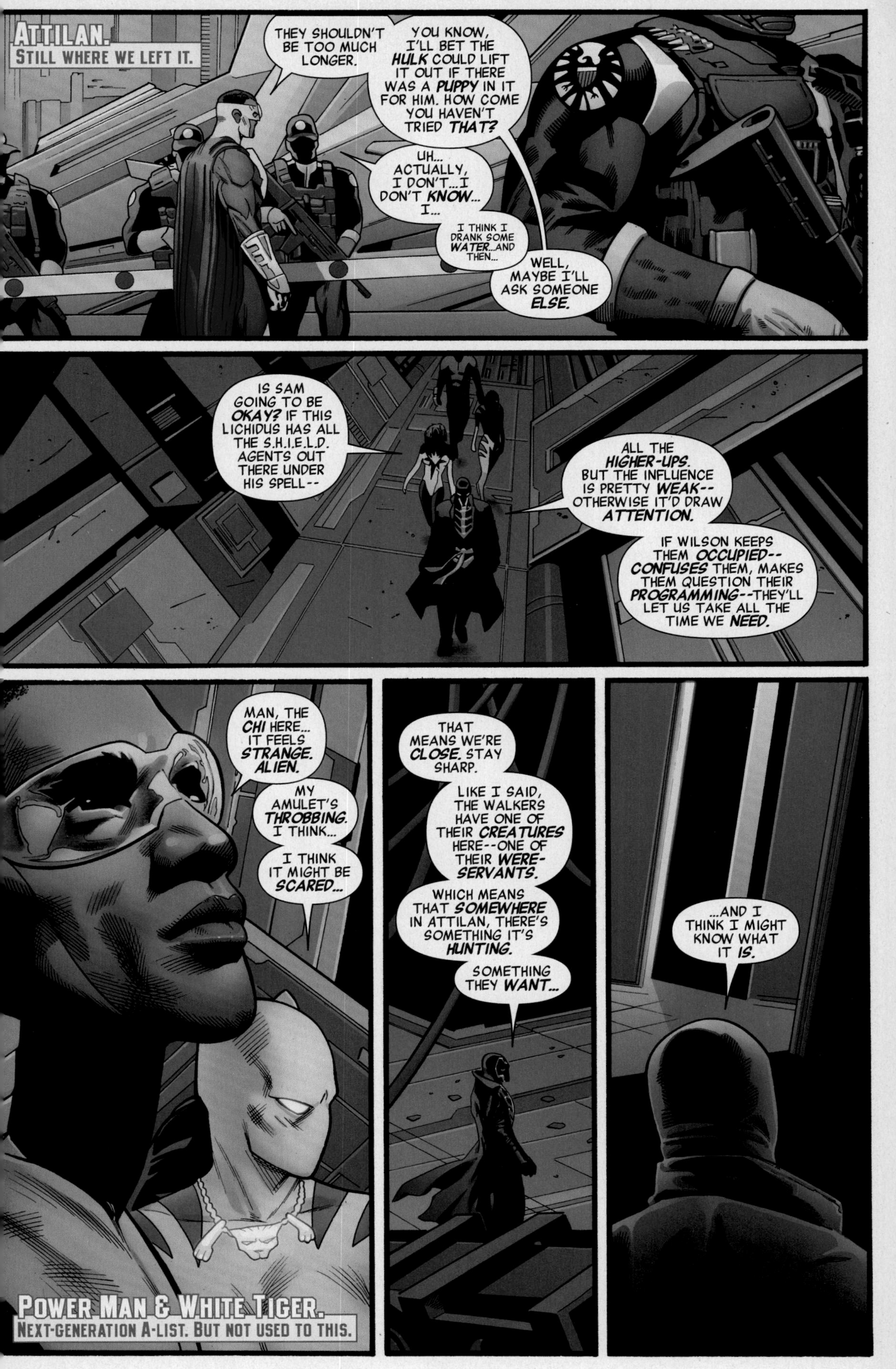
ATTILAN.
STILL WHERE WE LEFT IT.
THEY SHOULDN'T BE TOO MUCH LONGER.
YOU KNOW, I'LL BET THE HULK COULD LIFT IT OUT IF THERE WAS A PUPPY IN IT FOR HIM. HOW COME YOU HAVEN'T TRIED THAT?
UH... ACTUALLY, I DON'T...I DON'T KNOW... I...
I THINK I DRANK SOME WATER...AND THEN...
WELL, MAYBE I'LL ASK SOMEONE ELSE.
IS SAM GOING TO BE OKAY? IF THIS LICHIDUS HAS ALL THE S.H.I.E.L.D. AGENTS OUT THERE UNDER HIS SPELL--
ALL THE HIGHER-UPS. BUT THE INFLUENCE IS PRETTY WEAK--OTHERWISE IT'D DRAW ATTENTION.
IF WILSON KEEPS THEM OCCUPIED--CONFUSES THEM, MAKES THEM QUESTION THEIR PROGRAMMING--THEY'LL LET US TAKE ALL THE TIME WE NEED.
MAN, THE CHI HERE... IT FEELS STRANGE. ALIEN.
MY AMULET'S THROBBING. I THINK...
I THINK IT MIGHT BE SCARED...
POWER MAN & WHITE TIGER.
NEXT-GENERATION A-LIST. BUT NOT USED TO THIS.
THAT MEANS WE'RE CLOSE. STAY SHARP.
LIKE I SAID, THE WALKERS HAVE ONE OF THEIR CREATURES HERE--ONE OF THEIR WERE-SERVANTS.
WHICH MEANS THAT SOMEWHERE IN ATTILAN, THERE'S SOMETHING IT'S HUNTING.
SOMETHING THEY WANT...
...AND I THINK I MIGHT KNOW WHAT IT IS.

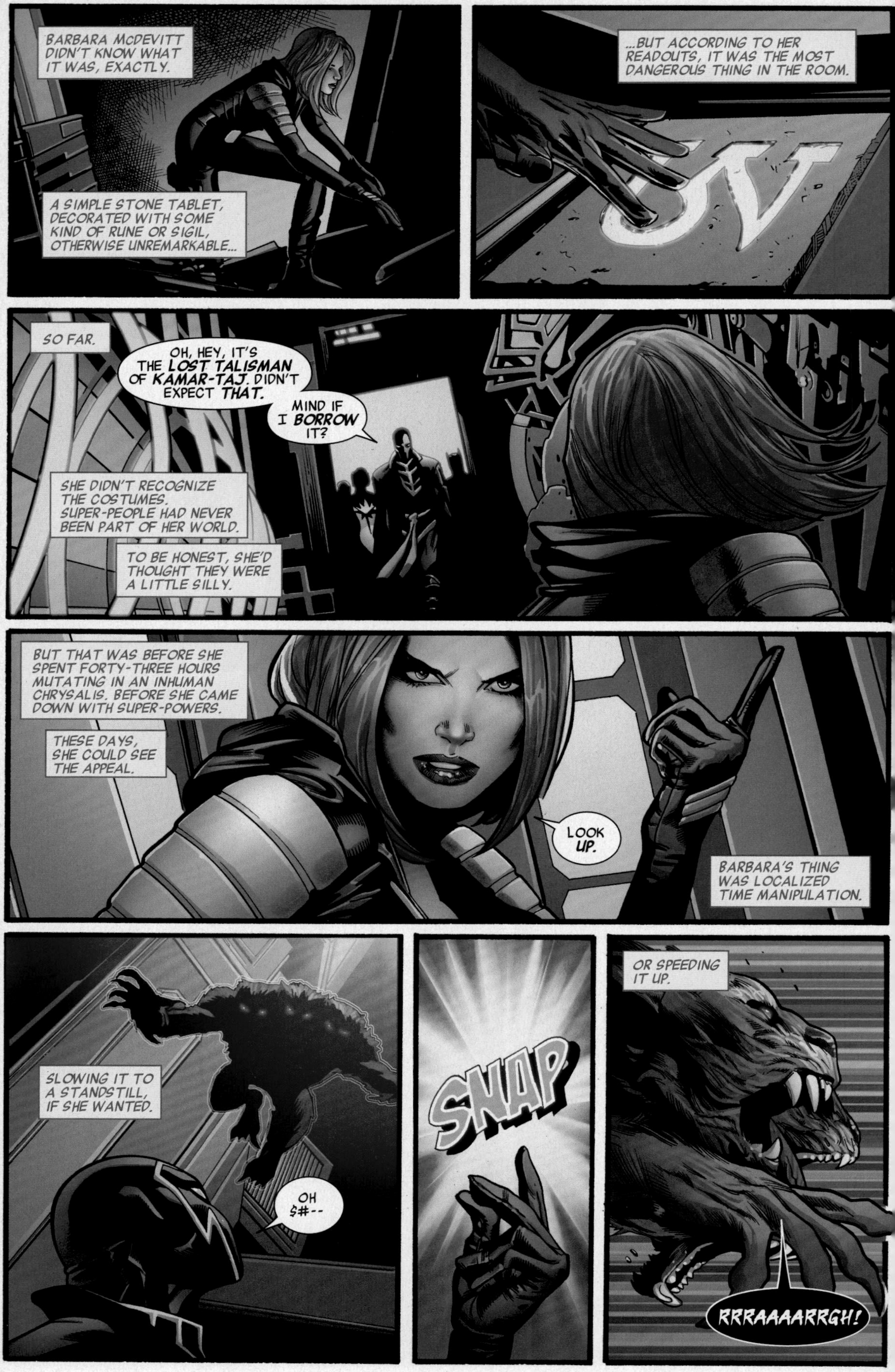
BARBARA McDEVITT DIDN'T KNOW WHAT IT WAS, EXACTLY.
A SIMPLE STONE TABLET, DECORATED WITH SOME KIND OF RUNE OR SIGIL, OTHERWISE UNREMARKABLE...
...BUT ACCORDING TO HER READOUTS, IT WAS THE MOST DANGEROUS THING IN THE ROOM.
SO FAR.
OH, HEY, IT'S THE LOST TALISMAN OF KAMAR-TAJ. DIDN'T EXPECT THAT.
MIND IF I BORROW IT?
SHE DIDN'T RECOGNIZE THE COSTUMES. SUPER-PEOPLE HAD NEVER BEEN PART OF HER WORLD.
TO BE HONEST, SHE'D THOUGHT THEY WERE A LITTLE SILLY.
BUT THAT WAS BEFORE SHE SPENT FORTY-THREE HOURS MUTATING IN AN INHUMAN CHRYSALIS. BEFORE SHE CAME DOWN WITH SUPER-POWERS.
THESE DAYS, SHE COULD SEE THE APPEAL.
LOOK UP.
BARBARA'S THING WAS LOCALIZED TIME MANIPULATION.
SLOWING IT TO A STANDSTILL, IF SHE WANTED.
OH $#--
SNAP
OR SPEEDING IT UP.
RRRAAAARRGH!

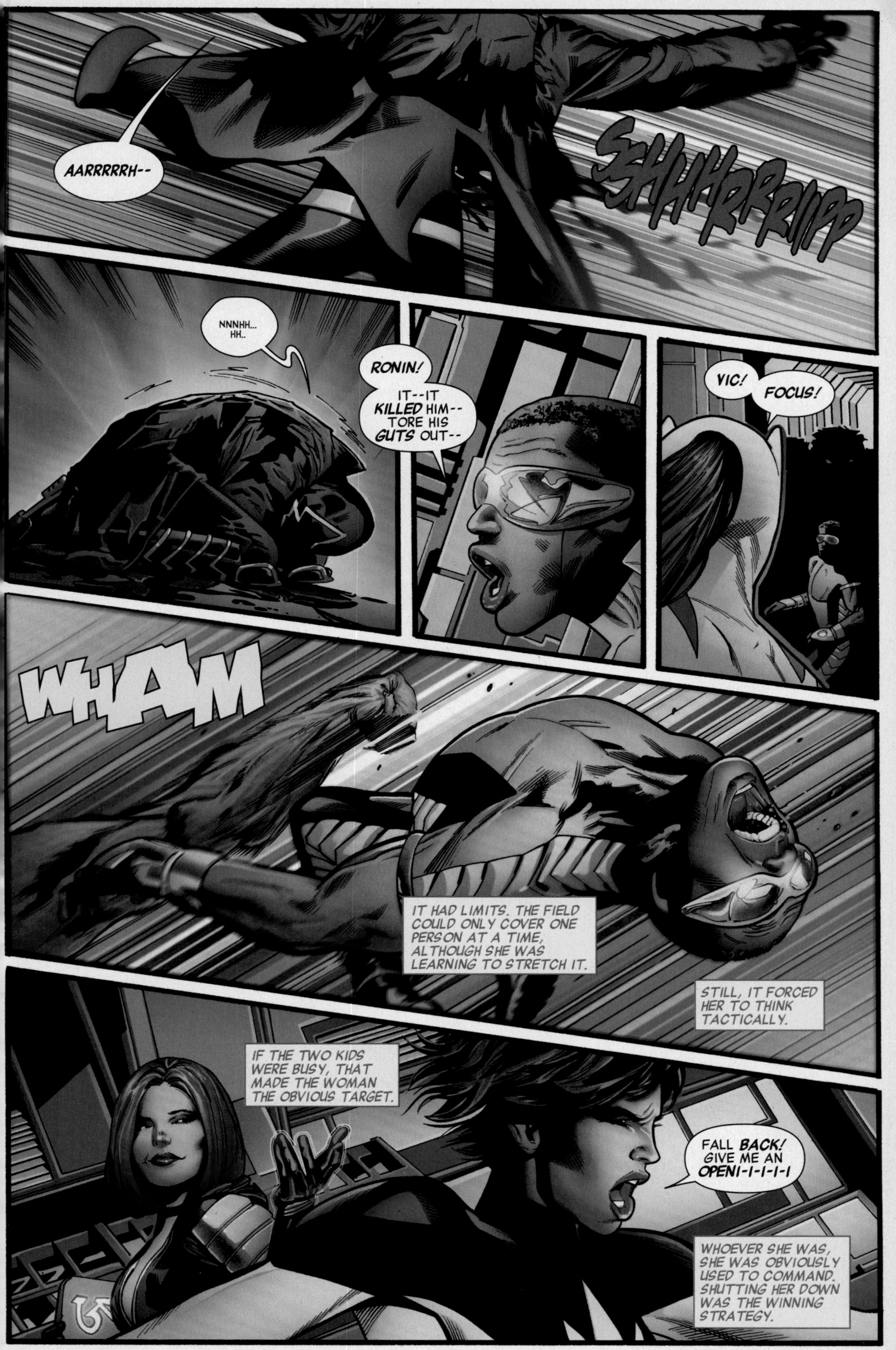

AARRRRRH--
SSHHHRRRIPP
NNNHH... HH..
RONIN!
IT--IT KILLED HIM--TORE HIS GUTS OUT--
VIC!
FOCUS!
WHAM
IT HAD LIMITS. THE FIELD COULD ONLY COVER ONE PERSON AT A TIME, ALTHOUGH SHE WAS LEARNING TO STRETCH IT.
STILL, IT FORCED HER TO THINK TACTICALLY.
IF THE TWO KIDS WERE BUSY, THAT MADE THE WOMAN THE OBVIOUS TARGET.
FALL BACK! GIVE ME AN OPENI-I-I-I-I
WHOEVER SHE WAS, SHE WAS OBVIOUSLY USED TO COMMAND. SHUTTING HER DOWN WAS THE WINNING STRATEGY.

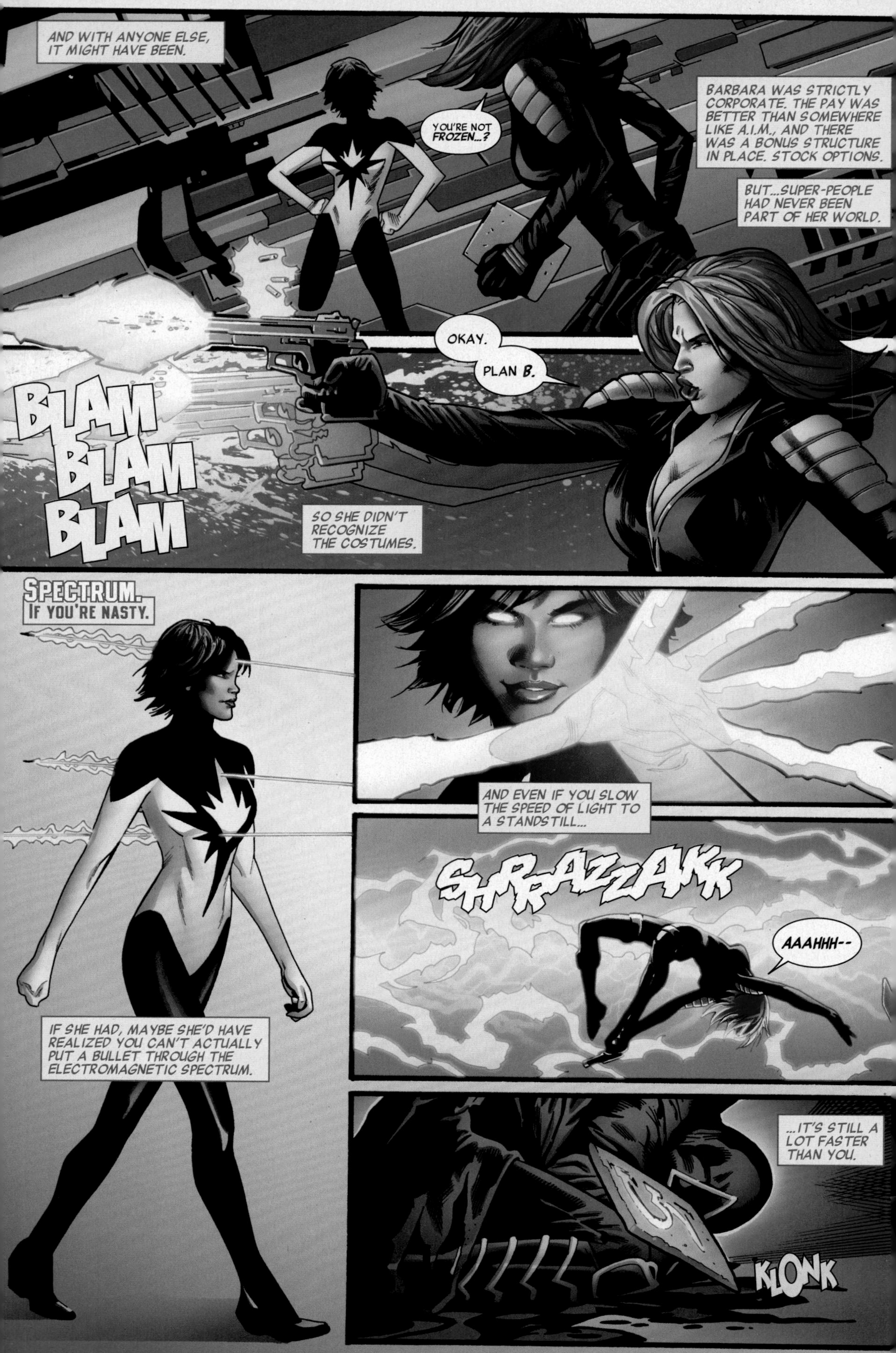
AND WITH ANYONE ELSE, IT MIGHT HAVE BEEN.
YOU'RE NOT FROZEN...?
BARBARA WAS STRICTLY CORPORATE. THE PAY WAS BETTER THAN SOMEWHERE LIKE A.I.M., AND THERE WAS A BONUS STRUCTURE IN PLACE. STOCK OPTIONS.
BUT...SUPER-PEOPLE HAD NEVER BEEN PART OF HER WORLD.
OKAY.
PLAN B.
BLAM BLAM BLAM
SO SHE DIDN'T RECOGNIZE THE COSTUMES.
SPECTRUM. IF YOU'RE NASTY.
IF SHE HAD, MAYBE SHE'D HAVE REALIZED YOU CAN'T ACTUALLY PUT A BULLET THROUGH THE ELECTROMAGNETIC SPECTRUM.
AND EVEN IF YOU SLOW THE SPEED OF LIGHT TO A STANDSTILL...
SHRRAZZAKK
AAAHHH--
...IT'S STILL A LOT FASTER THAN YOU.
KLONK

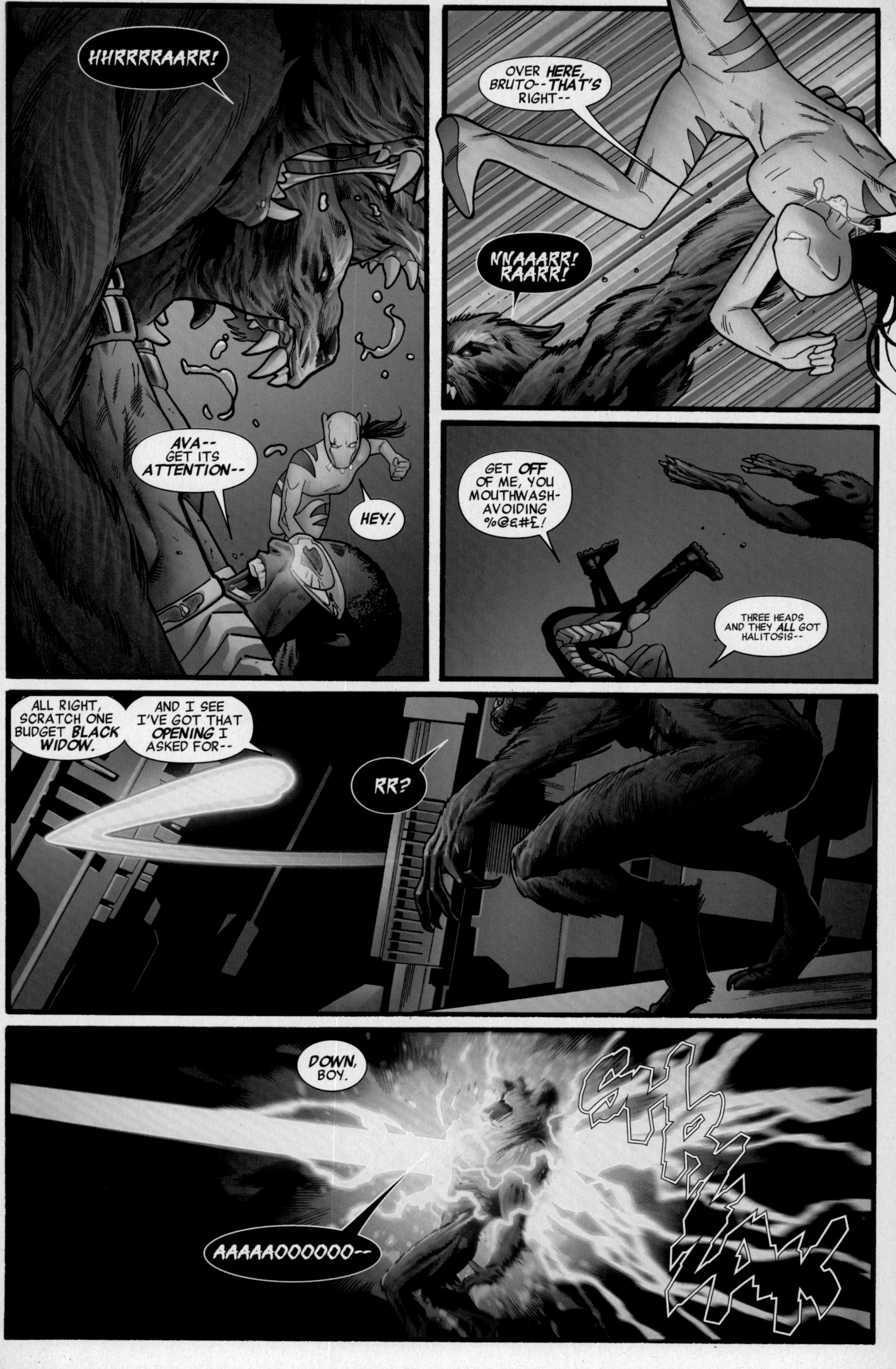
HHRRRRAARR!
OVER HERE, BRUTO--THAT'S RIGHT--
NNAAARR! RAARR!
AVA-- GET ITS ATTENTION--
HEY!
GET OFF OF ME, YOU MOUTHWASH-AVOIDING %@€#£!
THREE HEADS AND THEY ALL GOT HALITOSIS--
ALL RIGHT, SCRATCH ONE BUDGET BLACK WIDOW.
AND I SEE I'VE GOT THAT OPENING I ASKED FOR--
RR?
DOWN, BOY.
AAAAAOOOOOO--

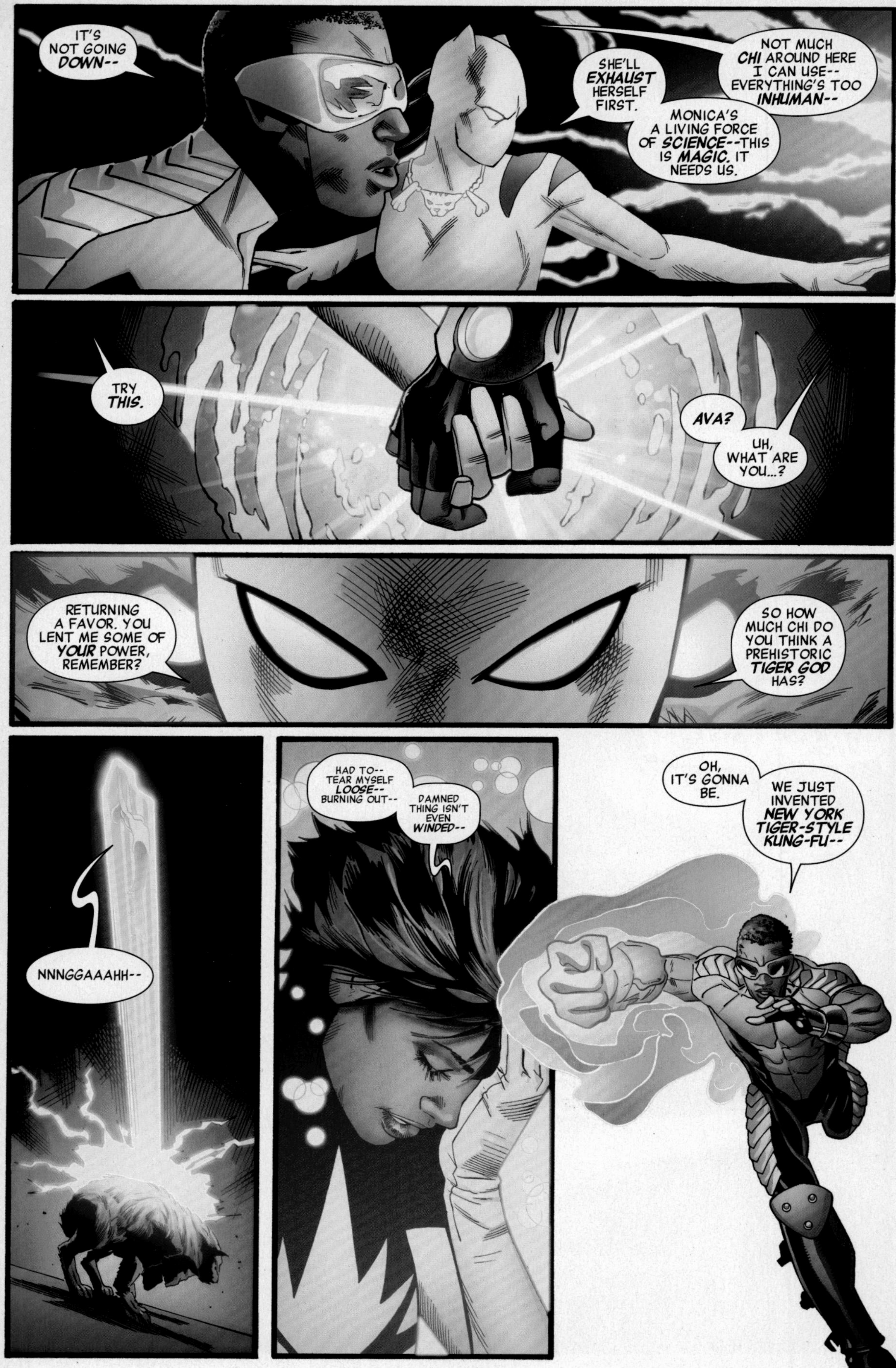

IT'S NOT GOING DOWN--
SHE'LL EXHAUST HERSELF FIRST.
NOT MUCH CHI AROUND HERE I CAN USE-- EVERYTHING'S TOO INHUMAN--
MONICA'S A LIVING FORCE OF SCIENCE--THIS IS MAGIC. IT NEEDS US.
TRY THIS.
AVA?
UH, WHAT ARE YOU...?
RETURNING A FAVOR. YOU LENT ME SOME OF YOUR POWER, REMEMBER?
SO HOW MUCH CHI DO YOU THINK A PREHISTORIC TIGER GOD HAS?
NNNGGAAAHH--
HAD TO-- TEAR MYSELF LOOSE-- BURNING OUT--
DAMNED THING ISN'T EVEN WINDED--
OH, IT'S GONNA BE.
WE JUST INVENTED NEW YORK TIGER-STYLE KUNG-FU--

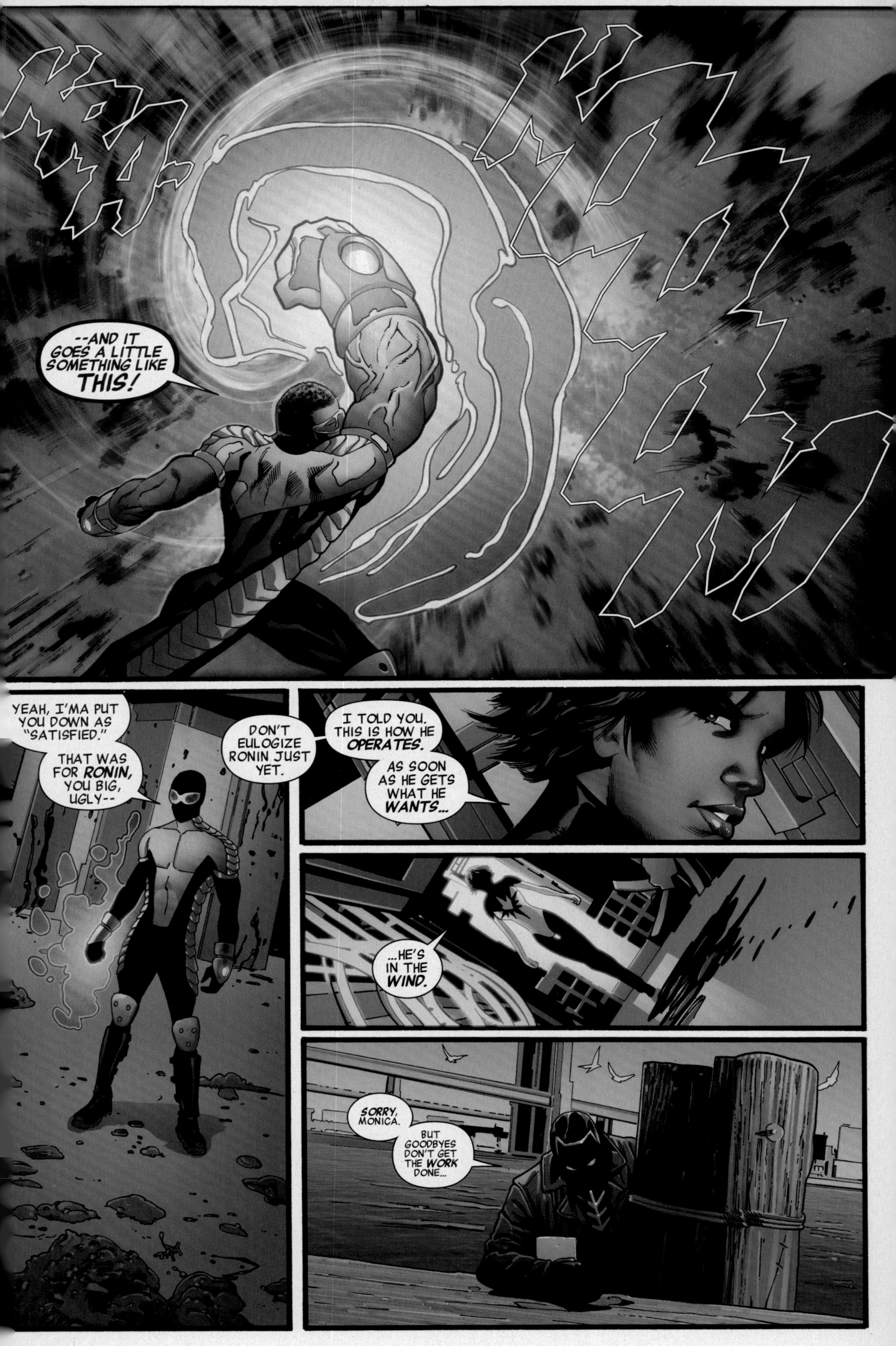
--AND IT GOES A LITTLE SOMETHING LIKE THIS!
YEAH, I'MA PUT YOU DOWN AS "SATISFIED."
THAT WAS FOR RONIN, YOU BIG, UGLY--
DON'T EULOGIZE RONIN JUST YET.
I TOLD YOU. THIS IS HOW HE OPERATES.
AS SOON AS HE GETS WHAT HE WANTS...
...HE'S IN THE WIND.
SORRY, MONICA.
BUT GOODBYES DON'T GET THE WORK DONE...

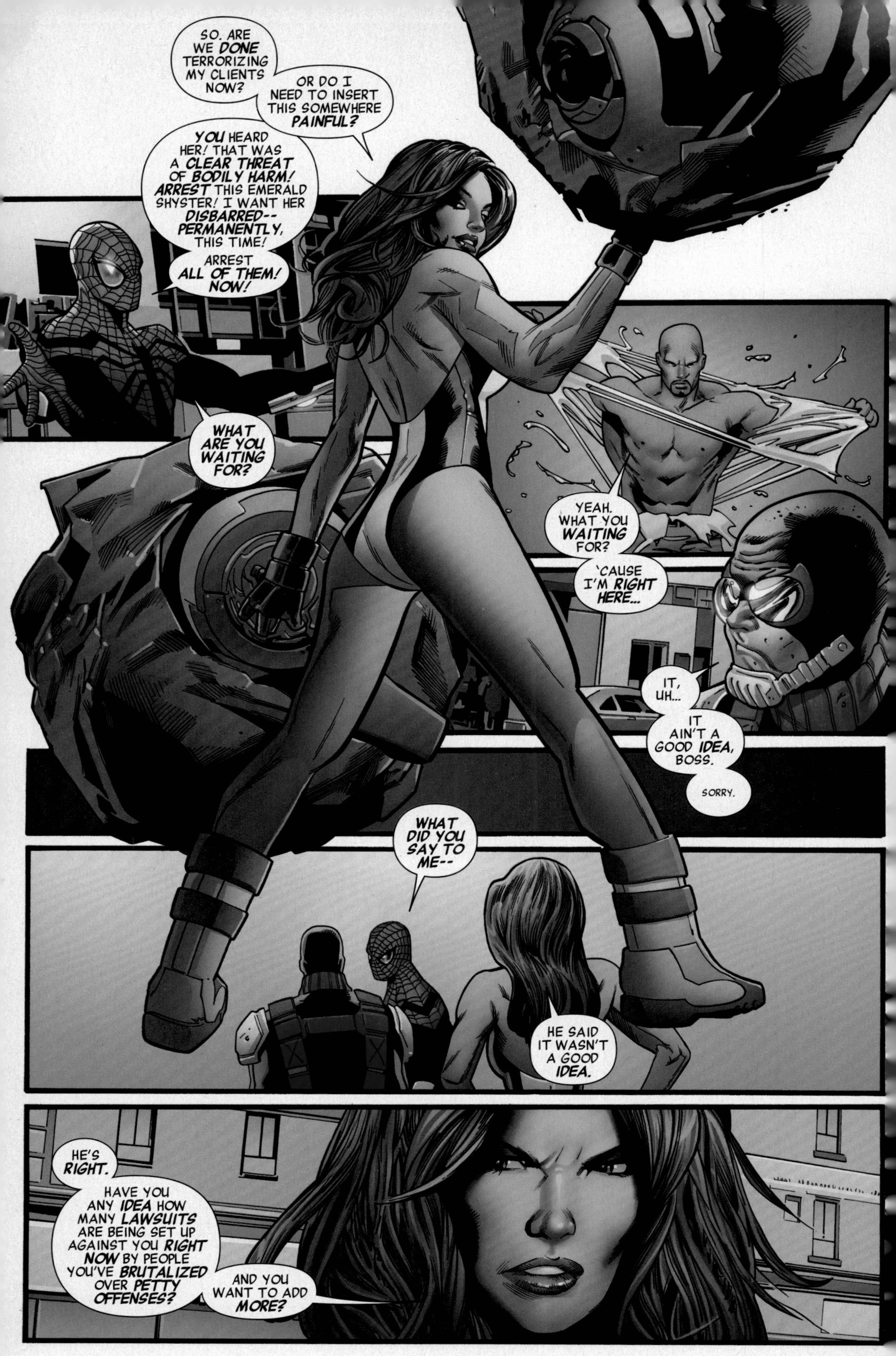
SO. ARE WE DONE TERRORIZING MY CLIENTS NOW?
OR DO I NEED TO INSERT THIS SOMEWHERE PAINFUL?
YOU HEARD HER! THAT WAS A CLEAR THREAT OF BODILY HARM! ARREST THIS EMERALD SHYSTER! I WANT HER DISBARRED--PERMANENTLY, THIS TIME!
ARREST ALL OF THEM! NOW!
WHAT ARE YOU WAITING FOR?
YEAH. WHAT YOU WAITING FOR?
'CAUSE I'M RIGHT HERE...
IT, UH...
IT AIN'T A GOOD IDEA, BOSS.
SORRY.
WHAT DID YOU SAY TO ME--
HE SAID IT WASN'T A GOOD IDEA.
HE'S RIGHT.
HAVE YOU ANY IDEA HOW MANY LAWSUITS ARE BEING SET UP AGAINST YOU RIGHT NOW BY PEOPLE YOU'VE BRUTALIZED OVER PETTY OFFENSES?
AND YOU WANT TO ADD MORE?

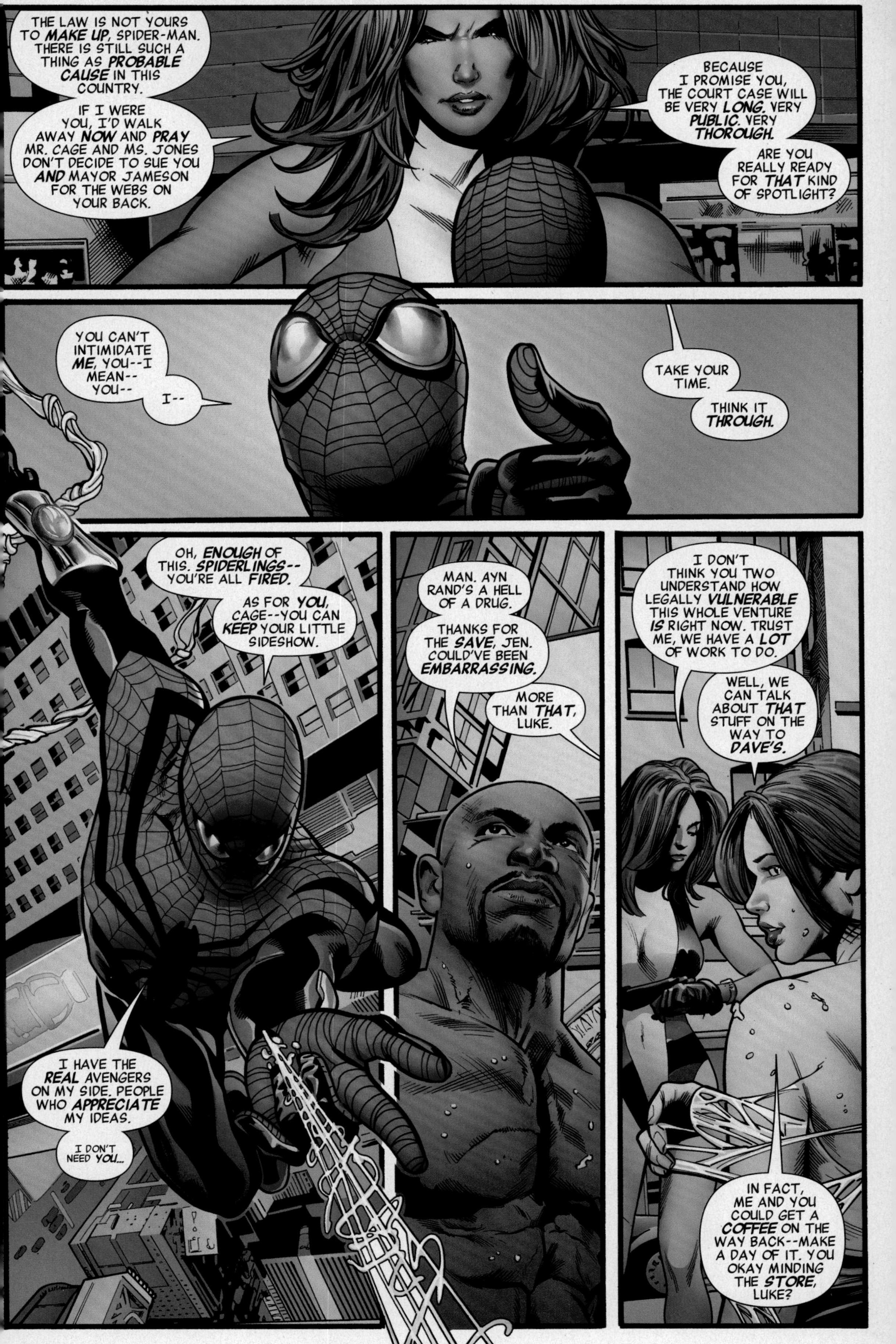
THE LAW IS NOT YOURS TO MAKE UP, SPIDER-MAN. THERE IS STILL SUCH A THING AS PROBABLE CAUSE IN THIS COUNTRY.
IF I WERE YOU, I'D WALK AWAY NOW AND PRAY MR. CAGE AND MS. JONES DON'T DECIDE TO SUE YOU AND MAYOR JAMESON FOR THE WEBS ON YOUR BACK.
BECAUSE I PROMISE YOU, THE COURT CASE WILL BE VERY LONG. VERY PUBLIC. VERY THOROUGH.
ARE YOU REALLY READY FOR THAT KIND OF SPOTLIGHT?
YOU CAN'T INTIMIDATE ME, YOU--I MEAN-- YOU--
I--
TAKE YOUR TIME.
THINK IT THROUGH.
OH, ENOUGH OF THIS. SPIDERLINGS--YOU'RE ALL FIRED.
AS FOR YOU, CAGE--YOU CAN KEEP YOUR LITTLE SIDESHOW.
I HAVE THE REAL AVENGERS ON MY SIDE. PEOPLE WHO APPRECIATE MY IDEAS.
I DON'T NEED YOU...
MAN. AYN RAND'S A HELL OF A DRUG.
THANKS FOR THE SAVE, JEN. COULD'VE BEEN EMBARRASSING.
MORE THAN THAT, LUKE.
I DON'T THINK YOU TWO UNDERSTAND HOW LEGALLY VULNERABLE THIS WHOLE VENTURE IS RIGHT NOW. TRUST ME, WE HAVE A LOT OF WORK TO DO.
WELL, WE CAN TALK ABOUT THAT STUFF ON THE WAY TO DAVE'S.
IN FACT, ME AND YOU COULD GET A COFFEE ON THE WAY BACK--MAKE A DAY OF IT. YOU OKAY MINDING THE STORE, LUKE?

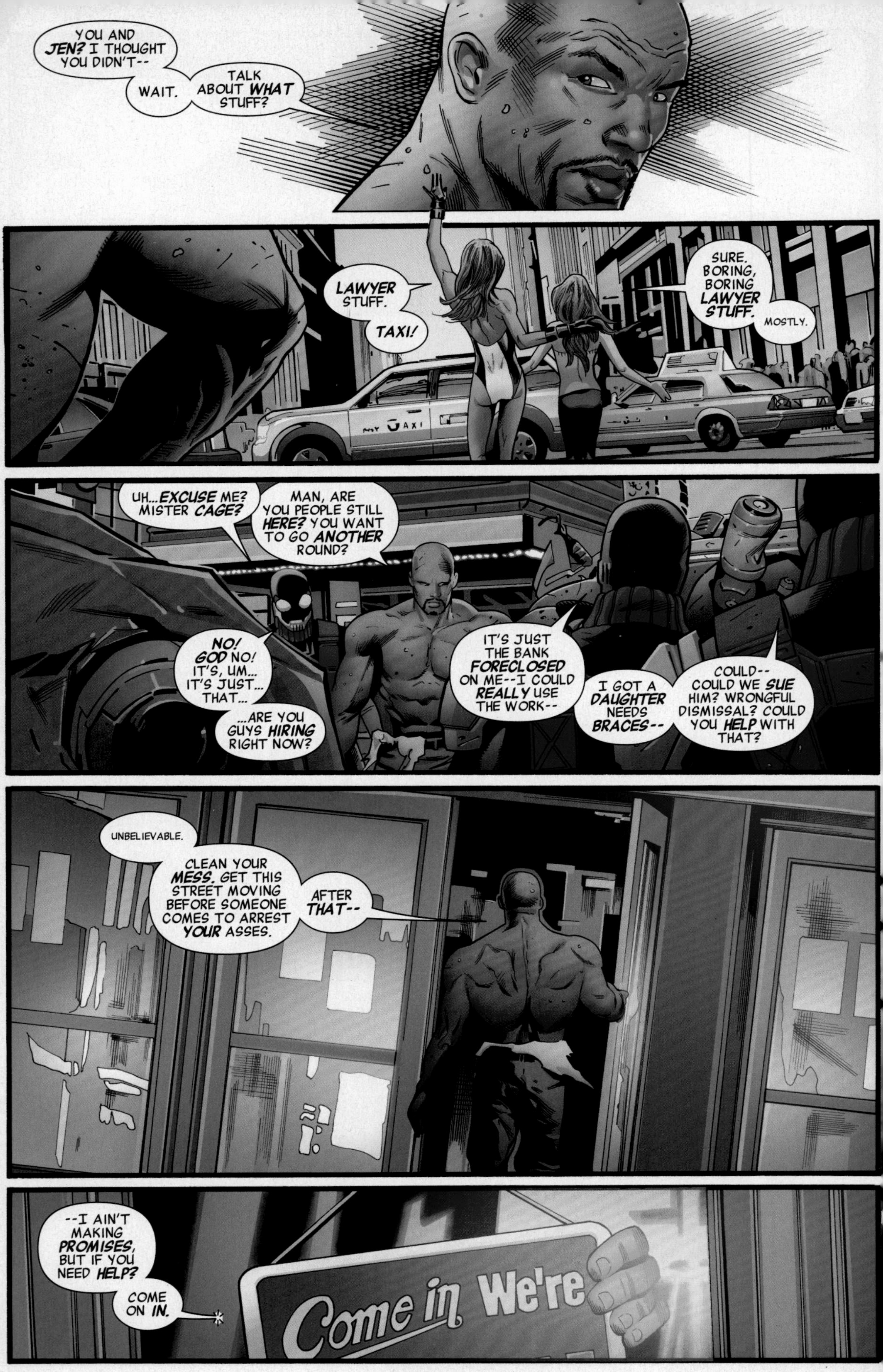
YOU AND JEN? I THOUGHT YOU DIDN'T--
WAIT.
TALK ABOUT WHAT STUFF?
LAWYER STUFF.
TAXI!
SURE. BORING, BORING LAWYER STUFF.
MOSTLY.
UH...EXCUSE ME? MISTER CAGE?
MAN, ARE YOU PEOPLE STILL HERE? YOU WANT TO GO ANOTHER ROUND?
NO! GOD NO! IT'S, UM... IT'S JUST... THAT...
...ARE YOU GUYS HIRING RIGHT NOW?
IT'S JUST THE BANK FORECLOSED ON ME--I COULD REALLY USE THE WORK--
I GOT A DAUGHTER NEEDS BRACES--
COULD-- COULD WE SUE HIM? WRONGFUL DISMISSAL? COULD YOU HELP WITH THAT?
UNBELIEVABLE.
CLEAN YOUR MESS. GET THIS STREET MOVING BEFORE SOMEONE COMES TO ARREST YOUR ASSES.
AFTER THAT--
--I AIN'T MAKING PROMISES, BUT IF YOU NEED HELP?
COME ON IN.
Come in We're

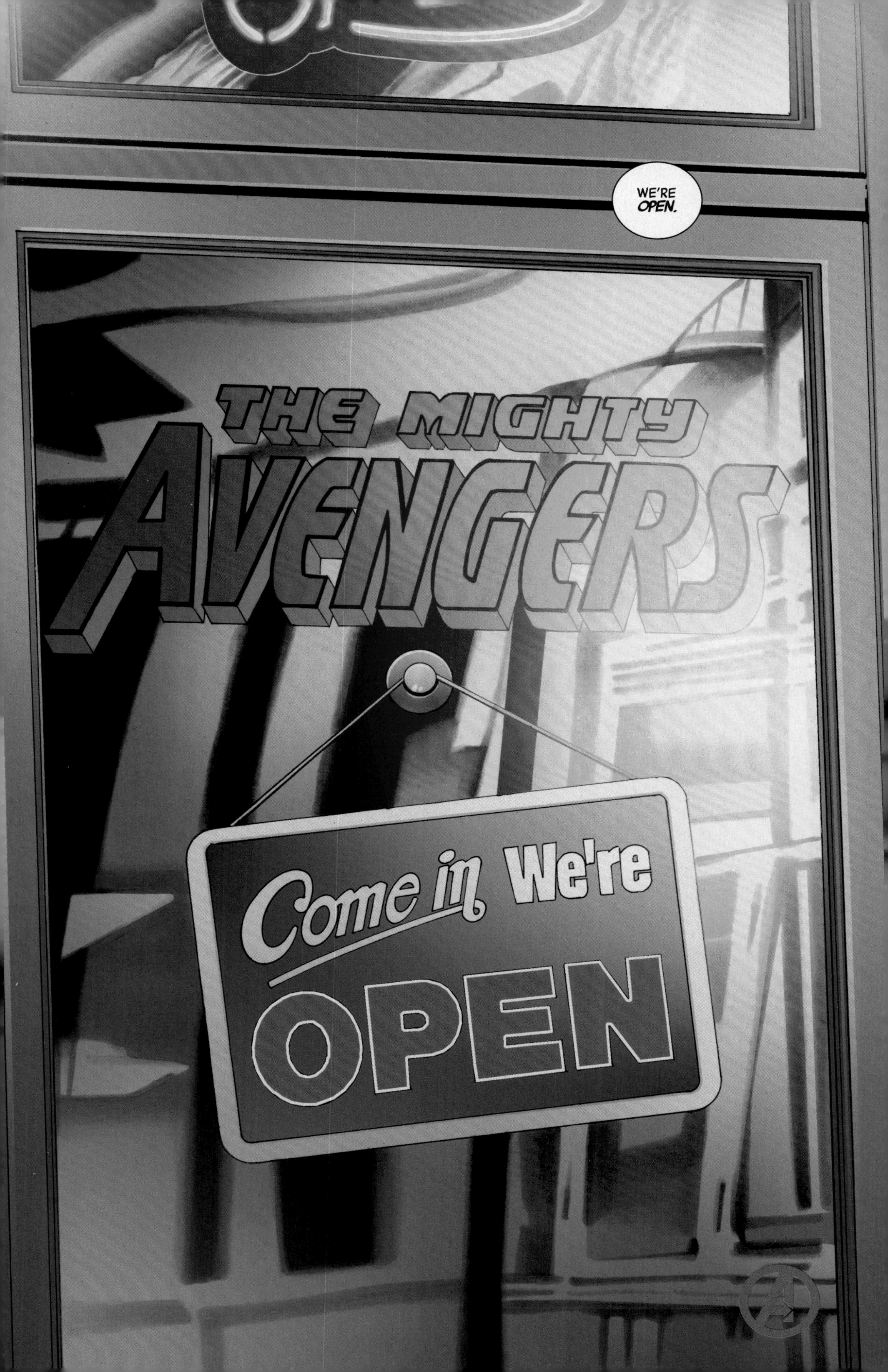
WE'RE OPEN.
THE MIGHTY AVENGERS
Come in We're OPEN

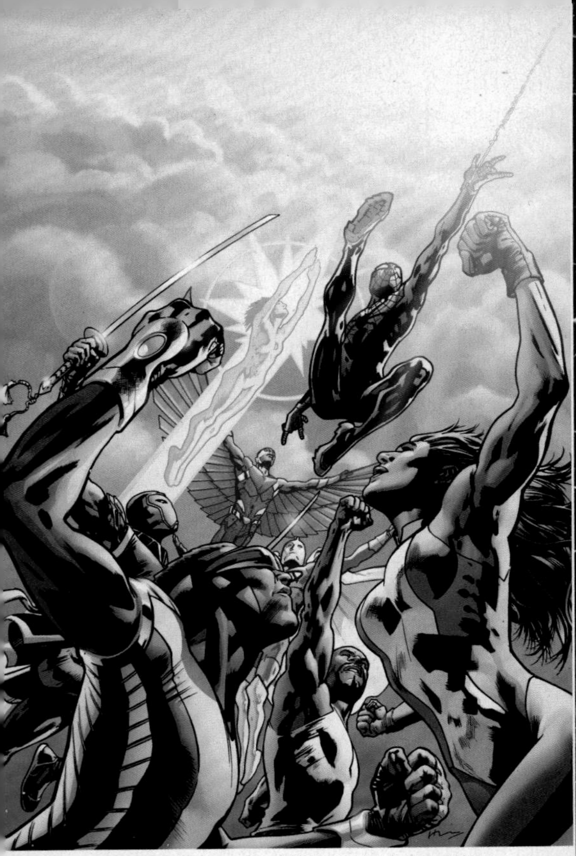

#1 VARIANT BY BRYAN HITCH & LAURA MARTIN

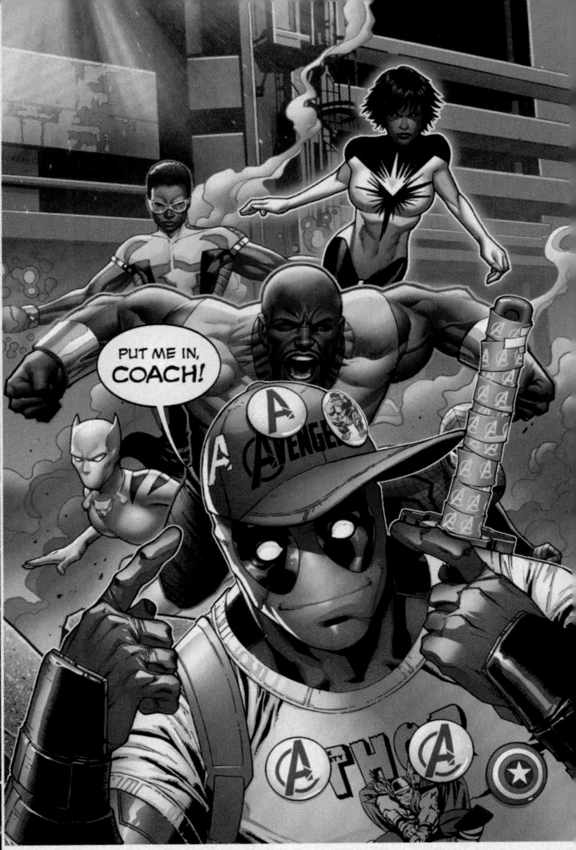
PUT ME IN, COACH!

#1 DEADPOOL VARIANT BY CARLO BARBERI & EDGAR DELGADO

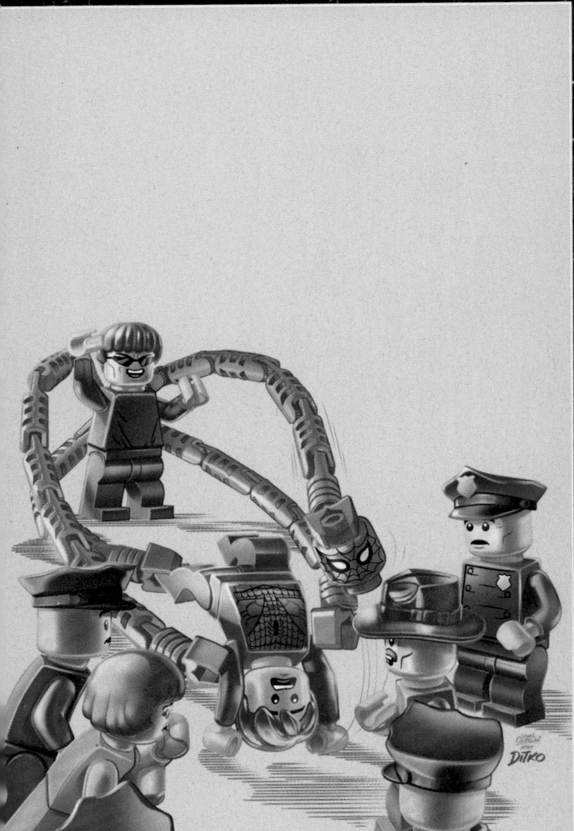

#1 LEGO VARIANT BY LEONEL CASTELLANI

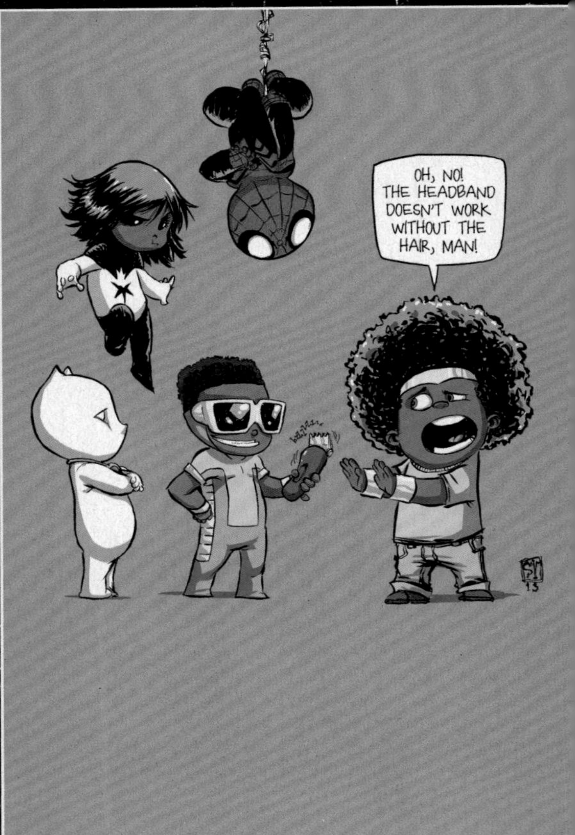
OH, NO! THE HEADBAND DOESN'T WORK WITHOUT THE HAIR, MAN!

#1 VARIANT BY SKOTTIE YOUNG

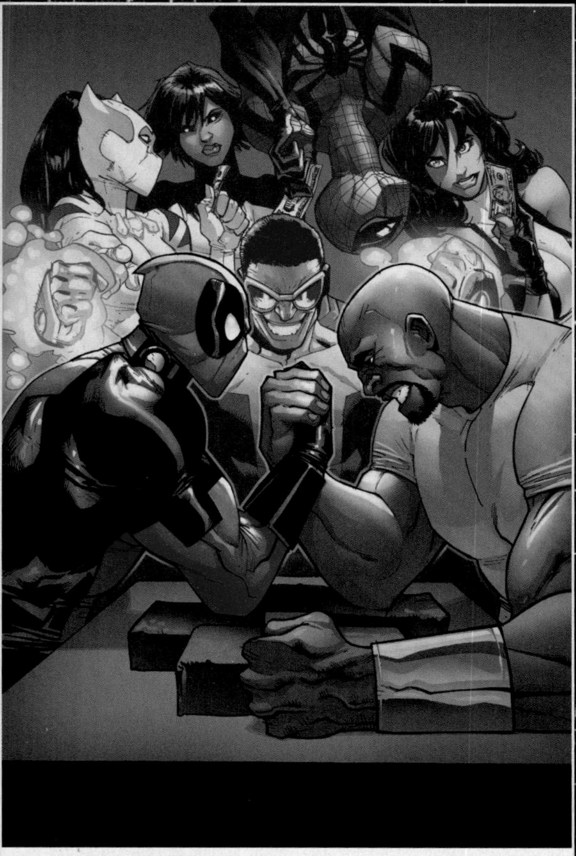

#1 HASTINGS VARIANT BY HUMBERTO RAMOS & EDGAR DELGADO

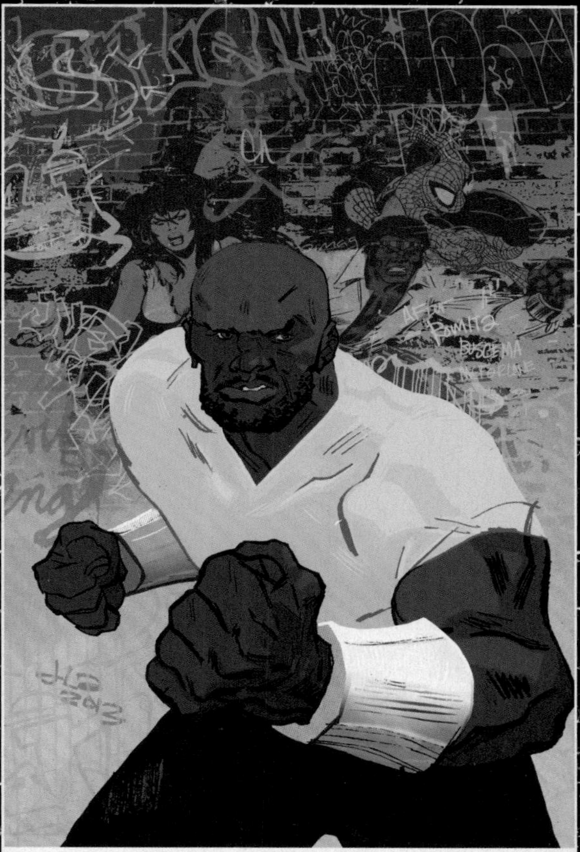

#1 CBLDF VARIANT BY JASON LATOUR

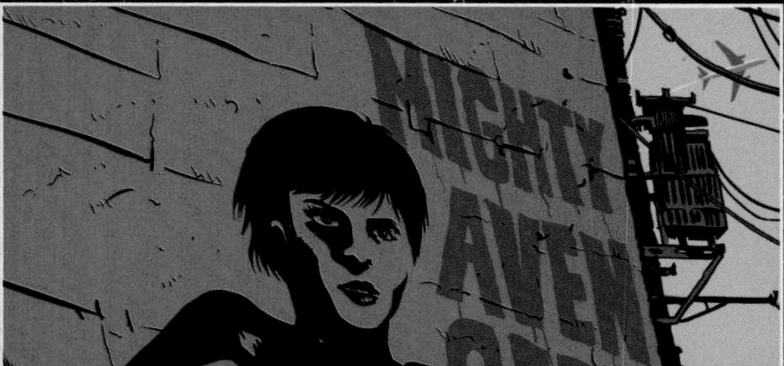

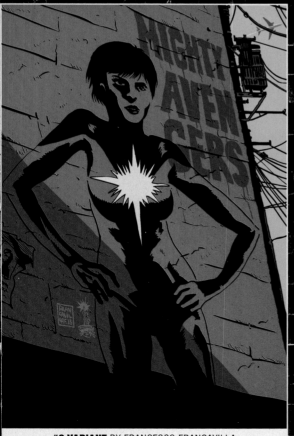

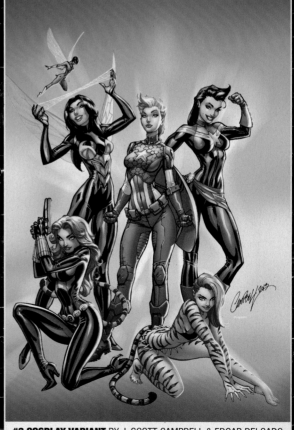

#2 VARIANT BY FRANCESCO FRANCAVILLA

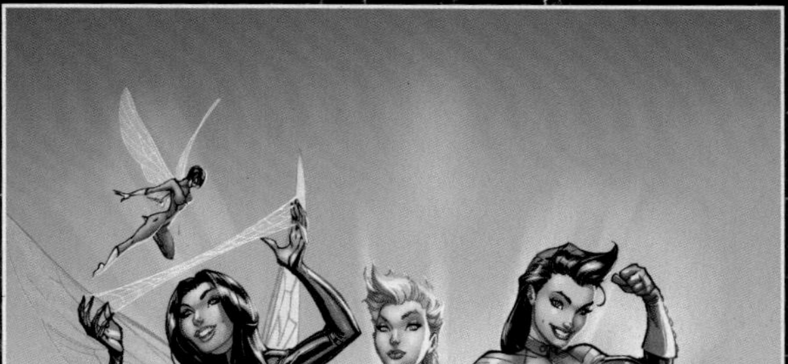

#2 COSPLAY VARIANT BY J. SCOTT CAMPBELL & EDGAR DELGADO

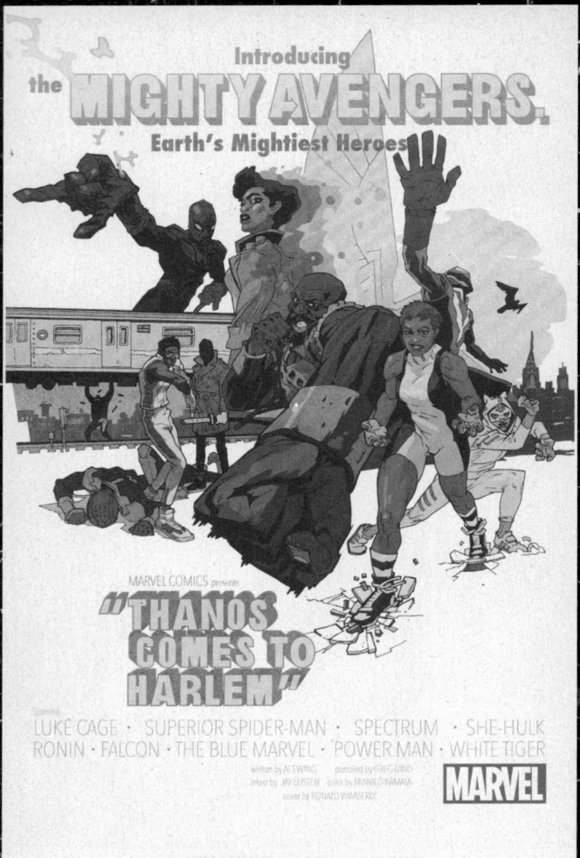
Introducing
the MIGHTY AVENGERS.
Earth's Mightiest Heroes
MARVEL COMICS presents
"THANOS COMES TO HARLEM"
LUKE CAGE · SUPERIOR SPIDER-MAN · SPECTRUM · SHE-HULK
RONIN · FALCON · THE BLUE MARVEL · POWER MAN · WHITE TIGER
MARVEL

#3 VARIANT BY RON WIMBLERLY

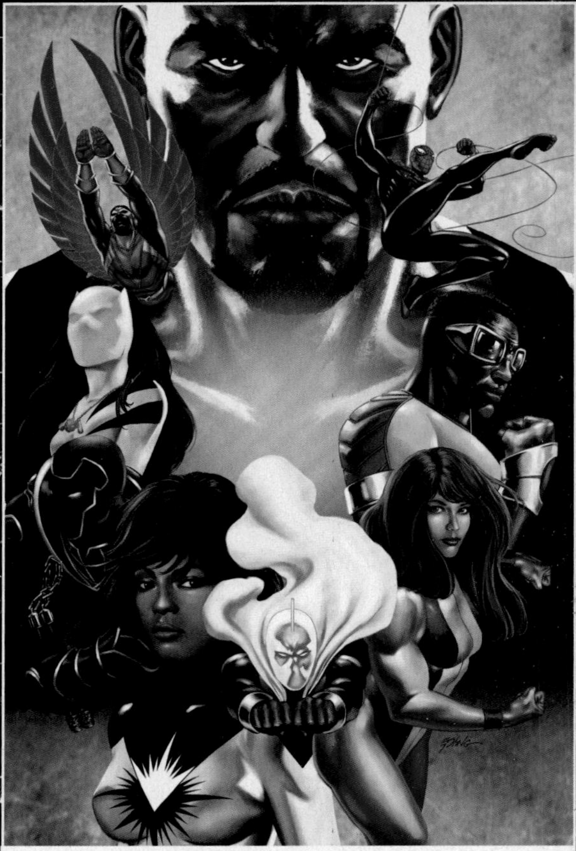

#4 VARIANT BY STEVE EPTING

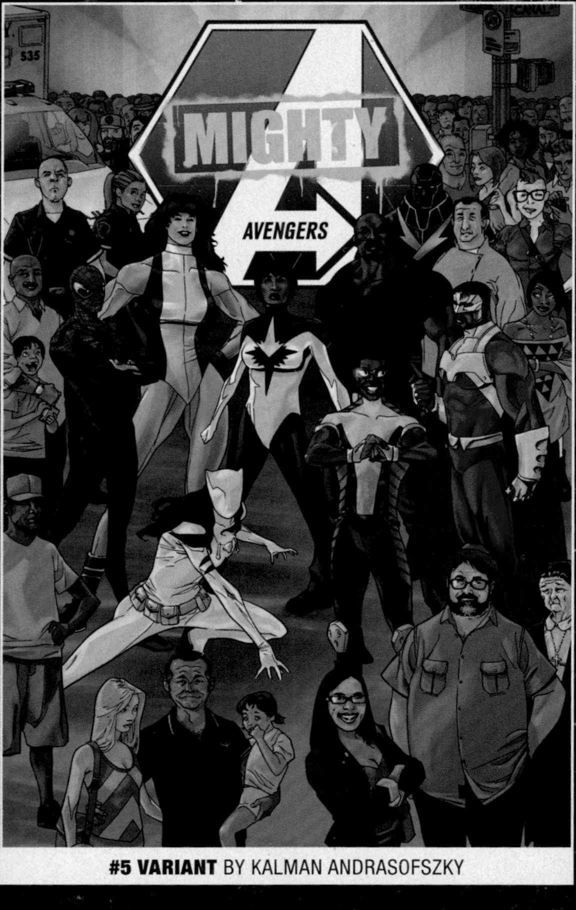
MIGHTY
AVENGERS

#5 VARIANT BY KALMAN ANDRASOFSZKY